THE
AFRICAN-AMERICAN
BOOKSHELF

THE
AFRICAN-AMERICAN
BOOKSHELF

50 Must-Reads From Before
the Civil War Through Today

CLIFFORD MASON

CITADEL PRESS
Kensington Publishing Corp.
www.kensingtonbooks.com

To Margaret May Johns, 1914–1978.
"Lady Luck"—*the Immortal Mommy*

CITADEL PRESS BOOKS are published by

Kensington Publishing Corp.
850 Third Avenue
New York, NY 10022

All Kensington titles, imprints, and distributed lines are available at special
quantity discounts for bulk purchases for sales promotions, premiums, fund-
raising, educational, or institutional use. Special book excerpts or customized
printings can also be created to fit specific needs. For details, write or phone the
office of the Kensington special sales manager: Kensington Publishing Corp.,
850 Third Avenue, New York, NY 10022, attn: Special Sales Department, phone
1-800-221-2647.

First Printing: January 2003

10 9 8 7 6 5 4 3 2 1

Printed in the United States of America

Library of Congres Control Number: 2002113375

ISBN: 0-8065-2204-6

CONTENTS

Books 7 through 16:
THAT ALL SHALL BE FREE   37

Books 17 through 25:
WHAT RACISM COULDN'T KILL—
THE ACCOMODATING AND THE ANGRY   95

Books 41 through 50:
THE EMPEROR'S NEW CLOTHES 217

PREFACE

The story of how this book came to be goes back almost fifteen years, to when I had to return to the New York City Board of Education for $15,000 a year, after an absence of over twenty years, or stand on a breadline. Since I had taught college in and around New York during the time that I was away, I was able without much difficulty to get tenure as soon as I applied for it. So there I was, at a high school in Manhattan, fifteen minutes away from my Upper West Side apartment, at a job I could keep for as long as I wanted, for the rest of whatever teaching life was left to me. Within six months of being retenured, my agent, Bob Markel (we'd been together for longer that either of my two marriages had lasted), got me a contract with a major nonfiction publisher to write a book on black America. It was to be an amalgam of history and literature, a survey of the field.

The editor of the book left her job before we even got to work, so as soon as the ink was dry on the contract, things fell apart. The new editor wanted to publish a book of her own that just happened to be about African-American something or other, which left me adrift without anyone actually wanting to say so. Since I had walked away from my tenure as soon as I had signed the contract, I was literally out in the cold. The tome I ended up writing, mostly for myself, since I no longer had a publisher, I dubbed *Burning the Confederate Flag*. Needless to say, Markel could find no takers.

I had sauntered back to sharecropping in the colleges, teaching drama and creative writing courses to graduate students at Columbia and New York universities, when my agent called with what seemed like a firm offer from Carol Publishing to write a book that was not too far removed in scope from the original project. My new editor, Jim Ellison, met Markel and me in Greenwich Village, not far from NYU, where I was teaching a course in freshman composition for the Higher Education Opportunities Program (HEOP). Ellison and I got on well enough for Bob to leave us alone before we had finished the first round of drinks. But Jim soon left my new publisher to work for himself.

My next editor, Linda Regan, was a charming young woman whom I never met in person. We talked over the phone and via e-mail, and mailed drafts of the manuscript back and forth. But we got on splendidly. By now the project, which originally had the provocative title *100 Must-Reads for Every African American,* had been redubbed *The African-American Bookshelf: 100 Must-Reads.* It was to be a book about books, my personal canon. All the books would deal with black America, so names like Pushkin, Alexandre Dumas, and Robert Browning couldn't be included. The list became a mix of history, biography, poetry, fiction, and drama, and I had a personal attachment to each and every one. Then came the blow. My publisher ceased operations just as I was about to make my final submission. Stranded again.

To make a difficult situation tragic, my agent's wife of forty-five years died. Pushing him to find another buyer for my book was, of course, out of the question. So the almost completed manuscript gathered dust for most of a year and a half; then a phone call came from Donald J. Davidson at Kensington Publishing Corp. I didn't know either—him or it. My book, he informed me, had been bought by Kensington, and they were ready to honor the contract and publish it under the Citadel Press imprint, as long ago intended.

I called Markel and he told me the offer was legitimate, so I met Davidson at Kensington's offices on Third Avenue and a very rocky relationship was launched. To say that we fought about what would and would not be included in the book would be to understate the case. The volume presented here is not totally un-like the original; rather it is both an abridged and an expanded version.

It was decided soon after our first meeting that the project should now comprise fifty must-reads instead on one hundred. All the poetry was excised, primarily because of the difficulties of getting permissions. All the James Baldwin titles went, as did three of my Richard Wright favorites: *Native Son, Black Boy,* and his mar-velous collection of short stories *Uncle Tom's Children. Raisin in the Sun* vanished from the list. I fought for and lost on the inclusion of both Earl Warren's *Memoirs* and Mumia Abu-Jamal's *Live From Death Row.* My biggest defeat was the loss of W. E. B. Du Bois's *World and Africa,* which the editor objected to on the grounds that it was not about black America. That may or may not be the case; nevertheless, I consider that book to be crucial to the under-standing of the black man's importance to world history.

With a much shortened list, I had room for wider-ranging commentary on each book and the inclusion of introductions to the sections that the book was eventually divided into. This espe-cially benefited the final section, books forty-one through fifty, which deal with the 1960s and include three titles from the nineties as well.

Again, a disagreement about Du Bois's work threatened to de-stroy the project. Davidson wanted *The Souls of Black Folk* in-cluded; I did not. Since I couldn't include *The World and Africa,* I wanted to use *The Autobiography* instead. We agreed on a clumsy compromise. We would include *Souls* and *The Autobiography,* but I would write about both in one entry. However, since the pub-lisher, Bruce Bender, insisted that I get permission for all ex-cerpts over 250 words, I began to look for ways to reduce the number of quotes and thus reduce the number of permissions that I had to get. Since I had quoted copiously from *Souls of Black Folk* and not from *The Autobiography,* and since *The Autobiography* was my preferred choice, *Souls* became an honorable mention.

In the final analysis, the spirit of the book has not been vio-lated. Throughout I have criticized racism, as I planned to do originally, and I have included works by George Jackson, Malcolm X, Eldridge Cleaver, and Randall Robinson toward that end. The primary aim of the book, which is much broader than the issue of racism, is discussed in the general introduction, so I won't repeat any of that here.

Black women, however, are underrepresented. Gone are Lorraine Hansberry's play, Phillis Wheatley's poetry, Charlotte Forten's journals, and Shirley Chisholm's autobiography, all cut from the final selection. I was able to salvage Ida B. Wells and Zora Neale Hurston. Male favorites such as Jean Baptiste Paul Du Sable, the man who founded Chicago, the famous cowboy Jim Beckwourth, and Muhammad Ali were lost as well, as was Benjamin Bannekar. Again, those were my calls, and I accept full responsibility for making them.

This preface, which started out as a tirade against the gods of publishing, is, I suppose, ultimately about creating a book that both my editor and I could live with. It's not as flamboyant as I would have wished and not as filled with bibliographic detail and old-time nostalgia as he would have. A compromise, not failed and not broken, rather one with a heart "made glad," if not too soon, not too late either.

ACKNOWLEDGMENTS

Besides my editor and my agent, who procured my contract with Citadel Press in the first place, the only person I have to thank (other than my dead mother who whispered words of encouragement into my ear from time to time) is the director of the Higher Education Opportunities Program (HEOP) at New York University, Param Chawla. As a consequence of my being on staff at HEOP and making a documentary for Dr. Chawla on the history of the program he granted me the use of some of my former students as research assistants, for which they were paid a small stipend. The help of LaJune Barnes, Aisha Ude, and Chrystal Vergara was invaluable to the success of the writing of this book. I am very grateful to them for their faithful fulfillment of all the tasks with which they were entrusted, for their loyalty, their research skills, and the level of professionalism that they brought to the work. They all started out as mere prefreshmen, and by the time they had finished their assignments, they were seasoned freshmen. Their accomplishments are certainly a tribute to the Opportunities Program and to Dr. Chawla. I was also ably assisted early on by another freshman from the program, Shannon Effinger. And don't forget my dead mother. She deserves double mention!

INTRODUCTION

The world of African-American culture—the culture of black America—is rich and varied and vast. It is a culture that has flourished from the beginning of the European settlement of the North American continent and is inseparable from whatever history has come from that settlement. It's a culture that began four centuries ago in the rich soil of its African origins.

Since the beginning of the American Republic, more than two hundred years ago, African-American culture has been resplendent in its many manifestations in time of both peace and war. In poetry and prose, in drama and painting and the plastic arts, in music, history, biography, sociology, black America has been nothing short of brilliant. It has thrown down a challenge to anyone, anywhere, at any time who dared to deny its majesty, its unending humanity, and the genius of its originality—an originality that has accounted for classic jazz, which may be the only original art form America has contributed to world culture.

The primary objective of this book is to show, through a selection and discussion of fifty books, the richness of black America's history and culture. I compiled *The African-American Bookshelf* to open the way for all Americans to share that history by reading it hopefully coming to a better understanding of it. The choices I have made form a personal canon and were to a large extent made on the basis of emotional appeal.

I am a playwright by profession. I have had ten Off and Off Off

Broadway productions. Some of the theaters where I've been produced include Café La Mama, Theater Row, Henry Street, and Intar II. My out-of-town credits include the Eugene O'Neill Conference in Waterford, Connecticut, and the Mark Taper Forum in Los Angeles. I've been reviewed favorably in the *New York Times,* the *Washington Post,* the *Daily News,* the *Afro American,* and the *Amsterdam News.*

As a critic, I have written articles on the arts for the *New York Times, Life, New York* magazine, and *Black Digest,* and on politics for the *Wall Street Journal,* and *GEO* magazine. I've published three murder mysteries, two with St. Martin's Press. I have taught graduate school at Rutgers, Columbia, and NYU, and undergraduate courses at Manhattanville, CUNY, and again at NYU, and received several grants from the NEA and the NEH.

Concomitant with showing the beauty of the African-American contribution was the need to shed light on the racist attitudes black America has faced and continues to face. I have tried to do more than repeat the many eloquent and voluminous statements on this subject and have avoided echoing the many solutions that have been offered (all too often) to combat that racism.

Black America has, throughout the centuries, taken an aggressive stance in response to racism: racist attitudes, racist violence, racist laws, expressions of racism on film, in the theater, on television, and in literature. It has also fought racism in our academic institutions, which are supported by huge endowments that bring with them an insistence on teaching the history of the ancient world as if it were a Teutonic dream; a Hollywood movie as presented in academia's version of history. The black persona, by contrast, is suffering, noble, sexless, avuncular, or a violent, unhinged racist. We pity the ones we can feel sorry for and run from the ones who frighten us as we would from anthrax. To view black America as a saga, as in *Up From the Ghetto,* albeit with many success stories to its credit, is paternalism.

I have concentrated instead on the fighters, those who couldn't and can't be patronized, who don't elicit white guilt from any quarter of the political spectrum, such as Harriet Tubman, Nat Turner, W. E. B. Du Bois, Adam Clayton Powell, Jr., Malcolm X,

George Jackson, and Eldridge Cleaver. As a result, many old favorites have not been included. That, however, does not mean that a militant lurks behind the cover of every book on this bookshelf. That would be a distortion, and it would falsify the history of black America. No, Booker T. Washington is included here, because his obsequiousness can still instruct us in what is manly in the face of the continuing denigration of racism. And the importance of other selected books lies beyond the pale of politics, such as Jean Toomer, Zora Neale Hurston, and the painters of the Black Renaissance.

This nation has generated a plethora of law but very little order. We have many attempts at trying to serve justice, to do what can be done within the bounds of what is legally permissible, but the ability to do what is right still escapes us. In another era, those who hide behind the law's failure to protect black America from racism would have used the law to plead that slavery had to be enforced because it was legal. Those who work to remove a law or dilute one that has been put on the books expressly to help black America rise from the ashes of slavery and Jim Crow racism would also have endorsed "separate but equal" as morally sanctionable.

Slavery has been dead for 137 years (as of this writing), yet its symbol—the Confederate battle flag—still flies proudly in some former states of the Confederacy. That black people have to live under that flag over a century later is similar to asking the Jewish race to live under the swastika. Mississippi, a sovereign state, did not ratify the Thirteenth Amendment (the one outlawing slavery) until 1997. In a poll taken in the Deep South in 1996, one fourth of the adults queried said they favored a law banning marriage between the races. Black America cannot be half equal, or almost equal, or better off than it was ten years ago. Black America is either equal or it is not. What this means, sadly, is that in the year 2003, when this book is published, black America will not be equal.

Many of the writers of the fifty selected books* have their solu-

---

* Many of these books have been through more than one printing. Rather than include all this information in the chapter headings, I have added an extensive Bibliography (see page 277).

tions for gaining that equality, from the separatism of Marcus Garvey to the self-reliance of Carter G. Woodson to the fiery eye-for-an-eye attitude of the Black Panthers. What is needed is efficacy. When a black man was dragged to his death in Jasper, Texas, in 1998, neither the black men who showed up with guns nor the ministers who came with a message of healing offered efficacy.

Efficacy means changing public opinion, at least it does in America, which is why the fight to control people's minds is such a vicious one, endlessly fought. Efficacy means meeting racism quickly and effectively wherever it shows its ugly head—in the pocketbook or in the gladiatorial arena of public opinion, through outrage expressed in film, on television, in the arts, and the press and in the bars and restaurants of the towns and cities across the nation. When black America can do that, or when white America is willing to do it, racism will die a quick death. Until then it will flourish.

The books presented here also offer a panorama, a sense of the big history of America. From the horrors of the slave trade holocaust that saw 200 million black souls transported to America or killed in the process, with disease and degradation their constant companions, to the rousing exploits of the frontier cowboys and soldiers to the black scientists and inventors without whom our version of the industrial revolution would have been much more stunted and halting, *The African-American Bookshelf* presents a saga filled with adventure as well as disquieting history.

It tells how the Federal Bureau of Investigation tried to use forged audiotapes to force Martin Luther King, Jr. to *commit suicide* the day before he was to accept the Nobel Peace Prize. It proves *prima facie,* that without the heroism and sacrifice of black men and women, on the battlefield and off, the North could *not* have won the Civil War. It tells about the salons and the wealth of the black millionaires of Harlem in the twenties. It recounts how Southern racists fought over a burnt finger or an ear from the corpse of one of the five thousand men and four hundred women burned alive or otherwise lunched over a bloody hundred-year era in American history. It also describes the black elite of the nineteenth century who sent their children to the best colleges and universities in America and abroad, and whose servants came from the elite of *their* class. It offers a feast of America's riches and holds up a mirror to its horrors.

Black America's fight against racism is a story whose ending still has to be written. When that work is finally finished, it will most certainly be part comedy and part tragedy. But let us hope, at least, that the ending has the possibility of being a happy one.

THE
AFRICAN-AMERICAN
BOOKSHELF

Books 1 through 6:
FIGHTING FOR THE FIRST FREEDOM

---

*T*HE FOUNDING FATHERS had done the dirty deed with no apologies. They had allowed slavery to pass into the legal system of the new nation. At the same time, they were using Thomas Jefferson's declaration that made the equality of *all* men the first principle upon which the nation would be founded. This compromise was made, scholars say, to appease colonies such as South Carolina and Georgia that would not have come into the new nation if they had not been allowed to keep their system of human slavery. The contradiction was monumental: A new nation had created itself without a royal bloodline to legitimize it decades before the Congress of Vienna in 1815 reasserted royalty as a prerequisite for any nation's existence. And yet it had done so by making chattel slavery, human slavery, legal.

Congress never said all *white* men are created equal, but that's what their laws implied. They acknowledged human slavery's existence in the Constitution. Congress not only gave the slave states the legal right to practice slavery but also allowed them to gain political advantage through it, since they could legally increase their population base by counting slaves as three-fifths of a whole man. The Founding Fathers had made a choice: They put the greed of the Southern slavers above the humanity of anyone unlucky enough to be a slave.

The slaves themselves, whether they were indeed the equal of three-fifths of a whole man or worth more, or worth less, received no direct advantage in this peculiar system. Congress allowed the slave trade to stand until 1808, when it made that trade illegal, but did nothing to enforce its prohibition until 1862. As a consequence, the slave trade flourished much more vigorously when it was illegal than it did while it was legal. (Congress had also enacted the first fugitive slave law in 1793 that allowed for escaped slaves to be returned to their masters.)

However, none of these laws stated that slaves had to be black. Since the country had grown up with vestiges of feudalism such as indentureship, in which white men had to work for seven to fourteen years without compensation because they had been convicted of a crime, often a petty one the argument could be made that slavery was color blind. The fact that, in practice, it was nothing of the kind is only half the point. The liberating forces and euphoria that swept across the new nation following the War of Independence went only so far for *all* men, no matter how they were created. In both the South and the North, a white man couldn't vote in most states if he didn't own property. In New York State, this law making owning property a prerequisite for voting stayed on the books until 1860. There was no free public education, no free health care in most of the country. Divorce was illegal in many states.

As a consequence, a de facto class system was built into the fabric of the nation from the outset. Money divided men in very meaningful ways that created different castes in America during the period from 1783 to 1865. A white man who wanted to run for president of the United States needed Western European bona fides to do so. And of course he had to be a Protestant. Still, the *idea* that all white men should belong to a single class called Americans with all the rights and privileges of citizenship was the eventual intent of the nation.

The same assumptions did not apply to the black man. In addition to being counted as three-fifths of a man, a distinction that he alone held by the end of the eighteenth century, there was the stated objection to his assuming the privileges and immunities of white men. In 1800 James Forten and Absalom Jones, two black men who were both free and prosperous, petitioned Congress to give them and their race relief from the slave trade and from the institution of slavery itself. The petition was not objected to on economic grounds, which was the basis most apologists of slavery used to argue that slavery was not an exercise in racial prejudice. Rather, Representative John Rutledge of South Carolina said, "The petition is a product of the newfangled French philosophy of liberty and equality." Lest it be assumed that only representatives of the South were expected to reply in such manner, Harrison Otis, a Massachusetts congressman, went even further. Said he, "To encourage a petition of this kind would be mischievous to America very soon. It would teach blacks the art of assembling together, debating and the like." The petition died in committee when the chairman declared that it would have the effect of creating disquiet and jealousy. In other words, the idea of black men exercising the rights and privileges of white men was objected to in principle. Not everyone felt this way, of course. And many of the early giants of American history thought that slavery would eventually "pass into history" as had many of man's other brutalities: human sacrifice, the whipping post, the stocks.

Nevertheless, in 1800 the black man was faced with the incontrovertible fact that he had just fought for the independence of a country that didn't want him to learn the art of assembling. Not only was he legally a dead letter as a citizen, but if he even tried to learn how to function as one, it would be dangerous—"mischievous to *America* very soon." The very idea that it would be dangerous for black men to learn to do what they had just fought to make possible *for all men created equal to do* was probably no worse in effect than the reality of chattel slavery itself. Still, blacks owned property, owned slaves, sailed their own ships from Boston to Africa and back, invented machines and mechanisms that proved crucial to the industrial development of the nation, wrote books on leading issues of the day, and fought for the country before and after it came into being. Yet, in spite of all this, the curse that was visited on the sons and daughters of Africa would not be lifted.

Although Paul Cuffee, a black man born in Massachusetts, owned his own ships and was a successful merchant sea captain worth a considerable amount of money in the late seventeenth and early eighteenth centuries, he couldn't vote—but was expected to pay taxes. "No taxation without representation" may have been a rallying cry of the American Revolution, but Cuffee was jailed on four occasions when he and his brother refused to pay their taxes until they were given the right to vote. They never got it, nor did any of the other blacks or Native Americans living in Massachusetts at the time, all of whom had to pay taxes. Rather than rot in jail, Cuffee gave in and paid.

Cuffee, whose sailors were both black and white, was so successful as a merchant seaman that he tried, unsuccessfully, to open a regular trade with Liberia in hopes of undercutting the slave trade. James Madison received him in the White House, treating him at first with punctilious courtesy. Later a genuine friendship developed between the two that became a propaganda tool in the hands of the Abolitionists, who used it to prove the intellectual equality of the black man. No matter, Cuffee died not being able to vote.

Jefferson thought blacks were inferior to whites, which makes him a racist by contemporary standards. Nevertheless, he was so filled with the euphoria of defining why America was declaring independence that he included a clause in the declaration that condemned the King of England for the slave trade. It read in part:

[He] has waged cruel war against human nature itself, violating its most sacred rights of life and liberty in the persons of a distant people who never offended him, captivating and carrying them into slavery in another hemisphere, or to incur miserable death in their transportation thither. This piratical warfare, the opprobrium of infidel powers, is the warfare of the CHRISTIAN [Jefferson's capitals] king of Great Britain. Determined to keep open a market where MEN [Jefferson's capitals] should be bought and sold, he has prostituted his negative for suppressing every legislative attempt to prohibit or restrain this execrable commerce: and . . . now exciting those very people to rise in arms among us, and to purchase that liberty of which he has deprived them, & murdering the people upon whom he also obtruded them; thus paying off former crimes committed against the liberties of one people, with crimes which he urges them to commit against the lives of another!

This clause never made its way into the final document. Congress's refusal to recognize the intellectual capacity of black men on any level led to the most appalling abuses, even though black men in servitude often showed intellectual and artistic superiority to many white men. Langston Hughes in *Black Magic* documents the case of Blind Tom, who had such total musical recall that he had the amazing faculty of playing back, on the piano, any composition that he heard on the instant. And not just jingles. He was such a phenomenon that he was taken all the way to Europe and presented to Franz Liszt. Liszt played what he considered a difficult piece and Blind Tom played it back for him flawlessly. All the money that Tom made, of course, went to his owner, Colonel Bethune, who advertised his gold mine as an "idiot." And black women inspired the manhood of white men almost without interruption until the civil rights movement of the 1960s, in the South certainly, and still skin color kept the black race in a rigidly separate, almost exotic category that simply got more rigid and maybe even more exotic as time went on and the country became stronger. Why the pathology regenerated itself no one can really say.

1

WORLD'S GREAT MEN OF COLOR, VOLUME 2

by J. A. Rogers, edited with an introduction by John Henrik Clark

NEW YORK: MACMILLAN, 1972

J. A. Rogers deserves a book all to himself, but no one's ever written his biography. He was an early pioneer of black history who went where no one else dared to go, into the belly and guts of the history of the world, where he found proof of how all pervasive has been the black imprint on world history. Carter G. Woodson (see Must-Read No. 26) has been called the father of black history, a title he deserves. But Woodson's primary focus was America. Rogers covered the entire ancient and modern world.

Of his many works, I have chosen the second volume of *World's Great Men of Color* for inclusion here. It runs to more than 560 pages in the Macmillan edition and has profiles of many key black Americans who are the main emphasis of the book. Volume 2 also includes black men from around the world whose exploits make black history illustrious, indeed; men such as St. Maurice of Aganaum, Benedict the Moor, Alessandro de Medici, Joachim Murat, the Chevalier St. Georges, Jean Louis, Alexsandr Pushkin, and the two Dumas—all from Europe, and eight entries from Central and South America.

Maurice and Benedict are both saints of the Catholic Church. Maurice was a Roman general during the twin reign of Diocletian and Maximilian Herculious. Rogers says he was canonized because he refused a command to slaughter Christians at Aganaum, Switzerland, and was beheaded as a consequence. Benedict the Moor was born in Sicily in 1524. As a priest, he led a life of such piety that he became a model for all men of the cloth.

Alessandro de Medici was the first reigning duke of Florence during the Renaissance. He was put in power by none other than Charles V of the Holy Roman Empire, who sealed the bargain by giving Alessandro his daughter in marriage. Alessandro's mother was a black woman from Colle Vecchio, Italy. He rose to power in part because he was the illegitimate son of Pope Clement VII.

Joachim Murat was the king of Naples under Napoleon. His lineage went back to the Moors who lived in the Auvergne region of France after they had been driven out of Spain. Napoleon did not bestow honors on a mere whim. Murat was one of his ablest cavalry leaders, the man who, at the head of sixty guards, had burst into the National Convention and dissolved it so that Napoleon could declare himself emperor.

Chevalier St. Georges, who was born in Guadeloupe in the West Indies in 1744, became one of the "most dazzling . . . figure[s] at the most splendid court in Europe [Louis XVI's]. As a violinist, pianist, poet, musical composer, and actor, he was phenomenal; as a swordsman he so far eclipsed the best of his time that in his prime none could match him . . . as a dancer, swimmer, horseman . . . he was the most graceful in a land supreme for its grace and elegance; in the matter of dress he was the model of his day, setting the fashions of England and France; a King of France, a future King of England, and royal princes sought his company."

Jean Louis, from Haiti, also became "one of the greatest swordsmen in France," according to Rogers. And for the uninitiated, Pushkin, the father of Russian literature, was black. The Dumas (father and son) need no introduction, and almost everyone knows *they* were black. In addition to Estevanico, the man whose profile I have chosen to focus on, Ira Aldridge also makes up the contingent from America.

Aldridge, who became one of the great classical actors of his day, was born in New York City in 1807. He went to England at the age of twenty because the police closed down the only black theater in New York, where he was developing his craft, under the guise that the performers were disturbing the peace. Othello was his signature role. He played in every major capital in Europe in addition to appearing at Covent Garden. He was considered one of the preeminent interpreters of Shakespeare in the first half of the nineteenth century, and he received medals and honors from the crowned heads of Europe the likes of which no other American actor has even dreamed of—and that's not hyperbole. Aldridge never returned to his native land.

Rodgers says that Estevanico was the first non-Indian to see the inner reaches of the American Southwest, in what is now New Mexico and Arizona, as early as the 1530s. John Henrik Clarke's excellent introduction to Volume 2 makes the claim, backed by the kind of historical proof that can't be dismissed, that black men from Africa sailed the Atlantic a thousand years before Columbus and shared their gold, their religions, and their language with the Plains Indians of the Americas. He also points out that Columbus admitted to finding a dark-skinned people trading with the native peoples in the Caribbean islands and inferred that they were from the coast of Guinea, in West Africa.

Little is known about Estevanico before his arrival in the Americas. He was a native of Azamor, Morocco, very black, with thick lips. He was part of the expedition of Spanish explorer Panfilo de Narvaez, who sailed up the mouth of the Mississippi River at least fourteen years before Hernando De Soto took the same route to search, unsuccessfully, for legendary cities of gold. De Narvaez's party was caught in a storm and ended up off the coast of present-day Texas. Of the three hundred men in the expedition, all but Estevanico and three white men were killed by Indians, who enslaved the four survivors. Writes Rogers: "For the next six years they were forced to do all the drudgery of the tribe.

Quite naked, they suffered from sores on their bodies caused by stones, thorns and bushes. Finally, [they] succeeded in escaping. Traveling westwards . . . they were the first from the Old World to see the buffalo. With their knowledge of Indian life they now became medicine men, and as such were well treated and even feared."

Estevanico returned with the others to Mexico City where they were celebrated after having traveled more than twenty-five hundred miles. The viceroy of Mexico City immediately sent out another expedition to look for the alleged cities of gold. He put Estevanico in charge and gave him three hundred Indians to command. Writes Rogers: "The journey proved a veritable triumph for Estevanico. Everywhere he was received with honor, thanks to his size and strength, his dark skin, his daring, bravery and bluff, as well as his good nature and ready wit, his reputation as a medicine man, and his knowledge of Indian life and lore. The most beautiful virgins were given to him as presents. These he accepted and incorporated into his retinue." He continued to win over all the tribes he came across until he reached the cliff-dwelling Zuni Indians of the Hawikuh. It was here, in 1540, that he met his fate. Rogers quotes from another historian, Herbert Bolton:

[Estevanico's] tall body flaunted robes dyed with the colors of the rainbow. Tufts of brilliant feathers and strings of bells dangled from his arms. He carried a magical gourd decorated with bells and with one white and scarlet feather; and sent it ahead . . . to awe the natives in each town. . . . [W]hen he presented it [to the Zuni] with the announcement that their lord had come to make peace and cure the sick, [they] became enraged. . . . Disdaining fear, Estevanico went on. Just outside the walls of Cibola, he was seized. The sun was about a lance high when the men of the Hawikuh suddenly launched upon his followers. Some of those, fleeing, looked back, [and] thought they had seen Estevanico fall beneath the thick hail of darts.

Rogers adds that the legends of the Zuni Indians confirm Estevanico's arrival as having predated any white men. One of the priests in his entourage, following several days behind him, got as far as the land of the Hawikuh himself. But he went no farther. Returning to Mexico City, he related all that Estevanico had accomplished, and an army was sent out several months later that overwhelmed the Hawikuh. Although no cities paved with gold were found, because of Estevanico's pioneering journey, this vast region was now on the map, and there were further forays into the interior, as far as present-day Kansas.

World's Great Men of Color is a thrilling book that reads like a novel, as do all of Rogers's works. Rogers's profile of Frederick Douglass, also in Volume 2, is among the many fine examples of the author's lucid though trenchant style.

J. A. Rogers was a truly remarkable man. He was a native of Jamaica, born on the west coast in Negril, a village that has become famous as one of the island's most popular tourist spots. Rogers also published a three-volume work, *Sex and Race,* and the one-volume *Nature Knows No Color-Line.* On the dust jacket of the latter is a picture of Charlotte Sophia, George III's queen and Queen Victoria's grandmother, which shows that she was clearly a woman of black ancestry.

A photograph of a coin picturing Jesus Christ, from Justinian II's reign, supports the claim that *he* was a black man. This illustration appeared in the original edition of volume one, published by Rogers himself, but not in the Macmillan edition, although most Jewish scholars will admit that Jesus was black by today's standards.

Rogers had to self-publish his books early in his career, but by 1930 he was a member of the Paris Society of Anthropology, the American Geographical Society, the Academy of Political Science, and the American Association for the Advancement of Science. He died in 1966 and was survived by his widow, Helga.

2

BLACK CARGOES: A HISTORY OF THE ATLANTIC SLAVE TRADE, 1518–1865

by Daniel Mannix in collaboration with Malcolm Cowley

NEW YORK: VIKING, 1962

Black Cargoes is the best book that I've come across on the subject of the slave trade. The other books that I've read were either thinly documented or verbose and dull and didn't give the well-rounded picture of the subject that Mannix provides. He begins with an account of the slaughter of the Indians of Hispaniola, or Haiti, in 1495 by Columbus and his Spanish dragoons. From there, he covers all the major periods of slave trading up to the mid-nineteenth century. It was the black holocaust: the account of hundreds of thousands of men, women, and children, chained, branded like cattle, beaten, starved, and put in the stinking hole of a sailing ship to be carried across the Atlantic. Upon arrival, they were beaten again and chained and sold in broad daylight, where their teeth were examined, and their ability to dance and sing and be happy in their work weighed in the balance before a price was paid for their body if not their mind and soul.

There were many Africans who didn't survive the infamous Middle Passage, as the journey from Africa to the New World was called. Some were whipped to death. Others died from suffocation and disease below decks, where upward of six hundred souls were packed, often having to lie in their own excrement. There's more than one recorded incident of the African prisoners jumping overboard in the middle of the night while on deck for an airing out, still chained to one another, before anyone could stop them. Many thousands gone, one way or another. Others starved themselves to death. But that wasn't always that easy to do in those boom years of America's first entrepreneurial miracle. One of the many doctors onboard these ships of death even wrote a book about how the slavers force-fed their African cargo, which Mannix quotes:

> Upon the negroes refusing to take food, I have seen coals of fire, glowing hot, put on a shovel and placed so near their lips as to burn them. If they still refused, they were flogged day after day until they agreed to take food. If this device proved ineffective, every slaver was provided with a special instrument called the *speculum oris*, or mouth opener. It looked like a pair of dividers with notched legs and with a thumbscrew at the blunt end. The legs were closed and the notches were hammered between the slave's teeth. When the thumbscrew was tightened, the legs of the instrument separated, forcing open the slave's mouth; then food was poured into it through a funnel.

But sometimes not even that worked. Those Africans! They were even more ingenious than their pursuers of the almighty dollar. They had a means of escape that nothing that the white man could devise could overcome. In the business of slave trading it was called "fixed melancholy." Mannix explains: "Even slaves who were well fed, treated with kindness, and kept under relatively sanitary conditions could often die one after another for no apparent reason; they simply had no wish to live." He then quotes an American medical student who witnessed the horrors first-hand:

> Each morning three or four dead would be found, brought upon the deck, taken by the arms and heels, and tossed overboard as unceremoniously as an empty bottle. Of what did they die? And why always at night? Among civilized races it is thought almost impos-

sible to hold one's breath until death follows. It is thought the African can do so. They certainly had no means of concealing anything and certainly did not kill each other.

As Mannix himself points out, it is impossible for a human being to hold his breath until he dies. Once he loses consciousness, his lungs will fill up with air and he will recover. After Mannix offers an absurd alternative explanation concerning the "shock" of being dragged through the "surf" in order to be put on the ship (as if Africans hadn't navigated all the waters of their continent since before the dawn of history), he presents a more plausible explanation: "The communal life of many tribes was so highly organized by a system of customs, relationships, taboos, and religious ceremonies that there was practically nothing a man or a woman could do that was not prescribed by tribal law. To separate an individual from this complex system of interrelationships and suddenly place him, naked and friendless, in a completely hostile environment was in some respects a greater shock than any amount of physical brutality." The thrust of this explanation is that these inexplicable deaths were not willful acts. Rather, the slaves simply fell victim to a disease brought on by a trauma that the mind could not deal with in any other way.

This explanation may have appealed to Mannix, but it doesn't say much for the emotional toughness of Africans. So how did they die? Most likely, they willed themselves to death. Some went mad—which may or may not have been an act of will, too. Writes Mannix, "Not surprisingly, the slaves often went mad. . . . Men who went insane might be flogged to death, to make sure that they were not malingering. Some were simply clubbed on the head and thrown overboard."

The slave trade was a business, nothing personal. Sometimes a slave was worth more dead than alive because he was covered by insurance if he drowned. *Black Cargoes* describes one captain who threw 133 black people in the ocean, even though they were still alive, *and* he was in sight of land, just to collect the insurance.

The "trade" lasted for three centuries. In its last thirty years,

America was the only country keeping it alive. It had been responsible for the forced migration of at least 150 million black men, women, and children out of Africa, and the killing of another 40 to 50 million.

As Mannix points out, America had passed laws that made the slave trade illegal as early as 1808. But like gun-control legislation and prohibition, illegality just whetted the appetite of traders. A governor of Georgia resigned from office in 1817 because he could make more money as an illegal slave trader. A governor of South Carolina complained that it was unfair that the North could keep increasing its population by taking in European immigrants without allowing the South to reopen the slave trade so its population growth could keep up! And Alexander Stephens, who became the vice president of the Confederate States of America in 1861, said, "Slave states cannot be made without Africans. . . . Without an increase of African slaves from abroad you may not expect or look for many more slave states."

Black Cargoes demonstrates that the slave trade, which had started out as a means of getting the new nation's economy growing, had become a permanent part of its social fabric, a way of life that men would fight to the death to preserve—it if came to that. If there was a war, said one Virginia congressman, then the fighting would be "between men contending for their firesides (the Southerner) and the robbers (the Northerner) who are seeking to despoil them of their rights, and degrade them before the world."

To the South the trade in human flesh was both a source of wealth and a symbol of pride in what the South stood for, what its way of life meant to itself and to history, which made the slave trade a matter of principle as well as pragmatic necessity. Mannix writes, "the two centers of the contraband trade were to be Georgia and the new state of Louisiana, where Negro fever raged as nowhere else in the country."

In 1862 Congress finally got around to appropriating $1.8 million to suppress the slave trade. It had taken them fifty-four years to get serious about a law that should have been a cornerstone of early American democracy. By the time the end came, bringing black people to America illegally was such an established tradition that slave ships scrambled to claim the honor of being the last one to cross the Atlantic.

Mannix tells the story of the *Erie*, which, while not the last slave ship, was the only one whose captain, Nathaniel Gordon, was hanged for an illegal crossing. Gordon, who was from Maine, had made at least three trips before he got caught, in 1860 (he should have been carrying lobster). Gordon's "cargo" of 890 Africans (106 women and 612 children) was landed in Liberia, and he was brought to New York to be prosecuted. His first trial ended in a hung jury, but by the time his second trial was convened, the Civil War had started. This time, Gordon was convicted and sentenced to hang. Someone slipped poison to him while he was in prison. He swallowed it, then gleefully told the guards that he had cheated the hangman. The doctor revived him however, and he was indeed hanged. His execution still didn't stop the lucrative trade. The *Huntress,* a slave ship out of New York, landed slaves in Cuba as late as 1864.

But it was all for a good cause—the building of America! It primed the economic pump in many ways: the Africans themselves were sold for money—cash profit. Once they were put to work on the plantations, they increased the South's political base because the Constitution counted them each as three-fifths of a man. They were a source of profit to the North as well, since shipping and the businesses it created, among them insurance, were all cornerstones of America's amazing growth during the first half of the nineteenth century.

The Africans were even more important to the South in these ways because they did all the work and they didn't have to be paid for it, and then could still be sold at any point, retaining their cash value even after their owner had made back his investment with a profit!

3

THE NEGRO IN VIRGINIA

*compiled by Workers of the Writers Program of
the Works Progress Administration (WPA)
in the State of Virginia*

NEW YORK: HASTINGS HOUSE, 1941

The Negro in Virginia was compiled in the 1930s by the only all-black unit of the Virginia Writers' Project, which was part of the Works Progress Administration, one of Franklin Delano Roosevelt's many federally funded agencies that was created to fight the Great Depression. It's an emotionally wrenching oral testimony of former slaves who were old enough to remember what it was like "back then." They touch us memorably with their sadness, their simplicity, their willingness to endure. Through their eyes we get an unadorned look at the day-to-day reality of slavery. We hear the language of the slave, we see the foibles as well as the ferociousness of those who owned human beings, and we get a sense of how they dealt with the power that came with their proprietorship, often in almost routine fashion, making it simply a part of their diurnal round (when they weren't giving into the sadistic brutality that absolute power allowed them).

The book begins in the seventeenth century. The authors write that Anthony Johnson, the first free black man to be born in America, was also the first Virginian of either race to "hold as a slave for life a Negro who had committed no crime." In 1653, the man in question, Casor, complained that Johnson had kept him in bondage for twice as many years as he was originally indentured, which had been only for seven years. Two white men took Casor's side, threatening to help him recover Johnson's cows as damages if Johnson didn't honor the original contract. So Johnson released him, only to renege a year later and go to court to get Casor back. The court found in Johnson's favor, and Casor was forced to end his days as Anthony Johnson's chattel slave.

This is the first case of "judicial support given slavery in Virginia except as a punishment for crime." Of course, the case of Johnson, while it is unique in many ways, was not free of racial partiality. Johnson may have been black, but then so was Casor. If Casor had been white and the master-slave relationship had worked both ways from the start, and then become a strictly white on top, black at the bottom affair, the idea that race was not really an issue in the earliest days of slavery might be argued.

Besides the singular *Johnson-Casor* case, the book presents the usual history of black America before the Civil War. The Virginia plantocracy so loved courtly music that they were willing to let black musicians play it for them. One man had a servant who "'fiddled' for the whole neighborhood." The perks for such accomplishments were sometimes handsome indeed. Sy Gilliat, the body servant of Lord Botetourt, was the official fiddler at state balls. "Gilliat [wore] 'an embroidered silk coat and vest of faded lilac, silk stockings . . . shoes decorated with large buckles . . . and a powdered brown wig.' His wardrobe consisted of fifty suits, and his 'manners were as courtly as his dress.'"

In the chapter "Slave Artisans," the authors write: "The ability of Thomas Fuller, the 'African calculator,' to answer 'all questions of time, distance, and space,' although he could neither read nor write won fame for the slave. . . . When . . . a noted mathematician posed to fuller the problem of calculating the number of seconds a person had lived who was seventy years, seven months, and seven days old, the slave gave his answer after a minute and a half of mental gymnastics. The mathematician, figuring on paper, obtained a different answer, but Fuller reminded [him] that he had neglected to count leap years."

The book also discusses the story of Christianity and slavery, which is revealed to be a study in national sophistry. At first, blacks couldn't be both Christians and slaves. Then they could be, but they couldn't have their own services. (Several black preachers were whipped and excommunicated for starting their own congregations.) Next they were allowed to form their own churches, but they had to have a white preacher. Then it was acceptable for blacks to have their own preachers. "But the gains made in the first quarter of the century were . . . all lost. Following Nat Turner's insurrection . . . Governor Floyd told the . . . legislature that the 'public good required that the Negro preacher be silenced.' " But "if whites were 'close by' their slaves" then it was all right for the latter to pray. A former slave describes how that was accomplished:

> When we git to de church, de white folks would go inside, an' de slaves would sit round under de trees outside. Den de preacher git de white folks to singin' an' shoutin', an' he start to walkin' up an' down de pulpit an' ev'y once in a while he lean out dewinder an' shout somepin' out to us black folk. . . . Den . . . ole nigger would git up outside an' start to preachin' right 'long wid preacher [inside] . . . wid a lot of handwavin' an' twistin' of his mouth widdout makin' no noise. We . . . laugh when he say just what de white preacher say.

The following episode from the chapter "Thirty and Nine" is a powerful example of existential sadism suffered by a young slave in a domestic situation. It's the story of Henrietta King and the deformity that she had to live with for the rest of her life because she was hungry and ate a piece of candy. She was ninety-eight when the WPA writers interviewed her.

> Her face is a hideous mask—her mouth horribly twisted across one cheek with jagged fangs of rotted teeth protruding. One cheek is speckled with lumps—"ends of de jawbones," she explains. She says she has no idea what she looked like before her face was

smashed. "I musta been a good lookin' gal. . . . Wanta know 'bout slave days? I'll tell you what slave days was like . . . ole Missus was a common dog. [She] was so stingy-mean dat she didn't put enough on de table to feed a swallow.

See dis face? See dis mouf all twist over here so's I can't shet it? See dat eye? All red, ain't it. Been dat way fo' eighty-some years. Well, ole Missus made dis face dis way.

Here's how it happened. She put a piece of candy on her wash-stan' one day. I was 'bout eight or nine years ole. . . . I seed dat candy layin' dere, an' I was hungry. Ain't had a father workin' in de fiel' like some of de chillun to bring me eats—had jes' little pieces of scrap-back each mornin' throwed at me from de kitchen. I seed dat peppermint stick layin' dere, an' I ain't dared go near it 'cause I knew ole Missus jus' waitin' for me to take it. Den one mornin' I was so hungry dat I can't resist. I went straight in dere an' grab dat stick of candy an' stuffed it in my mouf an' chew it down quick.

Nex' mornin' ole Missus say, "Henrietta, you take dat piece o' candy out my room?' 'No, mam, ain't seed no candy. . . .' 'You lyin' an' I'm gonna whup you.' 'Please, Missus, please don't whup me. I ain't seed no candy.' Well, she got her rawhide . . . an' she grabbed me an' she try to run me 'cross her knees whilst she set in de rocker so's she could hol' me. I twisted an' turned till finally she called her daughter. De gal come an' took dat strap an' commence to lay it on real hard whilst Missus holt me. [But] I twisted 'way . . . so ole Missus lif' me up by de legs, an' she STUCK MY HAID UNDER DE BOTTOM OF HER ROCKER, AN' SHE ROCK FORWARD SO'S TO HOL' MY HAID AN' WHUP ME . . . NEAR A HOUR WID DAT ROCKER LEG A-PRESSIN' DOWN ON MY HAID [emphasis mine].

Seem like dat rocker pressin' on my young bones had crushed 'em all into soft pulp. De nex' day I couldn't open my mouf an' I feel it an' dey warn't no bone in de lef' side at all. An my mouf kep' a-slippin' over to de right side an' I couldn't chaw nothing—only drink milk. . . . Ain't never been able to chaw nothin' good since. Don't even 'member what it is to chaw. Been eatin' liquid, stews, an' soup ever since dat day, an' dat was eighty-six years ago.

Unfortunately, the Old South didn't die. It just metamorphosed, or maybe it had lost the right side of the jawbone of its civilization.

4

David Walker's Appeal, in Four Articles, Together with a Preamble to the Coloured Citizens of the World, but in Particular, and Very Expressly, to Those of the United States of America

*edited, and with an
introduction by Charles M. Wiltse*

New York: Hill and Wang, 1965

One of the most remarkable literary efforts to come out of the period before the Civil War, *David Walker's Appeal* is a slight volume of less than eighty pages written by a black man who was born free in Wilmington, North Carolina, in 1785. He moved to Boston by 1825 because he couldn't stand to live in the South and watch the day-to-day depravity of a society with "a Bible in one hand and a bull whip in the other."

Walker penned what was, to that date, the most uncompromising attack on slavery by anyone, black or white. It was such a departure from anything that had been attempted before that it was in the true sense of the word a shocker. Four Southern states called special sessions to consider what to do about *David Walker's Appeal.* Even in Boston, it was denounced as incendiary. But as the mayor of Boston pointed out to the governor of Georgia when the latter asked that the Appeal be banned and Walker extradited, there was nothing he could do, no law of either city or state had been broken. But, of course, there was something that the South could do, and did.

Walker was self-taught. His Appeal, which was divided into a preamble and four articles by the time it reached its third printing, is quite an accomplishment for a man who made his livelihood as a second-hand clothes dealer. It's filled with allusions to writers like Thomas Jefferson, Plutarch, Josephus; quotes from the Bible; and contains commentary on the murder of Julius Caesar, the defeat of Brutus and Cassius on the plains of Philippi, the overthrow of Constantinople by Sultan Mahomed II in 1453, and the Spartans enslaving the Helots. It includes references to Oliver Goldsmith's *History of Greece,* to Carthage and Haiti, to the comparative value of the Protestant vis-à-vis the Catholic faith, the natural rights of man, Ferdinand and Charles V of Spain, Las Casas, Butler's *History of the United States* (with volume references in the footnotes) and an etymological discussion of the word "Niger," beginning with its Latin roots. He discusses or quotes the first edition of *Freedom's Journal,* the first black newspaper published in America; a breakdown of the number of blacks in Georgia and South Carolina (and comparable figures for whites); William Penn, Demetrius, Diana, St. Paul, and John Randolph (the owner who had all his human "property" manumitted upon his death); the Declaration of Independence and the *Common Book of Prayer.*

But Walker wasn't labeled a purveyor of revolutionary thought because of his smattering of knowledge. The strength of his Appeal was its simple and direct message. The black man was being degraded. He had been left no choice. He had to fight back, and with all his might, to destroy the evil that was destroying him. Walker wrote:

Can our condition be any worse?— Can it be more mean and abject? Can they get us any lower?

The Indians of North and South America—the Greeks—the Irish . . . the Jews . . . the inhabitants of the islands of the sea—in fine, all the inhabitants of the earth (except . . . the sons of Africa) are called *men,* and of course are, and ought to be free. But we, (coloured people) and our children are *brutes!!* And of course are, and *ought* to be SLAVES to the American people and their children forever!! To dig their mines and work their farms; and thus go on enriching them from one generation to another with our *blood* and *our tears!!!!*

How would they like for us to make slaves of, and hold them in cruel slavery, and murder them as they do us?

Now, I ask you, had you not rather be killed than to be a slave to a tyrant, who takes the life of your mother, wife, and dear little children . . . and believe this, that it is no more harm for you to kill a man, who is trying to kill you, than it is for you to take a drink of water when thirsty.

Now, to white America, that was incendiary. Walker had printed the Appeal (all three editions) with his own money, and he had devised a rather unique distribution system. His business in second-hand clothes served mostly sailors. He would smuggle copies of his Appeal into the pockets of their jackets, which is how they would get into the South. It wasn't long before money was being offered for Walker's head. Friends urged him to get out of the country. He refused, and was poisoned in 1830, just weeks after the third edition appeared.

From Article I:

Has Mr. Jefferson declared to the world that we are inferior to the whites, both in the endowments of our bodies and our minds? It is indeed surprising, that a man of such great learning . . . should speak so of a set of men in chains.

O! that the coloured people . . . instead of courting favour with, and telling news and lies to our *natural enemies,* against each other—would refuse to work with them no matter how much gold they were offered. Would they be able to drag our mothers, our fathers, our wives, our children and ourselves, around the world in chains as they do?

Never make an attempt to gain our freedom or *natural right,* from under our cruel oppressors and murderers, until you see your way clear. We have just as much right to hold them and their children in slavery . . . as they have to hold us. When that hour arrives and you move, be not afraid or dismayed; for be you assured that Jesus Christ will surely go before you so that you may vanquish those enemies who have stolen our *rights,* who cannot conceive how God can show mercy to us because it pleased Him to make us black— which colour, Mr. Jefferson calls unfortunate! As though we are not as thankful to our God, for having made us as it pleased himself, as they, (the whites), are for having made them white.

[A] South Carolina paper . . . speaking of the barbarity of the Turks . . . said: "the Turks are the most barbarous people in the world—they treat the Greeks more like *brutes* than human beings." And in the same paper was an advertisement, which said: "Eight well built Virginia and Maryland *Negro fellows* and four *wenches* will positively be *sold* this day, *to the highest bidder!"*

[T]here is an unconquerable disposition in the breasts of the blacks, which, when it is fully awakened and put in motion, will [not] be subdued. . . . [I]f you commence . . . do not trifle, for they will not trifle with you . . . therefore, if there is an *attempt* made by us, kill or be killed. . . . Now, I ask you, had you not rather be killed than to be a slave to a tyrant, who takes the life of your mother, wife, and dear little children? Is not God a God of justice to all creatures?

The South denounced *David Walker's Appeal.* The North denounced it. Everyone *white* denounced it. But Henry Highland Garnet, the black abolitionist preacher who later became minister to Liberia, reissued the Appeal after Walker's death, so they killed the man but not the idea. Walker had crossed the line—the great divide that separated black from white. Slavery was a terrible thing, intoned the white abolitionists, but none of them supported the idea that slavery should be abolished *by any means necessary,* certainly not by violent ones. The need to have black people really equal was never so great that one drop of white blood should be shed to bring it about! Walker obviously disagreed. What was the American Revolution all about, he was asking, if not about destroying tyranny in the most expeditious way possible—by getting the fellow off your neck. And if slavery wasn't tyranny, then nothing was.

Echoes of Walker are heard by Frederick Douglass, who broke with the white-dominated Abolitionist Society on the issue of using violence as a means of destroying slavery. The logic for a violent solution to ending slavery is undeniable in the context of American history. John Brown, who did so apply it, has been consistently portrayed as a madman. (Jesse James and Billy the Kid are folk heroes, Bonnie and Clyde romantic icons, but John Brown is considered a psychopath!)

Given the American response to anyone taking arms to defend the African American from white violence, it was the most dangerous thing that either Walker or John Brown could have done. America poisoned one and hanged the other—quicker than anyone could say "All men are created . . ." It wasn't until the nineteen sixties that a call for "by any means necessary" was once again made, and made with enough force to be heard, to make people react either with horror or with "Right on!" It would take the eloquence of Malcolm X to bring that about.

5

William Styron's Nat Turner: Ten Black Writers Respond

edited by John Henrik Clarke

Boston: Beacon Press, 1968

When William Styron's novel *Confessions of Nat Turner* was published, it created a storm of controversy, especially since the white literary establishment embraced it so wholeheartedly.

If a distinguished black novelist wrote a biography of George Washington, changing the facts of his life and maligning his character by portraying him as a whimpering, deluded, sex-starved psychotic instead of the stalwart hero, the champion of the people in the face of an oppressive regime—imagine the reaction. The general feeling among the black literati is that such a book would have been ignored, ridiculed, or never have seen the light of day. Whatever the reaction, the book would hardly have garnered the accolades awarded to Styron's *Confessions of Nat Turner*.

I suppose one can make the argument that a brilliant writer can take history and turn it on its head, creating great literature in the process. Possibly. But no one makes that claim for Styron. Nor has anyone from the white literati been critical of the way he played fast and loose with the facts. His racism is theirs, apparently.

The first of the ten writers to respond to Styron's novel is the redoubtable Lerone Bennett (see Must-Read No. 18). He says, in part:

> According to the historical data, the real Nat Turner was a virile, commanding, courageous figure. Styron rejects history by rejecting this image of Nat Turner. In fact, he wages literary war on this image, substituting an impotent, cowardly, irresolute creature of his own imagination for the real black man who killed or ordered killed real white people for real historical reasons. The man Styron substitutes for Nat Turner is not only the antithesis of Nat Turner; he is the antithesis of blackness.
>
> We are not quibbling here over footnotes in scholarly journals. We are objecting to something insidious, more dangerous. *We are objecting to a deliberate attempt to steal the meaning of a man's life.* And that attempt must be condemned in the name of the man whose name has been illicitly appropriated for a dubious literary adventure.

Bennett goes on to point out that Styron is reviving the Black Sambo type—the grinning, bootlicking plantation darkie. The fact that this type existed doesn't mean he had anything to do with Nat Turner, unless it's a case of guilt by color. Bennett also criticizes Styron for stripping Turner of his grandmother and his father, both of whom were important influences in his life. Turner told Thomas Gray, the man who took down his original confession after Nat had been captured, that he was very attached to his grandmother and that his father and mother taught him how to read and write. Styron eliminates the grandmother and the father, leaving a single mother, what Bennett calls "a proper ADC slave family" (as in Aid to Dependent Children).

Of course, Styron may have eliminated the grandmother and the father for economy. Or he may simply have not wanted to write about them. Novelists take these liberties all the time. But when the result changes the face of the man, reduces him in stature, then one has to suspect that the motive is other than artistic license.

Bennett goes even further. He makes the point that Nat's mother was so opposed to slavery that she tried to *kill him* at birth rather than add one more slave to the American democracy. Stryon makes her over as a house-nigger type who reminds her son that as such they "is quality." And Styron recreates Turner as a slave who feels toward his old "marsa" the way "one should [feel] only toward the divinity." He adds insult to injury by having Nat loathe black people "as creatures beneath contempt," adding, "my black, shit-eating people were surely like flies, God's mindless outcasts, lacking even that will to destroy by their own hands their unending anguish." Bennett seems to be saying that if there is a good novel in there somewhere, it probably needs a car chase to make it work.

Vincent Harding's response, "You've Taken My Nat and Gone," begins with a quote from a Styron interview that appeared in *Newsweek.* Said Styron: "I want the book to exist on its own terms as an American tragedy. . . . And I certainly don't mean to indiscriminately glorify the figure of the Negro rebel against society today. . . . You can see Nat Turner as an archetypal American tragic hero, but this doesn't make Rap Brown an archetypal American hero, nor does it make what he is preaching capable of anything but disaster." By dissociating his protagonist from one of the angry young leaders of the Black Power movement of the sixties, Styron wants to make it very clear that not all black heroes are equal. Some are "tragic" like Nat Turner (because he fought fire with fire, one has to assume); others, like H. Rap Brown, are doomed to disaster (one must go on assumption again) because they were trying to get the system to work for them and their kin, from within if possible, but work nevertheless.

John Killens and John A. Williams, both well-known authors in their own right, discuss Styron's style. Killens sums it up best when he writes: "What about the quality of the writing? . . . It is inspired, in spots, dull and repetitious oftentimes, tiresome even, jumping back and forth in time and space. And, in terms of getting into the slave's psyche and his idiom, it is a monumental failure. Then there was this contradiction of Nat, himself, sometimes thinking and speaking in biblical or Victorian English and at other times lapsing into an Amos-and-Andy dialect."

Ernest Kaiser, the longtime librarian emeritus of the Schom-

burg Center for Research in Black Culture, in Harlem, provides a
comprehensive response to the novel that covers many of the
racist views of white writers, from whom Styron drew inspiration,
and discusses Styron's earlier works. Then Kaiser adds:

> When Styron comes to write his fourth novel, *The Confessions . . .*
> which has haunted him since 1948, his talent really deteriorates
> and goes down hill. . . . He had read all of the works on Nat
> Turner and slave rebellions and rejected them. [The] novel is a
> witches' brew of Freudian psychology, [the] "Sambo" thesis on
> slavery and Styron's vile racist imagination that makes especially
> Will and Nat Turner animals and monsters. Styron has to rational-
> ize the oppression of [blacks] one way or another. . . . Having re-
> jected the Negro people's history, Styron cannot see Turner as the
> hero he was and as the [black] people see him; as a slave who led a
> heroic rebellion against the dehumanization of chattel slavery. This
> novel makes Styron look like a Rip Van Winkle who has slept
> through the Negro people's twelve-year struggle of the 1950s and
> 1960s.

Destroying black heroes under the guise of creative license
serves the needs of neither white nor black America, as these writers make perfectly clear. If the strength and pride that the black
man had throughout his long ordeal in America makes white
America uneasy about its role in that ordeal, when there is no
longer a need to deny the past, there will no longer be a need to
castigate black heroes such as Nat Turner. Yes, he did kill sixty
white men, women, and children in the space of two days. Yes, he
started out with just seven men and the group swelled to fifty. Yes,
they did desert him after their first loss, but before they did, he
vanquished at least one organized white attack. Yes, he was captured and beaten and eventually hanged. Yes, over one hundred
black people were killed that same day. And yes, Thomas Gray
wrote at the end of Turner's confession: "I looked at him, and my
blood froze in my veins." So what? Is that one effort, balanced
against the millions of black lives that the American democracy
destroyed in slavery and out enough to create panic 175 years later?
If so, the black man can never redeem his manhood.

6

THE TRAVELS OF
WILLIAM WELLS BROWN

by William Wells Brown,
edited by Paul Jefferson

NEW YORK: M. WEINER PUBLISHING, 1991

William Wells Brown was *the* black writer of the nineteenth century. He was an excellent stylist, equally at home writing fiction, nonfiction, and drama. He wrote a narrative of his life as a fugitive slave, a novel, three plays (two of which are extant), a travel book, a history of the black race, an account of the black contribution to the American Revolution, essays, reviews, and slave songs. He not only wrote the first novel by an African American, *Clotel; or, The President's Daughter,* but the first play, *The Escape; or, A Leap for Freedom.* (The "first novel" claim has a footnote to it. *Clotel* was published in 1853, in England originally, so it wasn't the first novel published in America by an African American; that distinction goes to *Our Nig* by Harriet Wilson.) His *Narrative* is included in the Jefferson edition of *The Travels of William Wells Brown* as is *The American Fugitive in Europe* (with deletions), but not Brown's novel or the plays.

Brown has not been given his due as a writer. Like Douglass, his prose is marked by intelligence and restraint and an accuracy that was rarely matched by other American writers of the day, white or black. Both his novel and his plays show him capable of creating memorable characters. *The Escape* is a brilliant dramatic satire of both slavery and the manners of the era, and the novel is an eminently readable story of one of Thomas Jefferson's daughters, who was born while he was in the White House, the issue of one of his many trysts with his female slaves. Jefferson sold both mother and daughter to more slave horrors in the cotton states, where they were separated.

Brown published the novel while he was in London. Editions that came out after his return to America were toned down. Writes Arthur P. Davis in his introduction to *Clotel,* as published by Collier: "In subsequent versions . . . Brown softened or eliminated entirely the Jefferson connection. In this original edition, however, he reflects the hostile attitude toward Jefferson held by the antislavery forces, particularly the Negroes. Jefferson had much to answer for: He fathered a large number of slave children; he spoke contemptuously of Phillis Wheatley's poetry; he stated in *Notes on Virginia* that he found the Negro inferior in body and mind."

Brown's mother was a field hand; his father, a relative of his owner, was white. He had five brothers and a sister. He was the youngest. The first whipping he remembers his mother getting remained etched in his memory for the rest of his life. As he relates in chapter 1 of the *Narrative*:

> My mother was . . . one morning . . . ten or fifteen minutes behind the others in getting into the field. As soon as she reached the spot where they were at work, the overseer commenced whipping her. She cried, "Oh. Pray—Oh! Pray—Oh! pray. . . . I could hear every crack of the whip, and every groan and cry of my poor mother. . . . The cold chills ran over me and I wept aloud.

When he was fifteen, Brown was hired out and treated so badly that he tried to run away. He was caught, brought back, brutally whipped, and put into a smokehouse with a fire made from tobacco stems burning near him and left there as punishment. Two of his brothers died early on, and two were eventually sold. Brown never saw them again. Both his mother and his sister were sold to the New Orleans slave markets, and he would never see either of them again.

In 1832, when he was eighteen, he was hired to a slave trader named Walker, whom he later made into a character in his play *The Escape*. The trader not only sold the children he sired by his slave women, along with the women themselves, but sometimes he even separated mother from child for the most trivial of reasons. Brown tells of one such incident. One of the women on the coffle had a baby four or five weeks old. The mother couldn't stop the baby from crying, so one morning Walker made a gift of the child to the woman in whose house he had spent the previous night and continued on with the mother and the rest.

On January 1, 1834, Brown managed to escape from a steamboat in Cincinnati and made it all the way to Buffalo, New York. There he became active in the Underground Railroad and as a speaker for the abolitionist movement. Because he had been forced to work in the slave trade, he was able to provide insight into an aspect of slavery that none of the other escaped slaves knew firsthand.

Indeed, Brown was such an asset to the abolitionists that he was sent to Europe in 1849 as an official delegate to the Paris Peace Conference, chaired by Victor Hugo. He held the world stage for an illustrious moment and created an international sensation by declaring, in front of the eight hundred delegates, twenty from America, that abolishing slavery would be a giant step toward abolishing the spirit of war, since slavery as practiced in America created a ceaseless state of war between master and slave. He also took Thomas Carlyle to task for declaring that the blacks of the West Indies should be whipped if they refused to raise sugar and cotton of their own free will.

Even though the trip to Europe was a wonderful experience for Brown, he knew that, in the final analysis, he could not abandon either his people's fight for emancipation or the land of his birth. He writes in *The American Fugitive in Europe*:

> I took passage in the steamship *Canada*... bound for Liverpool.... As we were passing out of Boston Bay, I took my ... last farewell ... of

my native land. . . . From the treatment that I had received . . . as a victim of slavery, and the knowledge that I was at that time liable to be seized and again reduced to whips and chains, I had supposed that I would leave the country without any regret; but in this I was mistaken for when I saw the last thread of communication cut off between me and the land, and the dim shores dying away in the distance, I almost regretted that I was not on shore.

Brown had this to say about the effect of being on English soil:

The prejudice which I have experienced on all and every occasion in the United States . . . vanished as soon as I set foot on the soil of Britain. . . . I was recognized as a man, and an equal. The very dogs in the streets appeared conscious of my manhood. Such is the difference, and such is the change that is brought about by a trip of nine days in an Atlantic steamer.

But no matter how much a sense of emancipation endeared Brown to England and the Continent, his artistic innards always belonged to his native soil and the fight for abolition that he, as a man of courage, had no choice but to join, heart and soul.

In addition to the Jefferson edition of *The Travels of William Wells Brown* there is an exhaustive though condescending biography of Brown by William Farrison. Farrison is almost academically anal, spreading his sics over every quote from Brown like so much weed killer, in a constant attempt to prove that he can spell words like Cleveland. But for the Brown enthusiast, it's worth wading through for the abundance of information about his life. William Wells Brown should be studied in every college course on nineteenth-century American literature. In addition to all of his other accomplishments, he was a barber, owned a bank in the West, and was a licensed doctor in the state of Massachusetts. He died in 1884.

Books 7 through 16:

THAT ALL SHALL BE FREE

---

*S*LAVERY FINALLY BECAME a national issue in the 1850s, catching the attention of the nation at large for the first time. John Brown, the Dred Scott decision, but probably most important of all *Uncle Tom's Cabin,* all helped create the new awareness.

Until then, practically nothing that black men had done (unless you give Dred Scott credit for the Supreme Court's decision against him, which wouldn't be totally inaccurate) had had anything but a parochial effect. The major slave rebellions were suppressed, as was the fact that they even happened. *David Walker's Appeal,* James Forten and Absalom Jones's petition to Congress, none of these had a nationwide impact.

One reason, and it still operates as a dynamic today, is that unless somebody white says or does it, no one cares or listens. Oh, there are exceptions, but these only prove the rule, since once the initial reaction has subsided, it's back to business as usual—which means white business. Blacks were a nonexistent class, psychologically, to be disposed of the way the Native American was. They were free labor, nothing more.

When Harriet Beecher Stowe wrote *Uncle Tom's Cabin,* about a poor suffering black man who was mistreated by a sadistic overseer, it inexplicably struck a chord. Like the millions of "good" Germans who almost a century later knew about the atrocities Hitler was committing, who saw Jewish shops vandalized and Jews beaten in the streets, heard about the concentration camps, even knew some specifics from relatives and friends who either worked in them or knew someone who did, yet didn't respond with righteous outrage or horror, so too America in the first half of the nineteenth century reacted to slavery as one might to a "minor" domestic disturbance. The transportation of black people, chained to a log and dragged endlessly through the countryside; the runaways who showed up at their back door in the middle of the night begging for food; the huge slave marts that did business in broad daylight in Charleston and New Orleans, just to mention two cities; the fortunes made in the slave trade, with slave ships coming and going continuously—none of this aroused the national consciousness.

Maybe, like the good Germans, many Americans made the excuse "I didn't really know how bad it was." Maybe being immigrants themselves was their excuse. Four million white immigrants came to America between 1830 and 1860. Many of them went to states such as Ohio, Indiana, Illinois, New York, Pennsylvania, and Massachusetts. They too wanted their share of the American Dream. Many of them had fled famines in Europe and Ireland, starvation in the streets, a hidebound Old World society with a caste system that would forever condemn them to the lowest rank of society if they stayed. What an ecstasy of abundant opportunity this New World must have seemed to them. The color of their skin would allow them to go anywhere and do anything with no regard for who their father or grandfather had been. A whole new world was there, literally, for the taking. All a man had to do was find the strength to go out and take it.

But there was one taboo. If the black man, whom they found when they arrived in the New World, was allowed to climb up the ladder, then that might well leave them at the bottom. And since the people who ran the country, the ones with whom they were trying to ingratiate themselves, had relegated the black man to the bottom rung, how could they, strangers in a new land, trying to establish themselves, grateful for the opportunity that American democracy was giving them, show ingratitude by in any way contravening the taboo?

No. The black man must stay at the bottom. Not only because that was a moré of the new, wonderful society that they had just been allowed to join, but also because their economic survival dictated it. There wasn't room for the black worker who knew the country better than they did and who had skills that they had yet to acquire if they were going to make it in this new land. It was a great country, but there wasn't that much of it to go around. Not yet anyway. And there probably never would be.

But immigrant and old American stock alike, they flocked to *Uncle Tom's Cabin,* both the novel and the play, like geese to the call of cackle. It was an amazing phenomenon: the book sold so many copies that it outsold every other book except the Bible. Howard Mumford Jones dubbed it, in his preface to the 1969 Merrill edition, "the greatest single fictional success of the American nineteenth century, one of the greatest fictional successes the modern world has ever seen." It sold half a million copies in the first five years and was translated into at least twenty-three languages. Everyone's heard of it a hundred years later, the lettered and the unlettered, the foreigner and the native. And as a play, it had an even more amazing career. There were so many translations to the stage, which resulted in so many productions in so many cities for so many years, that entire families were supported solely by performing a "Tom Show," as they came to be known. The first production of the play was at Howard's Theater in Troy, New York, in 1852. It was seen on Broadway in a revival as late as 1933. Now that's a long run! A musical version, *Deep River,* opened on Broadway in 1936. And it was made into a film at least four times, from the earliest days of the silents to the 1970s. Otis Skinner, in a Players Club production (carriage trade all the way), exhumed the Uncle in black face on Broadway at the Alvin Theatre and got good reviews in the 1933 production. One critic (the venerable Percy Hammond, who reviewed for the *Herald Tribune* at the time) said "the old idol glowed with a surprising luster."

Uncle Tom's Cabin was responsible for the long run, the single bill, and matinees, just to name a few of the staples of modern theater that it spawned. Some managers put on " 'Double Tom Shows' with two of everything—from two Toms to two Evas." But blacks never played any of the major parts (except for Topsy, of course), not even Uncle Tom—with the single exception of Sam Lucas in the nineteenth century.

One critic (the Southerner Stark Young) even said the mulatto parts had to be played by white actors because the characters had "the nervous system of white men"! That's a quote from one of his reviews in the *New Republic.*

America wasn't coming to grips with the sadism, the genocide, the indignity visited on four million black Americans except in terms that were convenient. To the nation at large, "fact was right," in the words of the seventeenth-century Dutch lawyer Hugo Grotius, that bête noire of Jean-Jacques Rousseau's assault on slavery.

As a consequence, there was no real human response to the holocaust within, certainly nothing that would actually break the chains of slavery. Abraham Lincoln and the North went to war to save the Union. The South went to war because slavery's hegemony was slowly being eroded with each new territory that became a free state.

Rather than sit by and see itself slip permanently into second place, the South decided that a permanent solution was the only way to reverse the trend. Before the war began, Alexander Stephens, who later became vice president of the Confederacy, warned his fellow Southerners that they had no legal argument to make in going to war. Andrew Jackson had already faced down John Calhoun on nullification, and the South was overrepresented in Congress, in the courts, and in government patronage. But the same arrogance that demanded a permanent slave class as part of the body politic also wanted complete parity with the rest of the country for its slavery.

George McClellan, one of Lincoln's early generals, whose great strength as a military commander was his ability to beat a fast retreat, made it very plain that if he caught any runaways, he'd return them forthwith to their *mastahs*. And Lincoln's solution to the race problem was to ship black people, wholesale, back to Africa. He convinced Congress to give him $600,000 to get the mass migration off the ground with millions more to come if all went well with his permanent solution.

"Malice toward none, and charity for all" meant malice toward none who were white, even if they had just tried to rip the nation apart. Proof of that was the Black Codes which sprang up all over the South in the first two years following the war's end, thanks to Lincoln's refusal to call any of the treasonous millions to account. If Lincoln had not been killed by Booth, the Republican Party, even with Sumner and Stevens leading, would probably not have been able to pass the Fourteenth and Fifteenth Amendments, which helped solidify the Northern victory and put the army in charge of the former Confederacy.

From the time the Federal government forced the South to let black men into the political process, in 1867, until they made the deal that led to the withdrawal of Federal troops a decade later, it was not business as usual. Instead of "malice toward none" there was plenty of malice, but for the first and only time, the playing field was level. And the fight was for men's minds, not to destroy them physically in order to break their spirit. And there was no charity for all, save what could be gained through the hard-fought battles of politics, American style. No one black was killed or burned out or lynched just for showing up at a meeting or to vote—all of which did happen once Reconstruction ended.

7

The Dred Scott Case:
Its Significance in American Law
and Politics

by Don E. Fehrenbacher

New York: Oxford University Press, 1978

To say that the Supreme Court violated the Constitution seems like a contradiction in terms. Yet this was certainly the case with the *Dred Scott* decision, which was named one of the five most important rulings in the entire history of the court by lawyers, judges, and law professors in a 1974 survey conducted by the *American Law Review,* the bible of the legal profession. What the decision said, or, more accurately, what Chief Justice Roger B. Taney, who wrote and read the majority opinion, said, was "the legal status of black people throughout the civilized world, at the time of the adoption of the Constitution, was so nonexistent, so far inferior, that the Negro (not that there should be surprise) had no rights which the white man was bound to respect." The South objected violently to this statement, supposedly out of context, since Taney first made it in 1839 and was making it again in relation to blacks at the time of the founding of the Republic. But since he was making the same argument as the basis for taking away black citizenship in 1857, it hardly matters when it was first uttered. Indeed, it might make it even more important since it shows the chief justice's previous state of mind: that is, that he was a racist throughout his life.

What Taney was trying to do was solve the slavery question all by himself. By the 1850s that question had threatened to tear the nation apart. Taney and his like-minded brethren thought that by coming down unilaterally on the side of the South, the North and the black man himself (Dred Scott and all the other Dred Scotts) would have no recourse but to acquiesce in the decision. It was an almost absurd miscalculation.

That Taney's decision brought disgrace on the Supreme Court there can be little doubt. Charles Evens Hughes called it "a self-inflicted wound," and Felix Frankfurter said the decision was never mentioned by members of the court after the Civil War "any more than ropes and scaffolds were ever mentioned in a family that had lost one of its number to the hangman." It was ignored the minute any legal, or even quasi-legal, transaction took place in which a white person, in a public or private capacity, accepted the rights of a black. And, of course, that happened in dozens of incidents throughout the nation, almost before the ink was dry on the document. For example, Connecticut immediately passed a law declaring that any slave who was brought into the state would be freed at once and went on to make blacks citizens of the state in unequivocal terms.

Taney, who came from slaveholding Maryland and had owned slaves himself, was eighty when he took on this legalistic gambit, trying to create a law where it didn't exist and certainly going far beyond the bounds of judicial review in the process. But he was encouraged by forces even more powerful than himself. The president, James Buchanan, had written a letter to one of the members of the court, arguing a pro-South decision after another member of the court had asked him to do so! Buchanan probably even saw a draft of the opinion before it was read in court, which allowed him to state in his inaugural address of 1857 that he expected the Supreme Court to rule on the slavery question soon and that "to their decision . . . I cheerfully submit, whatever this may be." Since everyone knew where Buchanan's sympathies lay, it wasn't hard to guess what he expected that decision to be. And prior knowledge of the ruling on Buchanan's part, of course, violated the ethics if not the rules of the Supreme Court.

Buchanan belonged to a wing of the Democratic Party that not only wanted to extend slavery within the territorial boundaries of the United States, but had its eyes on Cuba, all or a great portion of Mexico, and Nicaragua as well, either as states or territories in which slavery could be expanded. The idea of extending slavery to the Caribbean was so popular in the South during the eleven years that Dred Scott was trying to obtain his freedom through legal means, that entire books have been written about it. One such work, *The Southern Dream of a Caribbean Empire,* by Robert E. May, makes the point that the enthusiasm reached such effusive heights that it became erotic at times. Quoting from the *Congressional Globe of the 35th Congress,* May offers this bit of erotic enthusiasm for the tropics as a perfect paradise for slavery. "[Cuba] admires Uncle Sam, and he loves her. Who shall forbid the bans? Matches are made in heaven, and why not this? Who can object if he throws his arms around the Queen of the Antilles, as she sits, like Cleopatra's burning throne, upon the silver waves, breathing her spicy, tropic breath, and pouting her rosy, sugared lips?"

Franklin Pierce, who preceded Buchanan in the presidency, wanted to go to war with Spain when he heard that Spain planned on abolishing slavery in Cuba. He said he wouldn't allow Spain to create a "bad neighborhood" in the Americas by outlawing slavery. If Spain did, the "day of retributive justice must soon arrive. . . . The United States would not tolerate Negro rule in Cuba."

The Supreme Court decision against Dred Scott was seven to two, but only ostensibly. The court was deciding at least three distinctly different issues at the same time: (a) a black man's right to gain his freedom irrevocably by having lived in a free state, even if he subsequently returned to a state where slavery was legal; (b) whether or not blacks were eligible to become citizens of the United States; and (c) Congress's right to legislate for the territories, which in turn opened the door for a ruling on the constitutionality of the Missouri Compromise. Serious confusion occurred as to who was voting for what because the ruling didn't clearly indicate the conflicting opinions when each issue was considered separately.

Don E. Fehrenbacher, in his excellent study of the *Dred Scott* case, which won him a Pulitzer Prize, gives the box score version of what was, or more accurately what wasn't, decided, based on the actual opinions of the individual judges. According to him only four judges accepted jurisdiction for the case. That meant that a majority of the court didn't even think that the case should be before them. And when the final verdict was handed down, only three judges said that a black could not be a citizen.

Taney had to replace one of the judges in order to get the opinion to come out the way he wanted, and in doing so, he wrote an opinion that did not reflect the supposed seven-to-two opinion of the majority. The judge who was to have written that opinion originally, Samuel Nelson, waffled on the issue of jurisdiction, which would have made it rather difficult to proceed to any of the other issues, thus robbing Taney of his chance to invalidate the Missouri Compromise and in so doing, take away the right of black men to citizenship. So Taney replaced Nelson and *he* wrote the opinion.

But the confusion of the court, once they explored the merits of the case, was deep indeed. If only two judges thought that a black could not become a citizen, but seven thought that Missouri slave law should take precedent over Illinois or Minnesota free law, then not everyone who was willing to argue against Dred Scott's freedom wanted to take away the citizenship rights of all the blacks in the country. Taney's statement that the black man "had no rights that the white man had to respect" therefore went beyond what the majority of the court was willing to agree to.

Not only did Taney's opinion ignore this dissent, but he refused to release a copy of the opinion to the public for three months after he delivered it. Everyone sat in the courtroom while Taney droned on for over two hours, his voice almost inaudible toward the end. Judge Benjamin Robbins Curtis, one of the two dissenters, went public forthwith with a scathing dissent, putting Taney on the defensive. Taney decided to rewrite his own opinion before making it available to the public, even though it was now officially federal law. Fehrenbacher points out that Taney did so much rewriting of the opinion *after* he had read it in court that it was twice as long as the original by the time it did get into print three months later.

According to Taney not only didn't Congress have the right to pass *any* laws prohibiting slavery anywhere, since it had been guaranteed in the Constitution, but even if Congress wanted to grant the black man rights, they couldn't, since under the Constitution's definition of citizenship, the black man didn't qualify as a citizen, since he was only three-fifths of a man. However, Fehrenbacher points out there was no language in the Constitution to sustain Taney's decision. Taney had tried to create a *special* class of person who was entitled to citizenship. He called these the "sovereign people." Writes Fehrenbacher:

> [T]o be a citizen, said the Chief Justice, was the same thing as being one of the "sovereign people" of the United States, and at the time of the Constitutional Convention [blacks] had not been regarded as "constituent members of this sovereignty . . . whether emancipated or not." Before the adoption of the Constitution [he stated] every state had the right to "confer on whomsoever it pleased the character of citizen." But this character "was confined to the boundaries of the State, and gave him no rights or privileges in other States beyond those secured to him by the laws of nations and the comity of States." Somehow, in writing these mistaken words, Taney had managed to overlook the fourth article of Confederation, which declares: "The free inhabitants of each of these states (paupers, vagabonds and fugitives from justice excepted) shall be entitled to all privileges and immunities of free citizens in the several states."

Consequently, any black person who was a citizen of any state in the Union at the time of the ruling could not be excluded from Taney's sovereign-people club, at least not legally. Blacks were by then exercising the franchise on a par with whites in a least five states in the North: Maine, Massachusetts, New Hampshire, Rhode Island, and Vermont. And free blacks throughout the South could make contracts and own property even if they couldn't vote. That they were doing both is attested to abundantly by the wealth accumulated by black men such as Thomy Lafon and Cyprian Ricaud in New Orleans. The former has been called the richest black man in the antebellum South. He had a personal fortune of over half a million dollars in real estate. And Ricaud bought an estate worth $225,000 in 1851 that came with ninety-one slaves. Both men were certainly exercising citizenship rights in terms of residency, property owned, and contracts signed, all executed and legally certified.

The clearest rebuke to Taney came in August 1861, while he was still the chief justice, when the State Department issued a passport to the black minister and abolitionist leader Henry Highland Garnet. The passport stated quite simply that Garnet was a "citizen of the United States." While blacks could not become a sovereign people in Taney's order of things, corporations could, since the other constitutional basis for citizenship was the diverse-citizenship clause (Article III, Section 2), which gave citizens the right to sue not only other citizens of the same or other states, but the states themselves by giving them access to the federal courts.

Fehrenbacher challenges Taney's sovereign-people concept on strictly constitutional grounds: "[If Taney's citizenship was to mean] those active partners in a sovereign community who possessed all its civil and political rights and privileges . . . [then the] definition, strictly applied in the early nineteenth century, would have excluded not only women, children, and most free [blacks], but also many white male adults who could not meet religious and property-holding qualifications for voting." In his zealot's compulsion to exclude the black man from citizenship, Taney was within a millimeter of dismembering the body politic by excluding everybody who wasn't free, white, male, and a property owner. "In very strictest terms, it would also have excluded naturalized citizens," says Fehrenbacher.

Taney hopelessly confused the issue with the following explanation of a citizen's right and privileges by stating that while he may be a citizen of one state, that doesn't necessarily mean he's a citizen of every state. "It would be difficult," writes Fehrenbacher, "to formulate a more categorical contradiction of a specific clause of the Constitution . . . the one that declares: 'The citizens of each state shall be entitled to all privileges and immunities of citizens in the several states.' Before the adoption of the Constitution, Taney [said] every state had the right, 'to confer on whomever it pleased the character of a citizen.' But this character 'was confined to the boundaries of the State, and gave him no rights or privileges in other States.' "

If this is so, Fehrenbacher asks, then "What changes were wrought by the adoption of the Constitution?" And he gives Taney's answer: "None, as far as the rights of a state were concerned. It could still confer citizenship upon any class of person, even an alien. Yet he would not be a citizen in the sense in which that word is used in the Constitution of the United States, nor entitled to sue as such in one of its courts, nor to the privileges and immunities of a citizen in the other States. The rights which he would acquire would be restricted to the State which gave them."

How the rest of the country was going to function, since there were no citizens who had rights outside of their own states and none who could bring suit in federal court, was something that didn't seem to bother the chief justice. If he threw the baby out with the bath water, that was the baby's problem, not his. He was there to protect slavery, and protect it he would, come hell or high water or the Constitution. It was an astonishing performance, made even more astonishing because it was the first time in the history of the country that the court had used judicial review to declare a law of Congress illegal.

One more example of Taney's judicial absurdities will prove that his ruling attempted to create law where law didn't exist. In discussing the limits of naturalization, the chief justice insisted that it extended only "to persons born in a foreign country under a foreign government." Says Fehrenbacher of that section of the ruling:

Taney . . . had already excepted the Indians from this dictum. They could be "naturalized," while neither the states nor the federal government could confer citizenship on [blacks] "within the meaning of the Constitution." At the same time, no category of

foreigners, including black foreigners, was constitutionally incapable of being naturalized. *What this meant, though Taney never ex-
plicitly said so, was that* [Fehrenbacher's italics] *American [blacks],
free and slave, were the only people on the face of the earth who (saving
a constitutional amendment) were forever ineligible for American citizenship.*

Fehrenbacher concludes: "Taney's opinion . . . proves to be a
work of unmitigated partisanship, polemical in spirit . . . more
like an ultimatum that a formula for sectional accommodation
[between North and South]. Peace on Taney's terms resembled
the peace implicit in a demand for unconditional surrender." And
Fehrenbacher is by no means partisan. He apologizes for Taney
throughout his exhaustive study, which runs to over seven hundred pages. But he doesn't allow his reverence for a man whom
he says should be judged for a lifetime of work and not for ONE
decision to prevent him from using Taney's own words and reasoning in making Taney out to be a judicial ass.

In Dred Scott Decision: Law or Politics (Boston, 1967), Stanley
Kutler quotes a senator from Iowa who in 1887 had this to say
about the *Dred Scott* case and the Court's performance in it:

> When some future Tacitus shall record our annals, it will be diffi-
> cult for him to explain to the student of our government how it
> was possible for . . . [slavery] to attain such proportions under a
> free constitution, and such mastery over a free people; and espe-
> cially will he wonder by what process of alluring sophistry this
> [Supreme Court] . . . could have its eyes so dazed, and its intellect
> so blurred, as to seek to enthrone in the constitution the spirit of
> slavery, where the spirit of liberty had dwelt before.

Well, the senator, god bless him, should have extended the
question to cover the Supreme Court for the next sixty-seven
years, because the spirit of slavery that he talks about didn't die
when Roger B. Taney did. Not only were two of the seven men
who voted with Taney in the *Dred Scott* decision left to influence
the court after Appomattox (Samuel Nelson, a New York
Democrat, and Robert Grier, a Pennsylvania Democrat), but
Taney's racist philosophy itself survived. The odious, inhumane,

totally nonegalitarian, nondemocratic findings of that decision were cited throughout the rest of the nineteenth century and into the twentieth, reinforcing the gospel according to Roger B. Taney's hate.

Taney, whose pride didn't keep him from administering the oath of office to President Lincoln, said he wouldn't have administered it if William Henry Seward had been elected. In any event, he became a dead letter for the last four years of his life. Lincoln ignored him for the most part, and no one in Lincoln's administration even bothered to answer the chief justice's correspondence. He tried to get a fellow Marylander, who was engaged in treasonous activities during the war, released from jail (*Ex-parte Merryman,* it's an often cited case), but he was ignored by both Lincoln and the military.

In a letter written to an admirer after rendering his infamous decision, Taney offered this close observation of the Negro, which is quoted in Fehrenbacher: "[They are a] weak and credulous race . . . whose life in slavery was 'usually cheerful and contented,' and for whom a general and sudden emancipation would mean 'absolute ruin.'" Many slaves had been freed in Maryland, Taney wrote. "And in the greater number of cases that have come under my observation, freedom has been a serious misfortune to [them]." But Taney had freed his own slaves thirty years earlier and had this to say about their performance in freedom: "I am glad to say that none of those whom I manumitted disappointed my expectations, but have shown by their conduct that they were worthy of freedom, and know how to use it." Fehrenbacher then goes on to say, "If Taney noticed the glaring discrepancy in his words, he offered no explanation of it."

Of course he didn't, he was too far gone.

But he had been chief justice of the United States of America, and as such, he had to be rehabilitated for history's sake. Fehrenbacher notes that Taney has been discovered posthumously not to have really been against slavery! This benighted view of slavery's staunchest judicial ally begins with Charles Evans Hughes in the thirties, who called him a "great Chief Justice," and continues with Carl Swisher's biography in 1935, followed by Charles Smith's in 1936, who said Taney "regarded slavery as an evil institution." In 1971 Robert Spector gave that dictum an imaginative twist: "From the standpoint of morality he hated slavery as much as any abolitionist." But Fehrenbacher concludes these citations by saying "[Taney's] attitude on the bench was consistently and solicitously proslavery. By 1857 he had become as resolute in his determination to protect [it] as [the abolitionists were] in [their] determination to destroy it."

In the end, Taney became a pitiable figure as he wandered back and forth through the streets of Washington. The highest jurist in the land, he had become, simply, a ghost of slavery past. An entire race of people would have to travel through an orgy of violence and brutality once the war was over because those who had lost the war—the unregenerate progenitors of the Confederacy who lived on—had to have their revenge through blood lust.

Did Taney help to create the idea that a people, because they were black, could never gather the fruits of what force of arms and the law of the land had supposedly given them? Were black men, women, and children being slaughtered in the streets of the South in broad daylight, in genocidal proportions, by the end of the century because of the legacy that he tried to create? Did he manage to hand the sons and daughters of the Republic, America's future, a tradition of racism from which they would never be free? Was all of it, everything that came afterward, his fault? Of course not. But he helped.

8

HARRIET TUBMAN: CONDUCTOR ON THE UNDERGROUND RAILROAD

by Ann Petry

NEW YORK: CROWELL, 1955

Ann Petry, whose novel *The Street* became an instant classic when it was published in 1946, has done a wonderful job of recreating the legendary life of a legendary heroine. Harriet Tubman could neither read nor write, she was barely five feet tall and had a terrible scar on her forehead, but she managed to escape from slavery on the eastern shore of Maryland, at the age of twenty-nine, and returned at least nineteen times to lead three hundred of her people to freedom as well. Most of them she led herself, some she told how to do it. She became such a force that the South put a bounty of sixty thousand dollars (in 1862 money) on her head. No one ever collected.

There's a paucity of good books on Tubman. No first-rate historian has seen fit to do her justice. Maybe it's because her life reads like an escape novel or an old-time Hollywood movie. Although Petry's book is listed officially as a young adult biography, it's not. Not only is the book well researched, but Petry has given us the only readable work on the life of this great black American woman. It is not a novelization; it is a retelling, beautiful in its simplicity. Petry writes in such clear but compelling prose that we come away with a sense of the emotional beat of Harriet Tubman's life.

Tubman escaped in the summer of 1849. This was a time when America sold its soul for a cross of gold, even though William Jennings Bryan didn't make the expression famous until half a century later. True, there were white conductors of the Underground Railroad who gave their lives to see to it that black people were able to trickle out of slavery four or five at a time, but their contributions were not a national mandate. The mandate was better represented by Henry Clay, who importuned the Canadian government to send back all the "black gold" that it was allowing to live in freedom; by the arresting of several of Syracuse's leading citizens for "constructive insurrection" when they held a public meeting to oppose slavery; and by a group of two thousand of Boston's finest citizens who attacked an abolitionist meeting and almost lynched its leader, William Lloyd Garrison. Never mind the South.

Of course there were acts of heroism by many American citizens other than those actively involved in the Underground Railroad: in large numbers, in concert, and in public. But they represented a very distinct minority. Everyone knew that the horror of slavery was growing and everyone knew that it was immoral. Everyone knew that it violated the principles on which the country had been founded. But everyone who counted also knew that, because they were white, they need never worry about joining the wretched of the earth in their struggle to find life, liberty, and the pursuit of happiness.

Tubman becomes a huge symbol in that context since she illustrates all too clearly the monumental courage needed by anyone in America who wanted to take on the impossible task of fighting to rid the country of its racist, enslaving institutions in the nineteenth century. As Petry tells us, she started out by going back to Maryland to get her brothers and their families out. To finance each trip, she would work for almost a year as a maid in places like Cape May, New Jersey. Two years after she escaped, she went back for her husband who had turned against her before she even left because he was free, and it didn't bother him that she wasn't. He had his little warm cabin, could come and go as he pleased, and a wife who might be sold at any time, thus freeing him to get another one and another. When Tubman went back for him, she found that she had already been replaced. Having come that far for nothing—this was 1851—she decided to start rescuing strangers. And that's how her personal crusade became a public one.

Tubman's fight against slavery was so brilliant, so daring, so successful that it has given generations of African Americans something to point to with pride. In the land of "take what you're strong enough and bold enough to," her "taking" was an assault on the inhumanity of slavery, for which there was no other answer. That's why the South ended up offering sixty thousand dollars for her head. She threatened the billions of dollars that the South owned in human property. And yet, as huge as that sum was, it would never have grown to such an enormous amount if the property had been white. The economic reason was immense, but by itself it would not have won over the popular will, would not have become a mandate if the flesh had not been the unwilling victims of the African Diaspora.

Petry's book describes this little woman, returning again and again to the slave states, often, and incredibly, to the very plantation that she escaped from. As Petry describes, when she arrived, she called out in her husky but melodious voice, "Go Down Moses." And a cry from the slave quarters replied, "She's come back. She's here. We're ready to go."

Some of the slaves who went with her often wished they hadn't. She would fall asleep without notice, in broad daylight by the side of the road; recurring blackouts from a blow to the head that she received years before from an overseer who hit her with a two-pound iron weight. Her passengers couldn't go on without her because they didn't know where to go. (The railroad's routes had to be protected from would-be informers and spies, so they were a closely guarded secret.) Tubman would wake up as mysteriously as she'd fallen asleep, and the journey would continue.

And 135 years later, we have something to look back on other than words and speeches and failed attempts at rebellion, we have Harriet. She staked out her terrain, laid down the rules by which she would fight fire with fire and water. And she beat them all, all five feet of her. Before she was through, Tubman even rescued her mother and father. They were too old to make the journey on foot by the time she was ready to make the attempt, but that didn't stop Harriet. She simply stole a horse and buggy and drove them out.

But while the vast majority of white Americans, the ones who made no effort to stop the carnage, grudgingly admitted her greatness through varying degrees of indifference or hatred, the few who were her staunch supporters still made sure that she was kept separate and unequal.

During the Civil War, she was a nurse for the Union army and a guide who was allowed access to any battlefield she wanted to go into. But the army never paid her for her work in either capacity. Although they did give her free transportation wherever she went, she never got a penny from the government in back pay, no matter how many times she petitioned for it. Her second husband had been a soldier, and when he died, she got a small pension as his widow. According to Petry, the army didn't pay her for her work as a nurse because the black soldiers Tubman served protested.

As a result, she ended her days going from house to house in upstate New York (Auburn was her hometown), sitting in someone's kitchen and retelling her stories of heroism for a hot cup of tea and a handout. What was it about Harriet that men wanted buried even before she was? Was it simply because she was a woman or was it because nobody black could be a hero in America and get paid for it? Perhaps to reward a woman like Harriet Tubman, the public conscience would have had to think in terms of real equality (instead of a patronizing, liberal noblesse oblige) that would have made the superciliousness toward the race as absurd as the more arrant forms of racism are inhuman.

9

THE NEGRO IN THE CIVIL WAR

by Benjamin Quarles

BOSTON: LITTLE, BROWN, 1953

When President Lincoln finally got around to signing the Emancipation Proclamation in 1863, the North was losing the war so badly that he was seen crying in public upon reading the disastrous dispatches from his generals at the front. Washington itself had even been shelled, albeit from a distance. But Robert E. Lee had to turn back at Antietam because his men had no shoes and therefore couldn't walk on the roads of Maryland, which, unlike the dirt roads of Virginia and parts south, were paved. And Lee had blundered at Gettysburg. It seems his instinct for military maneuvers deserted him once he went any farther North than Virginia. But in spite of the dire straits that the Union army was in, Lincoln didn't want slaves doing anything as manly as shooting a gun. Under the proclamation, blacks were limited to drawing water, hauling coal, driving mules, and similar tasks.

In *The Negro in the Civil War*, Quarles describes how difficult it was to get blacks into the fighting initially. So much was Lincoln against it, that he fired his first Secretary of War, Simon Cam-

eron, when he pressed the issue too zealously. By the summer of
1863, only three weeks after General Hunter (who had tried as
early as 1862 to use black troops) was forced to throw in the towel
as well, his replacement, General Saxton, was finally authorized
to form regiments of black soldiers.

At Port Hudson, the black troops had scarcely been trained before they were thrown into battle. At Milliken's Bend, they had
been slaves a scant sixteen days earlier. One regiment didn't get
their rifles until the day before they had to engage the enemy.

Milliken's Bend had "the highest percent in killed and wounded
suffered by any unit in a single engagement during the course of
the war," writes Quarles. After six hours of hand-to-hand combat,
the enemy (a Texas outfit) had not been able to push the black
soldiers back one inch. By noon the Union navy arrived and
started shelling theTexans, so they had to withdraw, but with the
Boys in Blue in hot pursuit. One black soldier was almost killed
while chasing a Rebel whom he dragged back inside the fort.
When asked why he had risked his life like that, he said he had a
very good reason: the man had been his former owner. The battle
of Milliken's Bend was no sideshow. Without it, the Union Army
would have been hard pressed to take Vicksburg.

By the time the black units in the Army of the Cumberland
were used in the Battle of Nashville, in late 1862 and 1863, they
were well trained and fully integrated. Quarles gives a very detailed account of this battle and the contributions of black soldiers. What they accomplished here deserves far more of history's
praise than it has gotten. According to Quarles the battle "put an
end to effective Confederate resistance in the West."

In Virginia black units routed Confederate troops on more
than one occasion in 1864. In May they took Wilson's landing
and held it, in spite of a fierce counterattack by Major General
Fitzhugh Lee and his famous cavalry. Then, in mid-June, they
routed the enemy in front of Petersburg, the gateway to
Richmond. The town was theirs for the taking but General Smith,
the Union commander, bivouacked for the night instead of press-
ing his advantage, and the Rebels were able to refortify their posi-

tions. The resulting delay forced Ulysses S. Grant to lay siege to Petersburg, and the fiasco known as the Battle of the Crater was the result.

Even though a tunnel was dug under the Confederate fortifications, and even though the explosions went off after two hours' delay and Rebel men and munitions were blown sky-high, the order to let black troops go into the breach first was changed at the last minute. The white troops that went in panicked. When the black soldiers were finally sent in, they were sent in to a slaughter. In fact, Grant testified in Congress after the war that if the original plan had been followed, and the black troops had led the charge into the crater, he felt certain that the operation would have been a success.

The U.S. Navy was the most segregated of all the branches of the service by World War II. Not so up to and including the Civil War. There were so many black captains of navy vessels, and so many black seamen, that an accurate count prior to the war is not possible. But for the four years of fighting, one seaman out of every four in the Union navy was black. And the casualty list was 25 percent as well. Four black sailors received the coveted navy Medal of Honor.

In writing about the notorious Draft Riots of 1863 in New York City, Quarles gives the history of how the Irish in New York hated blacks, took away their jobs, went on strike to keep them jobless, and fought to get them out of their neighborhoods. When the manpower shortage became acute in the North and the draft law was passed, forcing Irishmen as well as others to fight what they dubbed "a nigger war," the Irish became savage. They rampaged and looted and killed by the tens of thousands, in howling, screaming wolf packs of up to a thousand or more, with no end to their hunger for blood: the blood of anyone black or anyone who aided or abetted, or was sympathetic to black people.

The killing and looting went on for four days. Thousands of black men, women, and children were killed on sight. Many were left swinging in the breeze in Union Square Park for days before anyone dared cut them down. The mob even burned down a black orphanage from which all but one black child had escaped. They found the child and killed her. And they torched the city.

Quarles skips over the brutal massacre of black soldiers at Fort Pillow, Tennessee, by ex-slaveholder Nathan Bedford Forrest with only a passing remark. Three hundred soldiers in uniform were shot in cold blood, nailed to logs, or buried alive, and black women and children were killed also, all to the cry of "Kill the niggers"—and that was after the fort had surrendered. Historians generally agreed that it was the worst violation of the code of civilized warfare by any army of Americans in uniform. Quarles's brushing it off as the exception to the way most black soldiers were treated is tantamount to someone dismissing the Battle of the Alamo as a minor incursion.

Blacks were crucial to the Union's success as spies. One of the most ingenious of these was the wife of a man named Dabney. The couple had escaped to the Union lines before she decided to cross back over the Rappahannock to work for a Confederate general. She sent Dabney detailed information of all Confederate troop movements in the area. Her system was a clothesline Morse code, which Dabney could read from the other side of the river without even leaving camp. The way she hung a blanket or a sheet, or the amount of pins she used were her dots and dashes.

As foragers who provided food and material for the Union army, blacks were without peer. Sherman could not have marched to the sea as quickly as he did were it not for the supplies they scavenged.

By the time the war was over, 180,000 black men had fought for the Union. A hundred of them were officers, and fourteen received the Congressional Medal of Honor. If they had been treated like men from the start and really allowed to fight to the best of their ability, as great as the record was, it would have even been greater. Over thirty-three thousand died for the cause. America has never fully repaid the debt it owes these men and their women.

There are several histories of this most important of all

American wars. Quarles, one of the pre-eminent black historians, has researched aspects of it not found anywhere else. His commentary, while often restrained, is never dull. For its overall comprehensiveness, *The Negro in the Civil War* is probably the best history of the black contribution to the war.

10

Captain of the *Planter*: The story of Robert Smalls

by Dorothy Sterling

New York: Doubleday, 1958

This is the story of a man who was born a slave in Beaufort, on St. Helena's Island, South Carolina, in 1839. He was never treated cruelly by either of his two masters (father and son), and in fact lived such a comparatively comfortable life as a young man that his mother made him visit the slave auctions in Charleston and the public whipping posts on the Sea Islands so he would not be confused about the reality of his status in life. Kind master or no, he was a slave according to the law of the land. But he found a way to escape from slavery that was so dramatic, so spectacular, that it made him famous for the rest of his life.

He would meet Lincoln, maintain a correspondence with Benjamin Harrison, work in the House of Representatives with James Garfield, and was supported by both Henry Cabot Lodge, Sr., and Robert La Follette, Sr. when the South contested his re-election in 1888. Horace Greeley would write a dozen editorials about him in the *New York Tribune*, Charles Nordhoff would do an article on him for the *Atlantic Monthly*, and the count of Paris would mention him in his dispatches to France. He would serve in Congress from 1876 to 1888, one of the last of the post-Reconstruction black congressman in the South. He was Robert Smalls, captain of the *Planter.*

Dorothy Sterling's book about Smalls's exploits, though written for a teenage audience, deserves a wider one. Why a man so important to history and so unique in his accomplishments should be so neglected that we have to turn to a young adult biography just to know who he was, what he did, and how he lived is a question that answers itself. He was black, he was heroic, he embarrassed the South by his bravery and daring, and he dramatically helped the nation to survive the assault from within to its freedom.

In 1851 Smalls, then twenty-three, was allowed to go to Charleston and find work on his own. He became one of the most skillful pilots and small-craft sailors on the waterfront. He married a slave named Hannah and decided that even if he was not free, he wanted his wife and whatever children they had to be. He convinced Hannah's owner to agree to sell her. The asking price was eight hundred dollars, a fortune for a slave to accumulate in those days.

In just two years, Smalls had saved seven hundred dollars, but the war came and South Carolina was the first to secede. In fact, the act of secession took place in Charleston. Both Smalls and his family were now trapped. His mother, at the age of seventy-one, stayed on St. Helena's Island when the whites left and joined the Union army as a cook, thus getting her freedom by not moving!

Smalls had been working as a pilot on a paddle steamer, the *Planter.* When the *Planter* became a flagship of the Confederate navy, Smalls and the rest of the crew were pressed into service under a Captain Relyea. Freedom was just seven miles away on the other side of the sand bar, where the Union ironclad, the *Onward,* was anchored ominously blockading the harbor. That gave Smalls the idea: steal the *Planter* and sail it across Charleston Bay, into the waiting arms of the Union navy as a prize of war.

Smalls knew where the Confederates had massed their men on

the Stono River. He knew the passwords for getting by the four forts that the ship had to pass in order to get up and down the river. And he was even the same height and size as its captain!

His day finally came. The ship had gone upriver to move cannon and ammunition from outlying areas to Charleston Harbor. With the aid of the men who were with him, Smalls made sure that the work went very slowly that day, May 13, 1862, so slowly that by the time the ship got back to port, it was too late to unload the extra cargo.

When the harbor watch rang thirteen bells and said "All's well" with "Dixie" playing in the distance, Smalls and seven other men boarded the *Planter.* He fired up the engines, and by three A.M. they had full steam. He sent a rowboat to another ship where the steward was hiding Hannah and the other women and children who were going to escape. When they got back to the *Planter* the steward decided to come along, too. In all they were nine men, five women, and three children.

At each of the first three forts Smalls successfully imitated Captain Relyea and was allowed to pass. And then came Fort Sumter, with guns powerful enough to blast the *Planter* out of the water with one round. Everyone onboard had agreed that they would blow themselves and the boat up rather than be captured, and that included the women and children. If anyone was still alive after that, Smalls had the small arms from the captain's locker to finish the job.

It was rather early for the *Planter* to be up and about, but Sumter also gave the signal to pass. Instead of turning upriver, the steamer headed straight for the open sea. By the time the Confederates at Sumter realized what had happened, Smalls was out of range of the fort's guns, but was sailing right into the guns of the *Onward.*

Sterling describes in detail how Hannah had brought as many things as she dared with the seven hundred dollars in savings, without raising suspicion. Now the biggest and best white sheet that could be purchased in wartime Charleston was unfurled. The stars and bars were run down and the white flag of truce run up. But the captain of the *Onward* thought he was being attacked and was ready to open fire. The sheet went limp because there was no breeze. Finally, Smalls swerved the *Planter* sharply to one side. That's when the breeze finally caught the white flag. Smalls sailed up and delivered a sixty-thousand dollar ship (in 1862 money) to the Union navy.

Everyone was astonished. Abolitionists in the North made speeches boasting that now there was proof that black men would not only fight, but that they could lead as well. Even Robert E. Lee sent a dispatch asking what the hell was going on. Smalls met Lincoln, but was disappointed when the boat was appraised at fifteen thousand dollars, which meant that his spoils of war commission would be one thousand, five hundred dollars instead of six thousand dollars. Smalls was further disappointed when he was made pilot of the *Planter* and the captaincy was given to someone else.

However, a year and some fifteen missions later, the captain, a man named Nickerson from Connecticut, got the ship trapped up the Stono. Attacked from all sides, Nickerson panicked and ordered Smalls to surrender. Smalls refused, saying that Nickerson, as captain, would be treated according to the conventions of war, but Smalls and the rest of the black crew would probably be hanged or worse. Nickerson abandoned the pilothouse, Smalls took over, and fought his way back out to freedom for a second time. At that point, he was made a U.S. Navy captain and given command of the ship.

At war's end, Smalls helped liberate Charleston and was present for the massive celebration that drew a throng of over ten thousand people. And that's where his story begins! He learned to read, was easily elected to public office after his wartime heroics, was in the thick of every political battle right down to the end of the century, and personally prevented a lynching from taking place in Beaufort in 1901.

The second half of Small's life is even more fascinating than the first half. At one point, Smalls was in the midst of campaigning for reelection to Congress when a group of ex-Confederates surrounded his platform and demanded the right to speak as well. He, of course, refused to share his platform with them—they certainly would not have shared theirs with him. A gun battle ensued, and Smalls and his followers retreated into a store that was behind the platform. Word got out that the general, as he was affectionately called, had been ambushed, and blacks from everywhere showed up to surround the "surrounders" and see that Smalls got safely out of town. The racists wired ahead to have him killed at his next whistle stop. But the blacks wired ahead as well, and everywhere he campaigned, the general was not only protected, but allowed to give his speech without interference.

Smalls died in 1915 at the age of seventy-six, still revered as the general and the man who long ago stole an entire boat from the Confederate navy and sailed it over to the Union side in the war to end slavery.

Sterling's book is well researched and an excellent read. The only time her writing style fails her is when she tries to create original dialogue for her characters: especially for Smalls and his wife and children. The bibliography is almost twenty pages long and in addition to ten pages of books, she lists several newspapers, magazines, and other brief biographies, plus unpublished material about Smalls.

11

THE LIFE AND TIMES OF FREDERICK DOUGLASS: HIS EARLY LIFE AS A SLAVE; HIS ESCAPE FROM BONDAGE; AND HIS COMPLETE HISTORY

by Frederick Douglas, with a new introduction by Rayford Logan

NEW YORK: COLLIER BOOKS, 1962

Frederick Douglass belongs everywhere in the nineteenth century. He lived for most of it and enjoyed an unparalleled position of power from the 1840s to the end of the century. He's a consummate example of a man of reason in an age when such men were at a premium. America was living the great lie that slavery could be justified within the context of the American experience. William Lloyd Garrison, the fiery leader of the Anti-Slavery Society, insisted in his newspaper, the *Liberator,* that violence could never be used as a means of abolishing slavery, even though slavery was using violence as the means of staying alive. Douglass not only disagreed but started his own newspaper, the *North Star,* in 1847, taking the position that "the man struck is the man to cry out." Garrison, who had been supported financially by blacks (James Forten, among others) still didn't expect a black man to contradict him. Didn't Douglass know that in the fight for black equality, only white men could make the really important decisions?

Douglass's was probably the biggest life that's ever been lived in public by a black American, certainly prior to the 1960s. He helped make slavery a national issue and abolition a rallying cry at home and abroad, and he didn't limit himself to the cause of his race only. He fought for women's rights as early as 1848, supported the temperance movement beginning in 1846 (he was a teetotaler), and fought for the rights of labor and against capital punishment. Once the war came, in 1861, he immediately became a recruiter of black soldiers. After the war, there was just as much to do: the elimination of the Black Codes, gaining the right for blacks to vote (he started that campaign as early as 1863), and stemming the tide of Jim Crow legislation wherever and whenever possible.

To this day, the dispute has continued—it's more of a compliment to Douglass than anything else—as to whether he was a better writer or a better speaker. When he first appeared on the platform as a living witness to slavery's horrors, he was so good that no one, even some who knew him personally, really believed that he had ever been a slave. He certainly couldn't have escaped from slavery just a few years before—not given his learning, his eloquence, and his courtly manner. So to prove that he was who he said he was, he wrote the story of his early years in slavery and of his escape.

In his *Narrative of the Life of Frederick Douglass,* published in 1845, the style was so serene, so well crafted, so eloquent in its understated condemnations of man's inhumanity to man that it became an instant bestseller. It sold eleven thousand copies and went into nine editions within two years, and it was translated into German and French. He subsequently published *My Bondage, My Freedom,* a second version of his life story. But these volumes are only part of the continuing story of his magnificent life. The final version, *The Life and Times of Frederick Douglass,* which is more than six hundred pages long, wasn't published until 1892.

Pick any page in the huge volume of *Life and Times* and you have a good read. The style is so modern, so accessible, so leisurely, that it is a pleasure throughout. It would be rare indeed to find a history of black America that did not include him. His is almost always one of the faces that adorns calendars every February in honor of Black History Month. It was his spirit as much as anything else that made him so huge, so outsized.

He had escaped from slavery in Maryland in 1838, a violation of the law in a slave state before 1850 and everywhere else afterward. Because he had to expose himself to establish his "credentials," he became a known fugitive, who had to leave the country to avoid being taken back into his former condition within the peculiar institution. He set sail for England, where he became a celebrity, and in Scotland and Ireland, as well. The Irish patriot Daniel O'Connell became a life-long friend and refused to take money for the Irish cause from slaveholders to show his support for the black cause of freedom.

During his overseas voyage, Douglass had to fight Southern slave owners who called him a liar when he gave a speech, at the captain's invitation, describing what slavery was really like when you had to live it day by day. The incident received such notoriety that the Cunard line quarantined him on the voyage back so he couldn't make any more speeches. But once the British press got hold of the item and attacked Cunard for being "racist" and an outrage to the British sense of "free speech," Cunard quickly regretted what it had done and apologized, saying it would never happen again.

By the 1870s, Douglass was a national figure. He served as Benjamin Harrison's ambassador to Haiti, and his opinion was influential enough to have an impact on public debates, such as the one between President Ulysses Grant and Senator Charles Sumner over the possible annexation of Santo Domingo (now the Dominican Republic). He was always ready to answer the call of the soldier, in the dirty business of trench warfare.

When a New England railroad company threw blacks out of their railroad cars, even though they had purchased first-class tickets, Douglass, who was one of the victims, refused to be budged. He held on to the seat with such determination that three men got him out only after he had ripped out three seats, which he dragged with him. The people of Lynn, Massachusetts, where Douglass was living at the time, supported him, so Stephen

Chase, superintendent of the railroad, ordered all passenger trains to bypass Lynn!

When the *North Star* began to have some impact, the *New York Herald* told the people of Rochester, New York, where the paper was based, to throw Douglass's printing press into Lake Ontario and banish him to Canada. They didn't but his house (which had been a station of the Underground Railroad) was burned to the ground. On a previous occasion, when a man named Parker and two others, escaping from slavery, shot and killed their pursuer and wounded his son, scattering the officers of the law who were assisting in the chase, arrived at Douglass's home seeking refuge, Douglass knew that he had more than just three runaways on his hands; he had men wanted for murder. In spite of the danger, he kept them in his house (while newspapers everywhere were filled with stories of what the men had done and where they might be headed) until he could get them safely to freedom.

When letters from Douglass were found in John Brown's possession after his capture at Harpers Ferry, a wire ordering his arrest was sent to Philadelphia, where Douglass was lecturing. No one doubts that, had he been caught, Douglass would have been returned to Virginia and hanged with Brown in 1859. Fortunately for him, the telegraph operator held up the telegram for three hours, which gave Douglass enough time to get out of town.

Throughout his life, Douglass had the wonderful ability to find the good in things. One of the best examples is his summation of the Emancipation Proclamation. When it finally came over the wires, Douglass was in Boston with a crowd of other hopefuls, waiting in anxious anticipation for what manna from man it could bring. He writes in *Life and Times* of the occasion:

> There was . . . no disposition . . . to criticize the proclamation. . . . [W]e saw only its antislavery side. But further . . . examination showed it to be extremely defective. It was not a proclamation of "liberty throughout all the land, unto all the inhabitants thereof," such as we hoped it would be, but was one marked by discriminations and reservations. Its operation was confined. . . . It only abolished slavery where it did not exist, and left it intact where it did exist. It was a measure apparently inspired by the low motive of

military necessity. . . . For my own part, I took the proclamation, first and last, for a little more than it purported, and saw in its spirit a life and power far beyond its letter.

Douglass died on February 20, 1895, at age seventy-eight. The legislature of North Carolina voted to adjourn for the day. In Indiana, Illinois, Massachusetts, and New York, the legislatures adopted resolutions of regret. And condolences poured in from all over the world. He was a special giant of the century.

12

THE GLORIOUS FAILURE: BLACK CONGRESSMAN ROBERT BROWN ELLIOTT AND THE RECONSTRUCTION IN SOUTH CAROLINA

by Peggy Lamson

NEW YORK: W. W. NORTON, 1973

Peggy Lamson's excellent biography of Robert Brown Elliott takes its title from history's assessment of Reconstruction as a flawed experiment. That Elliott failed in the end, there isn't any doubt. They all failed, the whole gallant band of men and women, black and white, who tried to make America a democracy in fact, finally—and for the first time. They failed because America failed them, not because they failed themselves.

Elliott's failure was more glorious than most because he was more brilliant than most in challenging the contention that blacks were in any way inferior to whites or incapable of participating in a modern democracy. And Lamson does an admirable job of demonstrating how superior Elliott was to many a white man who tried to best him in parliamentary debate, where the power of a man's mind is measured.

Her book is also important because she gives us a look at Reconstruction. It approaches the subject from the lives of Elliott and others who participated in the effort; how they went about making the great experiment work, how they did, in fact make it work. She makes it clear that only the South's refusal to accept the demise of slavery as a fact kept the Republic from moving forward to a new equality.

Elliott was a black man who was as educated as any man in America in the 1860s. He had one of the finest libraries in the South, and he may have been the only man ever to get elected to Congress and actually serve in the House who wasn't an American citizen. His country of origin has never been determined and there is no proof that he ever applied for citizenship as an alien. He was in turn a congressman, the speaker of the house in South Carolina, the state attorney general, the assistant adjutant general, and twice the chairman of the Republican Party state convention.

In 1871 he debated Representative Michael Kerr of Indiana, who was opposed to a bill to curb the Ku Klux Klan's slaughter of blacks throughout the South. Kerr was considered the most experienced constitutionalist that the Democrats could offer. He argued that the bill was unconstitutional because federal troops should not be allowed to intervene in a state matter unless the state asked for the intervention, citing article four, section four, of the Constitution: "The United States . . . shall protect [the States] against invasion . . . on application of the Legislature or the Executive. . . ."

Elliott replied that the clause was "not inhibitory but mandatory," designed not to "restrict the rights but to enlarge the duties" of the federal government. If a state made such an application, it was mandatory on the federal government to honor it, but that did not mean that the federal government had no authority to go in on its own when there was a clear case of widespread domestic violence. Elliott then used an anecdote, a favorite device of his, to ridicule the position of the strict Constructionists. Their point of view, Elliott said, reminded him of the "rigid etiquette of the Frenchman who, on being upbraided for not saving the life of a fellow passenger whom he saw drown before his eyes, attempted to justify himself by pleading that he had not been introduced to him."

The bill became law, due in no small measure to Elliott. He followed up that triumph with an equally brilliant defense of the Civil Rights Bill of 1874. It was the granddaddy of all attempts to give African Americans freedom of movement throughout the state, any state on par with everyone else. It provided that "no public inns or places of public amusement for which a license was required, no state coaches or railroads, no cemeteries or benevolent institutions, no public schools supported at public expense for public use should make any distinction as to admission on account of race, color or previous condition of servitude."

His opponent on that occasion was Alexander H. Stephens, who was no longer vice president of anything, but now just a congressman from Georgia. Stephens cited the Supreme Court's recent (1873) decision in the famous Slaughter-House cases to support his opposition to the bill. The Slaughter-House cases played a pivotal role in the long descent down to "separate but equal" that the court sanctioned officially in *Plessy v. Ferguson,* in 1891. Louisiana gave exclusive rights to livestock landings and slaughterhouses to specific individuals and corporations under its police powers. The Supreme Court upheld the lower court's decision, stating that Louisiana did, indeed, have the right to grant the monopolies under its "police powers."

Elliott insisted that the "decision of any court should be examined in the light of the exact question which is brought before it" and explained the context in which the Slaughter-House cases existed:

> What you give to one class, you must give to all; what you deny to one class, you shall deny to all, unless in the exercise of the common and universal police power of the State, you find it needful to confer exclusive privileges on certain citizens, to be held and exercised still for the common good of all. . . . Is it "pretended," anywhere that the evils of which we complain, our exclusion from the public inn, from the saloon and the table of the steamboat, from the sleeping coach on the railway, from the right of sepulcher in the public burial ground, are an exercise of the police power of the State? Is such oppression and injustice nothing but the exercise by the State of the right to make regulations for the health, comfort and security of all her citizens. . . . Does the gentleman . . . say that

my good is promoted when I am excluded from the public inn? Is
the health or safety of the community promoted?

Next came the issue of the rights of an individual as a citizen of
the state in contradistinction to that individual's rights as a citizen
of the United States. Said Elliott:

[It] is true [that] there are privileges and immunities which belong
to me as a citizen of my State. . . . But what of that? Are the rights
which I now claim rights that I hold as a citizen of the United
States or of my State? Or, to state the question more exactly, is not
the denial of such privileges to me a denial of equal protection of
the laws? For it is under this clause of the Fourteenth Amendment
that we place the present bill: no State shall "deny to any person
within its jurisdiction the equal protection of the laws." No matter,
therefore, whether his rights are held under the United States or
under his particular state, he is equally protected by this amendment. He is always and everywhere entitled to equal protection of
the laws.

As Lamson recounts, Elliott's speech was an overwhelming
success. Not only Republicans, but some Democrats as well
swarmed forward and formed a line to shake Elliott's hand. He
had carried the day in the House for the second day in a row.

In spite of the importance of his work in Congress, Elliott was
more interested in seeing that South Carolina remained protected against the red-shirt horrors of the Klan and their ilk, organizations which sprang up like weeds throughout the South.
The Straightouts, the Knights of the White Camelia, the White
League, Mother's Little Helpers, and the Baseball Club of the
First Baptist Church. Elliott helped form a black militia to protect black life and limb in South Carolina, and he was chosen by
labor conventions, black and white, to argue their causes. He had
as clients not one but two governors of the state.

Once the Hayes-Tilden deal was struck (see Must-Read No.
16), the federal troops were removed from the South in 1877.
After that, no one, not even Robert Brown Elliott, could survive
the tyranny that followed. He lost everything—money, homes, his

practice. It all disappeared, gone with the wind, although there was no Hollywood encomium to mourn its passing. From then on, he barely scraped together a living as a lawyer in a South that wanted black men barefoot and mindless. He died from malaria in 1884 in New Orleans at age forty-two.

Reconstruction is a much written about subject. W. E. B. De Bois's study of the period, *Black Reconstruction*, is so huge that it has even intimidated historians. John Hope Franklin's smaller volume, simply titled *Reconstruction*, is not only much more accessible, but has become quite popular because it doesn't deal as harshly with the South as one might expect it to.

The Old South view of Reconstruction, the view portrayed in the films *Birth of a Nation* and *Gone With the Wind*, has lost much of its stranglehold on historians and the populace in general. Nevertheless, nothing approximating proper credit to the black contribution for making the South a part of the country's development into a modern democracy has ever been forthcoming. While blacks are no longer seen as having done nothing but try to rape Lillian Gish and eat chicken in the houses of assembly, we still aren't looked upon as masters of the game of politics and nation-building, which we decidedly were for the brief period that we were given the chance.

13

PINCKNEY BENTON STEWARD PINCHBACK

by James Haskins

NEW YORK: MACMILLIAN, 1973

P. B. S. Pinchback, or Pinch as he was affectionately called, is a one-man answer to whether or not black people are lazy, shif'less, good-for-nothings without ambition, happy in a subservient position, unreliable, always late and unwilling to fight for their rights. Because his father, who was white, loved his mother, who was black, and didn't keep two families, just the one (although he couldn't marry the woman he loved as the law didn't allow that kind of conjugal bliss to be sanctified by either God or man), there was love, fidelity, and stability in the home, and that's what P. B. S. grew up with. When his father died, in 1848, the family had to flee the South or Pinch's white relatives would have disposed of them "as property."

So what did Pinch do with the rest of his life? He became a riverboat gambler, and officer in the Union army, fought at least two duels (killing one of his opponents), and married and loved and lived with the same woman all his life. He became one of the most important men in Louisiana politics during Reconstruction, serving as the governor of the state for almost two months, was

77

elected to the U.S. Congress and to the Senate (both bodies refused to seat him as he "warn't 'umble" enough), and ended up in
Washington, D.C., where his grandson, Jean Toomer, who later
became one of the most important American writers of the
1920s, watched over his dying.

James Haskins has done his research and puts more than
enough detail into this narrative. It's a solid volume, over 250
pages long, with copious annotation, and the only biography of
Pinchback worthy of the name. Haskins does have a penchant for
"must have" sentences: "It must have irked him that such men
[referring to the hypocrisy of many Republicans] were praised as
saviors of his people." Next sentence: "A great loneliness must
have touched him as he stared glumly at the sun-baked houses."
But despite this stylistic shortcoming, Haskins has done a com-
mendable job.

Pinchback wasn't quite twenty-four when the Civil War started.
When the order came to allow blacks to fight, he opened his own
recruiting office and raised an entire company of Corps d'Af-
rique, which included several black officers. He was commis-
sioned as a captain, but all the commissions were temporary, and
the black officers were subsequently replaced by white ones. By
September 1863, it became obvious that he would be a captain in
name only, so he resigned and got permission to recruit free black
men for a cavalry unit. He spent one thousand dollars of his own
money and had a full company ready by November. Then someone discovered that "the commissioning of Negroes as commis-
sioned officers [is] contrary to law." And that was that.

Blacks in Louisiana tried as early as 1866 to get the vote. At an
organizing meeting at the mechanics Hall in New Orleans, they
were attacked by a mob of whites led by the mayor. Of the nearly
forty men killed, all but four were black. When Philip Sheridan
stepped in and guaranteed that blacks would be allowed to exercise their civil rights without fear of death, Pinchback immediately formed a Republican club and was elected to the new state
convention to rewrite the state's constitution. He became a champion of Louisiana blacks when he authored an article granting

them "equal rights . . . and privileges" on public conveyances and in places of business or public accommodation.

Pinchback was elected state senator and then lieutenant governor, but the melodrama that is Louisiana politics was already a fact of life. In order to prevent Pinchback's confirmation, Democrats and some Republicans stayed away from the legislature so that a quorum couldn't be formed. These men were forced to return to the assembly so that they could carry out their legally mandated duties. But they were determined not to recognize Pinchback as lieutenant governor even though he was already functioning as president of the State Senate. The final vote to confirm him was a tie, and as president of the Senate, Pinchback couldn't vote. But he was also still a senator. So Senator Pinchback broke the tie that President Pinchback couldn't and made the honorable gentleman Lieutenant Governor Pinchback!

When Louisiana's governor was subsequently impeached for trying to buy elected officials for his own election and couldn't deny it, he had to step down until a trial either found him guilty or innocent. Thereupon, on December 9, 1872, Pinchback became acting governor. He signed ten bills during his brief tenure, but as Haskins describes, the threats on his life during that time were numerous and ominous. From New York came a letter from a detractor named Charles Taylor addressed to "Dead Beat Acting Governor Pinchbeck [sic] Sambo" that started with "you damb black niger . . . if we had you in New York, we would skin you like an ell you a niger of the Deapest Die. . . . The best thing you can do is sell out and go hunting gorillas in africa." From New Orleans came a threat that said in part: "If you do not resingn [sic] the office of Acting Governor within three days . . . from this date you will be dead, stabbed to the heart." Another suggested that "an organization of recent origin have sent to New York for som [sic] Italian brigans to dispatch [the] carpet baggers."

Undeterred, Pinch took control of the state, forcing the state militia, a rebel group still, to surrender when they refused to obey his commands. Once in the driver's seat, he showed his bi-partisanship by issuing commissions to able Democrats as well as Republicans. But the election of another Republican to the governor's chair that January meant that Pinch would be out of a job. That's when he ran for both seats in Congress at the same time. He got elected to both, but neither body would seat him. It took them three years to say no. During that time, he spent thousands of dollars fighting for the two seats to which he had been elected. His family lived well on an income of ten thousand dollars a year almost to the end. In 1880 he got legislation passed at a second Louisiana constitutional convention that created Southern University as an institution of higher learning for blacks.

When his legal battle was all over and the racists again had firm control of the state, he took his family first to New York and then to Washington, D.C. He had done all that men could do, "but a' s been done in vain, my love," as Robert Burns observed. It was left to Jean Toomer to write his epitaph after witnessing the "break up of Pinchback."

Haskins summarizes it well: "Pinchback died on December 21, 1921, at the age of eighty-four. His body was taken by train to New Orleans for burial in the family vault . . . Walter Pinchback [a son] and Jean Toomer [a grandson] accompanied the body home, and only a few local people were waiting at the railroad station when the train pulled in. Nina would follow her husband."

14

Buffalo Soldiers: A Narrative of the Negro Cavalry in the West

by William H. Leckie

Norman, Okla.: University of Oklahoma Press, 1963

Leckie's book does the buffalo soldiers proud. He gives them all the credit they deserve for having more to do with taming the West than any of the other cavalry units in what was by then a segregated army. His is by far the best study of the subject that I've come across, both for comprehensiveness and style. Even though he admires these men, he doesn't flinch from giving the gory details of their mistreatment.

The Civil War was over, and the Grand Army of the Republic, a quarter of a million strong, marched down Pennsylvania Avenue looking every bit the heroes they were. Among them, were some of the almost two hundred thousand black fighting men who had helped win the war and who had been the first troops to enter Charleston and Richmond. Now they, along with the rest, were receiving a nation's gratitude for saving it from the fratricidal conflict that an arrogant slave-owning South had plunged it into. No sooner had the peace agreement been signed, however, than the old attitudes reasserted themselves. Most of these black soldiers found themselves not only mustered out, dis-

armed and left to fend for themselves, but dwelling in a South
that was returned to the Bourbons who had brought about its
devastation.

Since most of these men had come from the South, when they
went home, their blue uniforms made them pariahs. The Native
American had had things his way during the war in the West and
Far West, which saw little of the fighting. Now the federal government wanted to reclaim that vast territory, larger than the area in
which the Civil War had been fought. So once again it turned to
the black soldier.

The law under which these men were to be made a part of the
army for the second time in the decade (and the first in peacetime) relegated them to second-class soldiership. They could
follow, but they couldn't lead. Black officers were specifically prohibited in the units that were reorganized. The only black officer
to serve from 1866 through the 1890s who was officially black
(besides Charles Young, who got his commission in the Ninth
Cavalry in 1889) was Henry Flipper, who graduated from West
Point and served with the Tenth Cavalry. Unfortunately for Flipper, he caught the eye of a young white belle. He was accused of
embezzlement and, though found innocent, was discharged from
the army for "conduct unbecoming an officer and a gentleman"
(whatever that meant), and that was that for the experiment in
black leadership.

The army created two cavalry regiments, the Ninth and the
Tenth, and four of infantry. Recruitment was not a problem. Even
though the black soldier earned less than a white soldier, still it
was a job, which was better than no job at all. Their horses were
older, their guns in worse repair, and their food often crawling
with worms and maggots. The abuse they had to take from their
superiors was probably without parallel in the history of men in
uniform, certainly in this country. An officer shot and killed two
troopers point blank over an argument. He was allowed to resign
six months later. For being drunk on duty, the black soldiers were
dishonorably discharged and given a year of hard labor. A common punishment that they had to endure was being tied up.
Leckie describes this torture device as consisting of a "grown

man being seated on the ground with knees up and feet flat with arms bound to the front. A stick was pushed across his arms and under his knees rendering him completely helpless. A piece of wood was commonly used as a gag. The normal time of such punishment was about half a day."

Buffalo soldiers, in turn, shot up San Angelo, Texas, not once but twice. First when one of their own was pistol-whipped by a group of Texas Rangers simply for enjoying himself as an emancipated male in a saloon, and the second time when an unarmed buffalo soldier was gunned down because he refused to dance for the amusement of a sheep man. In retaliation for the death of their comrade, they killed a Texan and destroyed a hotel.

They were segregated on one post by a Third Army general and left in the field longer than any other unit (sometimes for five years without extended leave). And they were often victimized by civilian justice as well. A Texan killed three troopers, one in cold blood. When he was finally caught and turned over to the civilian authorities, he was acquitted forthwith. On the other hand, during the Oklahoma land rush, a white officer of the Ninth ordered his troopers to fire on a group of homesteaders point blank—they were unarmed—because they were Boomers, trying illegally to homestead on what was still Indian land. The black soldiers looked at the white men and women and children and took pity on them, disobeying the officer's order and thus saving a lot of civilian lives.

And they had to rescue Custer's famed Seventh Cavalry from an Indian trap on one occasion, and the Ninth chased Billy the Kid out of town to end the Lincoln County wars. There's an ironic twist to the Custer rescue. To keep the much heralded Seventh Cavalry from being wiped out, the men of the Ninth had to make a forced march, covering a hundred miles in one day. All this to rescue a racist general: Custer had refused to serve in a black unit because he said he didn't lead "brunettes."

But the "brunettes" were such good fighting men that the Native Americans called them Buffalo Soldiers, a great honor, since they had made the buffalo a religion. They were an integral part of the final campaign that forced Victorio—the great warrior chief who ranks ahead of Geronimo as a strategist and the equal

of Crazy Horse and Sitting Bull—into Mexico, where he was finally cornered and killed. His death brought an end to the
Apache wars in the Southwest.

If these soldiers had been allowed to be more help to the civilian population, there would have been far fewer deaths in the
Old West. When the west was finally won, these men had won it.
None of them, however ever showed up in a Hollywood movie to
prove it.

Some of the buffalo soldiers whose exploits deserve to be remembered include Sergeant Stance of the Ninth, who was given
the Congressional Medal of Honor for five successful encounters
with the enemy in one year. Sergeant Ed Davis ordered his company of twenty men to attack a Cheyenne war party of seventy on
foot. They did and won the day. Private Filmore Roberts was
given the pony express pouch to carry from Fort Arbuckle to Fort
Gibson, a distance of two hundred miles. When he didn't show up
at Gibson, he was listed as a deserter. The following spring they
found his body, the pouch still strapped to his back. He had died
trying to ford the swollen waters of the Canadian River in the
dead of winter.

The soldiers also had time for play and for helping the army
experiment with new modes of transportation, notes Leckie. They
played baseball and rode bicycles before many other Americans
did. Abner Doubleday had commanded the Tenth briefly and introduced the game to them. And the bicycle was an early army
experiment—a possible complement to the horse.

The story of the buffalo soldiers was a thirty-year saga that saw
the black fighting man at his finest. The Ninth and Tenth
Cavalries continued on, after the West was won, serving with distinction in the Spanish-American War as well; they were the
troopers who really stormed San Juan Hill (Teddy Roosevelt was
on another hill, as Lanning documents in Must-Read No. 33).
These men were not only "the first line of defense," according to
Leckie, but a full 20 percent of the entire cavalry force in the
West. In other words, one cavalry soldier in five was black.

Leckie sums up their accomplishments as follows:

The experiment with Negro troopers . . . proved a success by any standard other than . . . racial prejudice. By 1891 the combat record spoke for itself. They had fought on the plains of Kansas and in Indian Territory, in the vast expanse of West Texas and along hundreds of miles of the Rio Grande and in Mexico, in the deserts and mountains of New Mexico and Arizona, in Colorado, and finally in the rugged grandeur of the Dakotas. Few regiments could match the length and sweep of these activities. . . . The Ninth and Tenth Cavalry were first-rate regiments and major forces in promoting peace and advancing civilization along America's last frontier. The thriving cities and towns, the fertile fields, and the natural beauty of that once wild land are monuments enough for any buffalo soldier.

Nevertheless, in 1992 an official monument to the heroism of these men was erected in the form of a bronze statue of a trooper astride his horse. The dedication site was Fort Leavenworth, Kansas, where the story had begun 126 years earlier. Colin Powell, then chairman of the Joint Chiefs of Staff, made the dedication address, and the 302nd Fighter Squadron, a unit of the Tuskegee Airmen, flew overhead. The monument was the creation of black sculptor Eddie Dixon.

15

THE NEGRO COWBOYS

by Philip Durham and Everett L. Jones

NEW YORK: DODD, MEAD, 1965

Durham and Jones create a context for their story of black cowboys that makes it clear history has been blatantly unfair in its treatment of these great American heroes of the Old West. Most of the Negro cowboys were already in Texas and Indian Territory at the end of the Civil War because they had been taken there as slaves. As slaves, they learned the skills of the cowboy.

According to *The Negro Cowboys,* by 1861 there were 182,000 of them in Texas alone, among a white population at the time of 430,000. (There would have been even more blacks in the West but by 1854, 200,000 had escaped to Mexico.) A few of them, including Aaron Ashworth, were free and owned cattle and land. Ashworth had a herd of 2,570, which made him the cattle king of his county. He also owned slaves. But as numerous as these black cowboys were and as active in making the West what it became, they are all lost to history. The authors write:

Now they are forgotten, but once they rode all the trails, driving millions of cattle before them. Some died in stampedes, some froze to death, some drowned. Some were too slow with guns, some too fast. But most of them lived through the long drives to Abilene, to Dodge City, to Ogallala. And many of them drove on to the farthest reaches of the northern range, to the Dakotas, Wyoming and Montana.

All the cowboys—black, brown, red and white—shared the same jobs and dangers. They ate the same food and slept on the same ground; but when the long drives ended and the great plains were tamed and fenced, the trails ended too. The cattle were fenced in, the Negroes out.

Years later, when history became myth and legend, when the cowboys became folk heroes, the Negroes were again fenced out. They had ridden through the real West, but they found no place in the West of fiction. That was peopled by tall, lean, tanned—though lily-white under the shirt—heroes. . . . Even the Chinese survived in fiction, if only as pigtailed caricatures who spoke a "no tickee, no washee" pidgin. . . . Although the stereotypes were sometimes grotesque, all but one of the races and nationalities of the real West appeared in fiction.

All but the Negro cowboy, who had vanished.

Since it is the legends of our history that define what we aspire to, what we hold most dear, the exclusion of the black cowboy from American myth makes perfect sense, according to Durham and Jones. The black man as hero has no place in American history, let alone American myth. The Gunfight at the OK Corral took about ninety seconds, and Ike Clanton, Hollywood's arch villain, wasn't even there, so Wyatt Earp made his reputation by shooting down the B team. As late as 1999, politicians were using Western myth as a metaphor for their political sallies, and candidates were riding into town "like Wyatt Earp" to win the gunfight. Real black gunfighters rode into town after town and won real gunfights. Here are a few of them, briefly discussed in *The Negro Cowboys* in more depth.

In 1876 Nat Love led his own crew to deliver three thousand steers to Deadwood, South Dakota, the day before the Fourth of July, in time to help celebrate the holiday. Love won the roping contest, and he wasn't the only black cowboy who entered. Said he: "I roped, threw, tied, bridled, saddled and mounted my mustang [three minutes faster] than the next nearest competitor."

Love also won the rifle- and pistol-shooting contests, thus earning the sobriquet Deadwood Dick. Durham and Jones spend a lot of time sneering at Nat Love; they find his bragging absurd and many of his claims inflated. Maybe they objected to the fact that he wrote his own autobiography rather than letting an "objective" historian do it.

Bill Pickett is given credit for having invented bulldogging, what is known today as steer wrestling and seen at rodeos throughout the South and West. His technique was unique to say the least. "The way Bill went at it, he piled out of his saddle onto the head of a running steer, sometimes jumping five or six feet to tie on. He'd grab a horn in each hand and twist them till the steer's nose came up. Then he's reach in and grab the steer's upper lip with his strong white teeth, throw up his hands to show he wasn't holding any more, and fall to one side of the steer, dragging along beside him till the animal went down."

The book also includes Stagecoach Mary of Montana, who could knock a man down with one blow. She ran her own stage and collected her debts at the end of a rifle. She liked her whiskey straight and her cigars long and black.

Ben Hodges was a supreme confidence man, whose base of operations was none other than Dodge City. He was there long before and long after both Earp and Masterson passed through. At one time, he passed himself off as the heir to a Spanish land grant. His schemes were so fantastic that he'd get the old-timers to back his story just for the fun of seeing him hoodwink the Easterners and other newcomers.

In spite of all these black cowboy exploits and many more, a second-rate white actor named Don Douglas played Deadwood Dick when it was made into a serial in the forties. And Rock Hudson played an honest John Wesley Hardin in the Hollywood version, who just wanted to work his piece of land and raise a family, even though he was known, and billed himself, as a "nigger killer," counting at least thirty black men he shot down to get even for Texas losing the war.

To be maligned throughout history is a terrible injustice. To be presented as a supplicant always on your knees when you were often the man standing tall is unconscionable. The only thing worse is to be torn completely from the book of history, so that even though you were there, you weren't. It's somewhat like looking into a mirror and seeing nothing.

16

THE BETRAYAL OF THE NEGRO: FROM RUTHERFORD B. HAYES TO WOODROW WILSON

by Rayford Logan

NEW YORK: COLLIER BOOKS, 1954

Rayford Logan makes the argument that the period from the close of the Civil War to the end of the century saw the demise of most of the rights of black America. He calls it the "nadir," and that's exactly what it was. The war was over. Reconstruction was over. Black men were now killed in the streets in broad daylight, shot and beaten in houses of assembly, hunted in the night like animals, burned out of their homes, their women and children left in complete desolation with no place to go and none to comfort them.

By 1877 the South had taken back control of every state except three: South Carolina, Louisiana, and Mississippi. Getting these states back seemed almost like mopping-up exercises once federal troops left. The South had also regained control of the House of Representatives by 1877, thanks to its wholesale disfranchisement of the black voter, and was ready to filibuster on a vote for the president if those troops were not withdrawn.

Logan argues that all of the violence, all of the intensity of purpose bespoke a combined national will to restore the country to a political status quo as similar to what it was before the Civil War as possible: all white, with North and South snarling at each other, and a black minority that was excluded from substantive participation in the political process.

Of course, there were changes. The Republican Party was here to stay and statutory slavery was not. Since the Northern victory in the war was consolidated and that section of the country wanted peace, Southern whites felt they now had the opportunity to get rid of the last vestiges of Black Reconstruction.

In three states, South Carolina, Louisiana, and Florida, both Democrats and Republicans claimed victory in the presidential election of 1876. The claim of the Republican candidate, Rutherford B. Hayes, was sustained by the electoral commission. Since Congress had to certify the results, a Southern filibuster in the House to prevent the counting of the votes was launched. At a hotel in Washington, D.C., called the Wormley (owned by a black businessman), the deal was struck that made Hayes president. He would agree to withdraw the troops and the south would agree to withdraw the filibuster.

It was Hayes, according to Logan, who was most responsible for the reimposition of white supremacy throughout the South after Reconstruction. Hayes did worry that there might be another war, and he did feel guilt over the fate of the "poor colored men of the South," writing in his diary: "The Southern people will practically treat the constitutional amendments as nullities, and then the colored man's fate will be worse than when he was in slavery." But he let the white people do with them as they may. Consequently his biographer wrote in 1914:

> [T]he experiment of permitting a newly enfranchised and ignorant servile race, led and dominated by unscrupulous adventurers, to govern American states in defiance of the intelligence, the culture, and the property interests of the Anglo-Saxon inhabitants, was bound to prove a failure.

There was a section in the Fourteenth Amendment that called for the reduction in a state's representation in Congress if that state violated the rights of any of its citizens. Under President

Benjamin Harrison (who followed Hayes after Chester A. Arthur), there was an attempt to enforce it. But his efforts just made the South that much more ornery.

One of the ideas behind all the extreme Jim Crow legislation was that the federal government couldn't protect the right of a citizen if the state had already taken that right away. By passing a poll tax of two dollars and barring anyone from voting who could not read a section of the state constitution (all of which was in clear violation of the Fifteenth Amendment), blacks lost the vote that they had used to help rebuild the South; this, even in states where blacks were a majority (56.9 percent in South Carolina, for example). By 1898, when McKinley was president and black soldiers were helping "to liberate Cubans from Spanish 'tyranny,' Louisiana adopted the 'Grandfather Clause' that set qualifications for voting." It stated that anyone whose grandfather could vote was excluded from the restrictions—which meant all whites, except for an occasional immigrant or two, from the North, if indeed the law was ever enforced in that regard. According to Logan, McKinley had no official reaction to this egregious violation of the Constitution.

The South had become so rabidly racist that Wade Hampton in South Carolina was defeated by Ben Tillman in the race for governor because Tillman was more of a white racist. "Hampton had not eliminated the Negro completely from politics as Tillman and his supporters demanded." In his inaugural address, Tillman said, "The triumph of Democracy and white supremacy over mongrelism and anarchy is complete." Proof of this was that he convinced the state Democratic executive committee to permit blacks who had been allowed to vote in the Democratic primary because of their loyalty to Wade Hampton in 1876, to be allowed "to vote [in the election] only when they would get ten white men to vouch for their loyalty."

In Congress, the entire race was vilified by the likes of David De Armond of Missouri, who described blacks as "almost too ignorant to eat, scarcely wise enough to breathe, mere existing human machines." By the time Woodrow Wilson was elected president, his opinion, as both a Democrat and a Southerner, was icing on the cake.

> Here was a vast laboring, landless, homeless class, once slaves . . . excited by a freedom they did not understand, exalted by false hopes, bewildered and without leaders, and yet insolent and aggressive; sick of work, covetous of pleasure, a host of dusky children put out of school.

But it took the whole country to create the climate in which the theft of civil liberties and the denial of respect for the race's human dignity took place. The white press in the North, whose readers "found delight in the lampooning of Negroes," showed itself to be as insensate as any Southern demagogue.

Harper's, Scribner's, Century, and to a lesser degree, the *Atlantic,* regularly employed derisive terms that are rarely used today. . . . [They] referred to Negroes as "nigger," "nigguh," "darkey," "coon," "pickaninny," "Mammy." Pralines were "nigger candy." Thomas Nelson Page published an article in *Harper's* titled "All the Geography a Nigger Needs to Know." And Charles Francis Adams Jr., Henry's brother and president of the Massachusetts Historical Society, wrote in *Century Monthly* in 1906: "The Negro had contributed nothing to civilization; Africa stood at its highest point of development because of the presence of the white man. The Negro mind did not expand—it promises fruit but it does not ripen." Oh, things would change—somewhat. Many a racist would die and his sons and daughters would grow up being racists themselves, but not being sure of why they were, knowing only that it was part of their heritage to be so. In time some of them might even lose the will to be a racist "when like their sires their sons are gone." But the long night of the nadir, which began in 1877 and didn't really lose its stranglehold on the African-American black throat until the Brown decision of 1954, would be the order of the day for those three-score years and twenty. Logan, for years a professor of history at Howard University and very well respected, has made this period his specialty, and no one understands it any better or has written about it more lucidly. Logan died in 1992.

Books 17 through 25:
WHAT RACISM COULDN'T KILL—THE
ACCOMMODATING AND THE ANGRY

ACISM BECAME so oppressive for blacks in the
South from 1877 to the end of Reconstruction
(what Logan calls the nadir, the dying days of
the century), that a huge exodus to Kansas and points
west took place. Close to two hundred thousand black
people left the only place they'd known since being
dragged to the New World to suffer Old World tyranny.
Carter G. Woodson, in his excellent study of the mass
exodus, *A Century of Negro Migration* (AMS, 1970),
puts the migration in its proper perspective as only he
can:

> Only a few intelligent Negroes [were] contented in the
> South. Negroes eliminated from politics could not easily
> bring themselves around to thinking that they should remain
> there in a state of recognized inferiority. . . . The murder of
> Negroes was so common that in 1875 General Sheridan said
> that as many as 3,500 persons had been killed and wounded
> in [Louisiana alone], the great majority of whom being
> Negroes; that 1,844 were killed and wounded in 1868, and
> probably 1,200 between 1868 and 1875. . . . As most of
> these murders were for political reasons, the offenders were
> regarded by their communities as heroes rather than as crim-
> inals. . . . Intelligent Negroes were either intimidated or
> killed so that the illiterate masses of Negro voters might be
> ordered to refrain from voting the Republican ticket.

In order to survive as something more than de facto chattel, blacks began to emigrate to Kansas, Missouri, and Indiana. Two men led this exodus: Moses Singleton of Tennessee and Henry Adams of Louisiana. Woodson says that Adams alone was responsible for organizing ninety-eight thousand blacks to move to Kansas. When a group of "leading whites and blacks" met to decide how to stop them, they decided that blacks were leaving because of the low price of cotton. Whatever errors had been committed, had been committed by whites and blacks alike! They also claimed that "the Negro race had been placed by the Constitution on a plane of absolute equality with the white race . . . and should be accorded the practical rights guaranteed by the said Constitution and laws."

By 1880 at least sixty-thousand blacks had made it to Kansas. Forty thousand of them were destitute when they got there, but they found employment and most were doing well within the first year. As to Kansas's reaction to all of this, writes Woodson: "The people of Kansas did not encourage the blacks to come. They even sent messengers to the South to advise the Negroes not to migrate. . . . When they did arrive, however, they welcomed and assisted them as human beings."

Southerners, who needed their black peons to survive well enough to keep up their tradition of Southern hospitality were forced to try to stop the exodus any way they could. They convinced the steamboat lines to stop furnishing blacks with transportation. When that didn't work, writs preferring false charges against blacks were obtained without much trouble. Some Southerners said "good riddance" to the blacks and insisted that importing Chinese and white labor to take their place would be better for the South in the end.

The issue eventually grew into a national debate and Frederick Douglass, for once, was on the wrong side.

He didn't think that blacks should leave: they were dissipating their potential voting power by going to a state where they would be a minority, and leaving one where they were in some cases a majority or close to it. But the great westward migration was the only means by which blacks could, to some extent, crawl up out of their lowly state. Kansas, fortunately, made that crawl possible.

The Autobiography of Ida B. Wells tells of a black man who was ascending the gangway on his way to Kansas, but his dog held back. The man turned and accosted the dog with, "Do you want to stay in the South and be lynched?"

The two histories covered in this section Lerone Bennett's *Before the Mayflower* [Must-Read No. 18] and *The Negro in New York* [Must-Read No. 19], edited by Roi Ottley, cover huge periods. Bennett's book begins when the title indicates and comes up to the present in the most recent edition (the ninth as of this writing). Ottley's book also begins before the *Mayflower*, when New York was still a Dutch colony, and continues through the decade before World War II. I've chosen to focus on Bennett's discussion of the 1850s to the end of the century, taking excerpts mostly from his work on the conflicts between the Irish and blacks in New York and on the Underground Railroad. A complete record of the work of the Underground Railroad was compiled by William Still (not to be confused with the well-known black composer William Grant Still, who helped Dvorak with his Ninth Symphony) who was in charge of the Underground Railroad in Philadelphia, the hub of that vast network of way stations out of hell. It runs to over seven hundred pages and is only available in research libraries so far as I know. Ottley's book is an excellent read, a treasure trove of the colorful and tragic history of blacks in New York.

Fighters like Ida B. Wells and Monroe Trotter [see

Must-Read Nos. 20 and 24] are, in effect, modern-day gladiators, and Woodson's *Mis-Education of the Negro* [Must-Read No. 25] is as contemporary as any book dealing with the problems of race that could be written today. With these volumes, we have turned a corner, moving from the post-Civil War era into the twentieth century.

One book about this era that deserves an honorable mention (and that would have been included if my list could have been a longer one) is James Weldon Johnson's *Black Manhattan*. *Black Manhattan* is a complete account of black activity in New York City from the Dutch days through the end of the 1920s. It is an excellent companion piece to *The Negro in New York* and includes sections on the theater and the nightclub life of blacks in nineteenth-century New York that I have not encountered elsewhere.

However, Johnson's *Autobiography of an Ex-Colored Man,* arguably the first successful novel, in modern terms, written by an African American, and his actual autobiography, *Along This Way,* are far more important works. *Along This Way* is the *one* volume by the inestimable Mr. Johnson that I've chosen to include here.

Similarly, of the many works of W. E. B. Du Bois, if any one must be chosen that's an accessible read for laymen, it would have to be either *The Autobiography* or *The World and Africa.* I have omitted *The World and Africa* with great reluctance. This important book introduces the immense subject of black African contributions to the culture of the entire world. In much the same way that America takes her cultural validity from Europe, and all formal, institutional learning in America is seen in a European context first, so too the black American can only get credibility as a cultural animal when the true story of Africa's impact on the world's history, and consequently on its culture, is told. And no one tells this story like Du Bois. So it's a Must-Read that isn't.

The achievements of black men and women in America in the nineteenth and twentieth centuries was nothing short of amazing. Black men crossed the continent, discovered passes, explored the territories, killed the Native American and the Mexican (may God forgive them), founded cities, and made their contributions to the practical sciences and to medicine. The books included here celebrate their accomplishments.

17

CREATED EQUAL: THE LIVES AND IDEAS OF BLACK AMERICAN INNOVATORS

by James Michael Brodie

NEW YORK: MORROW, 1993

In *Created Equal* James Michael Brodie has written a well-researched book that goes a long way toward establishing the bona fides of the black scientist and the black inventor. He makes black America proud of what it has accomplished in these two fields and should make white America ashamed of its failure to teach its sons and daughters about their homegrown history, of which they also should be proud, since it represents the American democracy at work. Sad to say, they didn't do it and they still aren't.

Brodie starts out with a bang. He tells us that "Massachusetts was the first state to recognize slavery in its Body of Liberties in 1641. Such famed landmarks as the House of the Seven Gables in Salem, were major headquarters for that state's deadly trade. . . . Until 1858 slavery laws made the inventions of slaves the property of their enslavers. It may never be known just how many inventions credited to Whites [sic] were actually created by their African captives."

The first chapter, "Slave Inventors," begins with the saga of

Ned, whose owner tried to patent Ned's invention in his name. He was turned down by the commissioner of patents even though he got Ned to sign a document stating that he was the creator of the invention—a cotton scraper. The commissioner argued that since Ned was not a citizen, he couldn't file for a patent. The owner marketed it anyway, encouraged by a planter who wrote "I am glad . . . your implement is the invention of a Negro slave— thus giving the lie to the abolition cry that slavery dwarfs the mind of the Negro. When did a free Negro ever invent anything?"

Onesimus, property of Cotton Mather, developed a cure for the smallpox virus. Henry Boyd did so well with a bed-frame design that he was able to buy himself and most of his family out of slavery and still have three thousand dollars by 1833. Ten years later, he had a staff of twenty-five to fifty employees. But even though his workshop was in Cincinnati, he was burned out twice. (You can't be that close to Kentucky and be black and prosperous.) Unable to get insurance after that, he retired and died three years later.

Early Inventors includes the big names: Benjamin Banneker, Norbert Rillieux, Jan Matzeliger, Lewis Latimer, Granville T. Woods, Elijah McCoy, Daniel Hale Williams, Charles Henry Turner, and Sarah Boone. Woods was so prolific and so successful that Thomas Edison, jealous of his accomplishments, sued him. Woods won in court. If Edison had been black and did what he did, no one would know his name, not any more than they know the name of Granville T. Woods. Born in Columbus, Ohio, Woods ended up holding over fifty patents on electrical and mechanical inventions: a steam boiler furnace, electric incubator (the forerunner of the machine that can hatch fifty thousand eggs at one time), an automatic airbrake, telephone receiver, the first device that made it possible to communicate between two moving trains—the Synchronous Multiplex Railway Telegraph, *and the third rail.*

Brodie opens the chapter called "The Twentieth Century" with a discussion of George Washington Carver, then goes on to Matthew Henson, Garret Morgan, and Madame C. J. Walker, then little known Annie Malone, Ernest Just, and Charles Drew.

His final chapter, "The Modern Era," includes Ralph Gardner, one of a dozen black scientists who worked on the Manhattan Project (the atom bomb). In all he tells the stories of over sixty inventors. And he's added additional names at the end of the book.

Henson carried Robert Peary in his arms to the spot that Peary claimed was the North Pole, and it was Henson who planted the flag. All he got for his efforts when they returned to America in triumph was a job as a messenger at two thousand dollars a year and no recognition as an explorer who helped make America proud of being the first country to reach the North Pole. I interviewed Henson for my junior high school newspaper in his apartment in Harlem thirty years later. He was still erect, dapper, with a wiry strength and a calm demeanor.

Garrett Morgan had to pretend he was a Native American in order to make his business thrive, when that didn't work he pretended that he worked for a white man who actually worked for him. In the end, he had to give up and sell out to General Electric for what ion Uptown parlance is called "chump change"—forty thousand dollars and no royalties. Born in Paris, Kentucky, in 1877, Morgan invented a gas inhalator mask (the precursor of the gas mask) in 1914 and used it to rescue twenty workmen trapped in a tunnel under Lake Erie. The city of Cleveland awarded him a gold medal for his heroism, and orders for the mask poured in from everywhere until it was learned that the inventor was black. Then many of the orders were cancelled. In 1923 he invented the stop light. It was the patent to that invention that he had to sell to General Electric for forty thousand dollars.

Elijah McCoy is the inspiration for the nugget in American jargon "the real McCoy." Born in Canada to runaway slave parents in 1843, he invented the drip cup that made it unnecessary to stop and restart engines (especially on the railroad) to lubricate them. It's still used in large industrial machines today. He filed over fifty-seven patents in his lifetime and started his own McCoy Manufacturing Company in Detroit. When inferior imitations of his products failed to do the job, a general complaint began to be heard, "We want the real McCoy." This didn't stop Irish railroad men from complaining that a "nigger" had invented a lubricating device that was taking away the jobs of honest Irishmen.

Madame C. J. Walker had made a million dollars by 1914. Annie Malone had made fourteen million dollars by the twenties. Both women made their money through the successful marketing of hair and skin-care products. But Walker is remembered because her daughter, A'Leila, to whom she left her fortune, became one of the shining lights of the Harlem Renaissance, entertaining European royalty and the literati of the day at her famous Dark Tower mansion cum salon on West 136th Street.

Ernest Just was a tragic figure. He was a pioneering marine biologist who gained recognition as the foremost expert on the egg development of sea life and was befriended by the white scientist Jacques Loeb. When he had the temerity to discover errors in Loeb's work, he was blackballed, never to get a major grant or an offer from a major institution again. He ended up in Italy where he tried, in desperation, to work for Mussolini. When the war broke out, he had to return to America. He died penniless. Drew discovered ways of preserving blood plasma in the thirties and became one of the world's leading authorities on "banking" blood. This work in plasma research saved hundreds of thousands of lives during World War II. As a consequence, the British asked him to supervise their blood bank during the war. Drew resigned from his appointment as head of the Red Cross when that organization insisted on segregating white blood from black. However, Brodie writes that his death was probably not due to his being refused a blood transfusion by a segregated hospital, as is so often reported. As to Ralph Gardner, he couldn't get a job after he helped create the atomic bomb. End of story.

18

BEFORE THE MAYFLOWER: A HISTORY OF BLACK AMERICA

by Lerone Bennett, Jr., 6th edition

NEW YORK: PENGUIN, 1998

Lerone Bennett's major opus is one of the bibles of African-American history. His has been a passionate voice of outspoken historical protest for over half a century. With a style that is so readable *Before the Mayflower* is now in its sixth edition. Along with John Hope Franklin's *From Slavery to Freedom* and Benjamin Quarles's *The Negro in the Making of America,* it is among the best of the comprehensive histories of black America. It is a good place to begin if you want to read a complete history of the black American experience.

Bennett is at his best when he transcends the facts of history and writes about what in his inspired hand becomes the high drama of the human condition. His treatment of the Underground Railroad, Reconstruction, and the added burden created by immigrants who took the bread out of the mouths of blacks throughout the nineteenth century are perfect cases in point. But he caused his greatest stir early in his career because of an article he wrote for *Ebony* magazine in which he criticized the limitations of the Emancipation Proclamation.

That article, published in the late fifties, argued that Lincoln freed the slaves he couldn't free and left in chains the ones he could since he freed only the slaves in the Confederacy over whom he had no control. The slaves in the border states of Kentucky, Maryland, Delaware, and Missouri (the states that remained loyal to the Union) were not the beneficiaries of this emancipation. Of course Lincoln argued that if he had attempted to end slavery in the border states, they might have joined the enemy. Nevertheless, Bennett's point was still well taken. And he made it at a time when Lincoln was still universally revered by most blacks in America.

His chapter on Reconstruction, titled "Black Power in the Old South," begins:

Never before had the sun shone so bright.

A former slave . . . was representing Mississippi in the United States Senate. Pinckney Benton Stewart Pinchback, young, charming, daring, was sitting in the governor's office in Louisiana.

In Mississippi, South Carolina and Louisiana, black lieutenant governors were sitting on the right hand of power. A black was secretary of state in Florida; a black was on the state supreme court in South Carolina. Seven blacks were sitting in the House of Representatives.

Nor was this all. Blacks and whites were going to school together, riding on streetcars together and cohabiting, in and out of wedlock. An interracial board was running the University of South Carolina, where a black professor, was teaching white and black youth metaphysics and logic.

So Reconstruction was making democracy a reality.

In his chapter "The Generation of Crisis," which covers the period that led up to the Civil War, when the conflict between immigrants and blacks was at its most intense, he writes:

The struggle between the . . . immigrants and black workers was particularly acrimonious. Most free blacks at this juncture lived along the docks and wharves and in alleys. Wherever they lived, people wanted them to go away. . . . Time and time again immigrants, fresh from the boats, cracked their skulls and burned their homes and churches. Some whites said openly that the only solution to the "Negro problem" was the "Indian solution."

In the chapter "The Life and Times of Jim Crow," Bennett has this to say about the genocidal attacks that blacks were subjected to when they tried to vote:

> Southern demagogues ... call[ed] for repeal of the Fourteenth and Fifteenth amendments. The U.S. Congress now became the major forum of racist propaganda.
>
> What this meant ... was spelled out in a revealing statement by Ben Tillman, [of] South Carolina. "We have done our level best," he said. "We have scratched our heads to find out how we could eliminate the last one of them [blacks]. We stuffed ballot boxes. We shot them. We are not ashamed."
>
> Shortly before the election of 1989 [in North Carolina], some fifty thousand rounds of ammunition and carloads of firearms were shipped [there] by whites in South Carolina and Virginia. ... [I]n Wilmington a white mob, including ... a former congressman, destroyed a black newspaper office, murdered eleven blacks and wounded scores.
>
> Nine Negroes massacred outright; a score wounded and hunted like partridges on the mountain; one man, brave enough to fight against such odds, was given the privilege of running the gauntlet up a broad street, while crowds of men lined the sidewalks and riddled him with a pint of bullets; ... another Negro shot twenty times in the back as he scrambled empty handed over a fence; thousands of women and children fleeing in terror from their humble homes in the darkness of the night. ... All this happened ... within three hundred miles of the White House ... within a year of the twentieth century.

And he has this to say about the Underground Railroad, quoted from *Boston Commonwealth*: "It was said long ago that the true romance of America was not in the fortunes of the Indian, where Cooper sought it; nor in New England character, where Judd found it; nor in the social contrasts of Virginia planters, as Thackeray imagined, but in the story of the fugitive slaves."

Bennett then goes on to say:

Fugitive slaves scaled mountains, forded creeks and threaded the forests. They came across the Ohio River and the Chesapeake Bay. They came with ailing women and sick children. Softly sometimes and sometimes imperiously they rapped on windows and begged help: a piece of bread, a spoon of medicine, directions to the next town. Wherever they rapped, wherever they stopped, men and women had to make a decision—either for or against slavery.

Was it true what they said about Dixie? This question was the core of the slavery dialogue; and no one could answer it better than fugitive slaves. . . . In the 1840s no abolitionist meeting was complete without a black speaker or a black exhibit (a fugitive slave).

In addition to his brilliant text, Bennett offers two reference sections at the end of the book that are quite useful: "Landmarks and Milestones" and "Black Firsts." "Landmarks and Milestones" covers the period from 1619 to 1992 and runs to over 200 pages in the sixth edition. Each year is broken down into months, and each landmark or milestone is descried in a short paragraph. "Black Firsts" is another thirty pages long, divided into categories that include everything from sports to the military.

Along with Benjamin Brawley, Franklin, Quarles, and J. A. Rogers, and of course, W. E. B. Du Bois, Bennett is among the preeminent historians of his race. His strident style, his refusal to turn the other historical cheek, has earned him many enemies among white editors and literati. Prominent among his other books is *Pioneers in Protest*, which presents short biographies of the black men and women who fought slavery with everything they had: Frederick Douglass, Nat Turner, Harriett Tubman, and Sojourner Truth—along with white heroes in the struggle, such as Thaddeus Stevens, Charles Sumner, and Wendell Phillips.

19

THE NEGRO IN NEW YORK: AN INFORMAL SOCIAL HISTORY

edited by Roi Ottley and William J. Weatherby

NEW YORK: NEW YORK PUBLIC LIBRARY, 1967

This informal social history, as the editors call it, is based on material originally put together by the Federal Writers Works Progress Administration (WPA) in 1940 but not brought together and published until twenty years later. It reads like a primary source with a good writing style, as it skips trippingly over the waters of the history of the most important city in the world, one to which black people have made a most important contribution, not least of which has been to help New York City grow into what it has become, since they have lived there from the very beginning.

The Works Progress Administration employed people to work for the government at jobs that they had skills in or were trained for. So the writers of this project went about the task of putting the book together in much the same way that a doctoral thesis is researched. They combed the archives and dug up as much as they could for one volume.

Ottley wrote screenplays (including *Knock on Any Door* starring Humphrey Bogart), which certainly explains why the book reads so well. While some of this material can be found in Black Manhattan, the pace of this volume and the editors' choices make it worth reading. I've described some of its content to people versed in black history, and they were surprised that this chapter in black America existed to such an extent, right here, under their very noses.

We learn, for instance, that there were probably black men in Henry Hudson's crew, and that the first blacks (eleven in all) arrived in America in 1626. They were put to work as the Dutch West India Company's Negroes. By 1644 other black men (also eleven) petitioned the council of New Netherlands for their freedom. The Dutch freed them and their wives for "long and faithful services." They were given land located far away from the village so they could provide for their own support. This area became the center of black activity in New York for the next two centuries and is known today as Greenwich Village.

The editors report that "at no time did the Dutch bar blacks from receiving the Word of God in their churches." Stuyvesant's Chapel in the Bouwerie had forty black parishioners at one time, who were given an education along with their Dutch brethren. The Dutch were not allowed to whip their slaves without official authority. The earliest free black living in the colony was probably Domingo Antony, who owned land by 1643.

England invaded the colony in 1664. One of the first things the English did was to send white Dutch soldiers to Virginia to be sold as slaves. By 1674 English law had decreed that blacks could not be freed even if they became Christians, and they were set apart from whites economically and socially. The English further decreed that "no Negro shall be buried in Trinity Churchyard."

Black retaliation for the harsher English rule came early. In 1708 an entire white family was wiped out by an Indian man and a black woman who were both slaves of the family. The woman was burned to death and the man hanged. In 1712 thirty blacks started a fire in Maiden Lane, and while whites were putting it out, the blacks attacked them with rifles and knives, killing nine white men and wounding six others. The reprisals were severe. The ringleaders, Clause, Robin, and Kuako, were tortured to death. The last man was burned alive. Wall Street gained its first notoriety as the place where "Negroes and Indians could be bought, sold or hired . . . and whites sold as indentured servants."

On the lighter side, Catharine Market became the place where blacks met and danced and sang in public together. But they were having too good a time, and in 1740 a law was passed prohibiting the sale of fruits and other produce by blacks or Indians. The most serious revolt came in 1741 when blacks set several fires to important business establishments and homes and there was general panic. The editors write that the hysteria was not unlike that found during the Salem witch-hunts. The innocent suffered with the guilty. Even a Catholic priest was thrown in jail because he seemed suspicious.

There was a trial during which an elaborate plot by three black men—Caesar, Cuffee and Prince—to burn the town and kill all the whites came to light. Blacks as far away as Long Island and Hackensack, New Jersey, were implicated. In the end, eighteen blacks were hanged, fourteen burned alive, and over seventy deported to Africa.

Whites involved in the plot were also severely dealt with. The white man who owned the tavern where much of the plotting took place was executed, along with his wife and Caesar's mistress, "the Irish beauty" Peggy Kerry, and a Catholic priest. But the spirit of blacks seems not to have been seriously dampened by any of this. One Tom was burned alive a short while later after he had set fire to a house and planned to burn down the whole town, with the help of blacks from Brooklyn and Long Island.

Industry and commerce were the keys to New York's growth, so slavery became unprofitable and primarily patriarchal. There were no slave rows because there were no plantations. Blacks lived under the same roofs as their owners. Sam Fraunces, who had come from the West Indies, was no slave, but he was black. He purchased a mansion on the corner of Broad and Pearl streets and turned it into his well-known tavern. It's still there today, but it's no longer owned by blacks.

Fraunces enlisted in the army during the American Revolution and served with distinction. He received a note of thanks from

Congress and two hundred pounds for the fighting he did. George Washington made his farewell address to his officers at Sam Fraunces's Tavern; he made Fraunces his steward after he became president, and Fraunces's daughter, Phoebe, actually saved Washington's life. An Irish agent named Hickey enlisted her help (after making love to her) in his attempt to kill Washington. He poisoned a plate of peas that Washington would have eaten had not Phoebe stopped him by throwing the peas on the ground. Hickey confessed and was hanged on June 28, 1776.

By 1809 Tom Molineaux had come to New York and joined in the Catharine Market festivities, which now included boxing. He became so proficient at it that he was the first boxer declared champion of America. After he had beaten everyone in America, he went to England, but lost there to the British champion Tom Cribb. (Cribb's second, said Molineaux, bit Cribb's thumb off and that's why he lost.)

The first black theater had come into existence at Bleecker and Mercer streets by 1821. It lasted for eight years. The owners of the African Grove, as the theater was called, segregated whites to the back of the house because they said the whites didn't know how to behave, but the police closed them down "for their own safety." This is the theater where Ira Aldridge got his start.

The first newspaper published by blacks was published in New York City on March 20, 1827. It was called *Freedom's Journal.* Following *Freedom's Journal,* many other black newspapers came into existence—eight in New York City and four more in the rest of the state. The Black Four Hundred had become so well established by 1887 that the *New York Sun* ran a story on them. They had an aggregate wealth of over three million dollars. In 1903 the *Sun* wrote that there were over three hundred families who could afford to buy houses priced from forty thousand to one hundred thousand dollars. These black families never hired black or Irish servants because they could not get them to show the proper respect. The children usually went to college abroad to escape American racism. However, many attended Howard University or Oberlin College in Ohio. Some went to Harvard and Yale. The black clubs that proliferated on West Fifty-third Street in

Manhattan were not frequented by these people, and they usually entertained at home, since Delmonico's and Sherry's were closed to them.

Race riots below Fifty-ninth Street became more serious and more frequent from 1890 to 1910. This was due in part to the fact that blacks dominated several neighborhoods downtown that whites wanted for themselves. "Nearly every house from Thirty-fourth Street and Forty-second Street between Eighth and Ninth avenues was occupied by blacks." The result of all this was that blacks had to move farther north. The only place "north" was north of Central Park. And that was Harlem.

The Negro in New York is a charming history of the city before 1940, with much that is not well-known about the part that blacks played in making New York City the chief reason why New York is called the Empire State.

20

CRUSADE FOR JUSTICE: THE AUTOBIOGRAPHY OF IDA B. WELLS BARNETT

edited by Alfreda M. Duster

CHICAGO: UNIVERSITY OF CHICAGO PRESS, 1970

She was one of the great African Americans, surely, yet her fame is muted compared to those whose position in the pantheon of stars is unquestioned. A fine figure of a woman, she was a well-respected journalist, with a strong presence and an immense fighting spirit. In spite of jealousy and chauvinist distemper, of which she faced her fair share, she made her mark and was in many ways the Martin Luther King of her day.

Ida B. Wells was born a slave in Mississippi in 1862. Both of her parents died in a yellow fever epidemic when she was fourteen. She began teaching school to take care of herself and her five surviving siblings. At twenty-two, she took her first official stand against segregation.

The U.S. Supreme Court had repealed the Civil Rights Bill of 1875 when it declared part of it unconstitutional and gave back to the states the power to determine who could ride in railroad cars and how—which was like sending the fox to protect the henhouse. That was the beginning of segregation of railroad cars and everywhere else. Wells was riding the railroad in the ladies' coach when the conductor tried to move her physically to the designated "colored" car. She retaliated by biting him on the hand. He went for help, and with two other grown men dragged Wells to the segregated car to the applause of the white passengers. She sued the railroad and won a five-hundred-dollar settlement. That was in 1883. But the state court reversed the decision and she ended up paying two hundred dollars in costs.

Her interest in journalism had her writing for the *Free Speech* and *Headlight* of Memphis by 1889. She soon bought a third interest and became one of its publishers. This was the period of wholesale lynchings and the exodus of black people to Kansas and points west. A particularly brutal double lynching of two prominent black men took place in Memphis, and Ida B. Wells made front-page copy of the incident:

> The city of Memphis has demonstrated that neither character nor standing avails the Negro if he dares to protect himself against the white man or become his rival. There is nothing we can do . . . as we are outnumbered and without arms. . . . The order was rigidly enforced against the selling of guns to Negroes. There is therefore only one thing left that we can do; save our money and leave a town which . . . takes us out and murders us in cold blood when [we are] accused by white persons.

For "telling it like it is" she almost got killed. After writing the editorial, she went to New York City to meet with T. Thomas Fortune, publisher of the *New York Age,* and while she was there, her printing press, the building it was in, and everything belonging to the paper were totally destroyed. Men and dogs were stationed everywhere to watch for her as soon as she came back to town, so she stayed in New York and went to work for T. Thomas Fortune. She begins chapter nine of her autobiography with: "Having lost my paper, had a price put on my life, and been made an exile from home for printing the truth, I felt that I owed it to . . . my race to tell the whole truth now that I was where I could do so freely. Accordingly . . . the *New York Age* had a seven-column article on the front page giving names, dates, and places of many lynchings."

This activity brought her national attention, and she soon became a celebrity. She was even asked to lecture in England more than once and fully a third of the book covers her sojourns there. By 1894 there were Ida B. Wells clubs in cities like Chicago, and several other anti-lynching clubs were formed as a consequence of her work. When she married an attorney, F. L. Barnett, in 1895, many black people were sorely vexed; they assumed that her marriage meant that she would no longer be a fighter for the cause and had abandoned them to seek a life of personal happiness. They needn't have worried.

In 1898 a black man, Frazier B. Baker, had been appointed postmaster of Lake City, South Carolina. His house was surrounded and set on fire by a mob of four hundred men. As members of the family ran out of the house, they were shot. Baker wasn't killed because he had been accused of raping a white woman—the usual excuse. He was killed because the Republican government of William McKinley had appointed him postmaster! Mrs. Barnett went to Washington, D.C., to meet with McKinley, who promised to get the secret service to investigate. All that happened was that a bill calling for compensation for the widow never even got out of committee, and the Spanish-American War took everyone's mind away from such trivia.

Of Booker T. Washington, Wells writes:

When Theodore Roosevelt became president... Booker T. Washington became his political adviser so far as the colored people of this country were concerned. There were those of us who felt that a man who had no political strength in his own state and who could do nothing whatsoever to help elect a president of the United States was not the man to be the adviser as to the political appointment of colored men from states which not only could, but did cast votes by which the Republican president had been placed in office.

W. E. B. Du Bois was persuaded to keep Barnett out of the founding inner circle of the National Association for the Advancement of Colored People (NAACP) by one of the white power brokers, Mary White Ovington, even though she had been invited to the opening ceremonies. So after being bumped from that august body, Barnett formed her own organization.

Her work included saving both Steve Green and "Chicken Joe" Campbell from death, which she describes in fascinating detail. Green sharecropped for a white man in Arkansas. When he decided to leave his life of peonage, the man tried physically to stop him. Green killed him and, with his new-found freedom, made it all the way to Chicago, but he was tracked down and jailed pending extradition. He tried to commit suicide by eating glass rather than go back to Arkansas, where certain death awaited him. In fact, the sheriff from Arkansas showed up and told him a thousand men would be waiting for him when he got off the train. Through her lawyer's maneuvers, Barnett managed to get another sheriff to "arrest" Green in transit and return him to Illinois. The sheriff from Arkansas returned with a second extradition order, but Steve Green had gone into hiding and the sheriff had to return to Arkansas empty-handed.

"Chicken Joe" Campbell was one of the trusted prison guards of Joliet prison. Someone killed the warden's wife, and of the forty trustees, Chicken Joe was singled out as the culprit and put in solitary confinement for forty days on bread and water. Mr. Barnett took the case at his wife's behest. It lasted six weeks and, of course, the defendant couldn't pay him. In addition, he lost several briefs and a small fortune in fees as well from other work he didn't have time for. But theirs was a solid marriage that brought them four children. Although Chicken Joe was found guilty and sentenced to the death penalty, the sentence was commuted to life. Both men escaped lynching, even if one was in hiding and the other in prison, thanks to Ida B. Wells Barnett and the efforts of her husband, family, and committee. If you want to know how she ended her days, it's all in her book.

21

UP FROM SLAVERY: AN AUTOBIOGRAPHY

by Booker T. Washington, with an introduction by Louis Lomax

NEW YORK: DOUBLEDAY, 1964 EDITION

In his 1964 introduction to *Up From Slavery*, Louis Lomax claimed "Booker T. Washington's impact on the destiny of the American Negro is unmatched, save by, perhaps Abraham Lincoln." Throughout his lifetime, Lomax was a strong advocate of militancy in the face of racism. At one point in the fifties, he took on William Buckley, that bright and shining star of the Far Right, one-on-one, and by all accounts bested him. When Buckley invited him on his television talk show, Lomax stated quite categorically that he is in the camp of those who are critical of Booker T. Washington and most of what he stood for. Given that stated position, the exalted place that Lomax reserves for Washington is nothing short of startling.

It's been almost a century since the man from Tuskegee held the black world in thrall and wielded more power in the land than most white men. Reading his autobiography this many years later is still an excruciating experience that the passage of time has not been able to ameliorate. Whenever Washington talks about the horrors of slavery, his approach is so obsequious that he always

manages to find a reason for excusing the dehumanizing subjuga-
tion. Two quotes from *Up From Slavery* will suffice to make the
point:

> I pity from the bottom of my heart any nation or body of people
> that is so unfortunate as to get entangled in the net of slavery. I
> have long since ceased to cherish any spirit of bitterness against
> the Southern white people on account of the enslavement of my
> race. . . . [W]hen we look facts in the face, we must acknowledge
> that, notwithstanding the cruelty and moral wrong of slavery, the
> ten million Negroes inhabiting this country, who themselves or
> whose ancestors went through the school of American slavery, are
> in a stronger and more hopeful condition, materially, intellectu-
> ally, morally, and religiously than is true of an equal number of
> black people in any other portion of the globe.

It's the same argument that Walter Winchel used to criticize
Paul Robeson after Peekskill: Robeson should have been grateful,
he said, that he was in America and not back in the jungle.
Washington also writes:

> Ever since I have been old enough to think for myself, I have en-
> tertained the idea that, notwithstanding the cruel wrongs inflicted
> upon us, the black man got nearly as much out of slavery as the
> white man did. The hurtful influences of the institution were not
> by any means confined to the Negro. This was fully illustrated by
> the life upon my own plantation. The whole machinery of slavery
> was so constructed as to cause labor, as a rule, to be looked upon
> as a badge of degradation, of inferiority. Hence labor was some-
> thing that both races on the slave plantation sought to escape. The
> slave system on our place, in large measure, took the spirit of self-
> reliance and self-help out of the white people.

These are the sentiments that account for Washington's great
popularity in his day. He's certainly right that there has always
been a need for the two races to work together to break down
racial barriers and open the gates of opportunity. But if, once the
gates are opened and blacks enter, they are still in a supplicant position, owning nothing of significance, never the ultimate decision-
maker, beset on all sides until whatever real gains they've made

are once again stripped from them, then we aren't talking about cooperation, we're talking about inequality. Without political power, no amount of respect for hard work, no amount of "owning your own" can ever make equality a reality.

But Washington's inner strength was impressive. He grew up in a log cabin, fourteen by sixteen feet, that he shared with an older brother, a sister, and his mother. Because his mother was the plantation cook, she was required to do all the cooking for everyone on the plantation—in her cabin. There were no windows, just openings that let in the cold in the winter and the heat in the summer. The floor was dirt and the bed was rags on the floor. Coming from such distressing beginnings, his success was worthy of a Horatio Alger story. Booker T. Washington didn't just succeed, he succeeded mightily.

Founding the legendary Tuskegee Institute was only one of his accomplishments. He became a national figure in 1895, when he made the famous speech in Atlanta that espoused separate but equal in social intercourse. "In all things purely social we can be as separate as the fingers, yet one as the hand [and he balled up his fist] in all things essential to mutual progress." Of course, such an absurd dichotomy isn't possible, and shouldn't have to be, in a modern democracy. But it is key to the understanding of why he was such a success.

If anyone had attempted, at any point in the life of the country, to put forth the idea that another ethnic group should accept a socially subordinate position in the society in order to get ahead economically, the rage that would have ensued would have probably created instant anarchy. Because a black man was advocating this compromise for black Americans, he was hailed as a hero and made HNIC (Head Nigger in Charge). To the extent that white America still looks for such leaders and advocacy, we, as a country, are holding on to our racist past. And only white America can cure the disease, because only white America is really infected by it. Most of black America, almost sadly, just wants to be left alone. Any hostility that we harbor, given the hate that surrounds us, is almost pitiable as a response to that hate.

The rewards that Booker T. reaped were immense. He became

the confidant of two presidents: Theodore Roosevelt and Howard Taft. He counseled both on domestic policy, whenever it pertained to race, rewrote the sections of their speeches that dealt with those issues, and had approval over every black appointment to any post of significance. Despite these powers, Washington couldn't stop either man from turning to the South and supporting racism in order to get votes. Not once when it really counted did either of them listen to him.

The infamous Brownsville Raid of 1906 is a case in point. Black soldiers in Brownsville, Texas, fed up with the insults and abuse they were constantly subjected to, went on a rampage. One white man was killed. The soldiers testified freely to white attacks against them but refused to testify against one another. Roosevelt discharged three entire companies of the Twenty-fifth Regiment as a consequence, without a trial, and that was that. Washington's attempt to intercede was flatly rejected.

His control of the black press, on the other hand, was practically monolithic. He gave money to and advertised in most black newspapers of the time. Whenever an unfavorable article appeared, a simple phone call handled the matter. He bought the *New York Age* in secret and had to deny the purchase in public, although he refused to sell his stock and blocked all attempts to buy him out. That was real power. At the time, the *Age* was one of the preeminent black newspapers in America.

In 1901 he dined at the White House with Roosevelt. The South was highly offended in spite of his public obsequiousness. And today many see his emphasis on self-reliance as an object lesson that black America would do well to emulate. Hiding underneath that "self-reliance" that seems to carry a message of social separateness with it is the fear that to try for anything else in a white-dominated society is foolhardy. Du Bois, in *Souls of Black Folks*, had this to say about Washington in 1908:

> His programme of industrial education, conciliation of the South, and submission and silence as to civil and political rights, was not wholly original. . . . It startled the nation to hear a Negro advocating such a programme after many decades of bitter complaint; it startled and won the applause of the South, it interested and won

the admiration of the North; and after a confused murmur of protest, it silenced if it did not convert the Negroes themselves.

That explains his popularity. He was "leading" his race into a position that both the North and the South wanted the black man in. And the black man went along with it because its proponent was so popular and so powerful. It was a case for them of "whatever is, is right." The Wizard of Tuskegee, as he was often called, died in 1915 at the comparatively young age of fifty-nine. But his "work" was carried on by his minions well into the twenties. At one point in the essay, Du Bois calls him "the most distinguished Southerner since Jefferson Davis." That's as good a dig as one can think of to hand Booker T. Washington.

22

ALONG THIS WAY: THE AUTOBIOGRAPHY OF JAMES WELDON JOHNSON

by James Weldon Johnson

NEW YORK: VIKING PRESS, 1933

James Weldon Johnson was a teacher; a lawyer; a professional musician and a lyricist with several Tin Pan Alley hits and Broadway shows to his credit; a poet who is included in most black American anthologies; a historian who published in that field; a novelist; a foreign service officer who was first consul in both Venezuela and Nicaragua; a journalist who wrote the editorials for the *New York Age* for ten years; and, for fourteen years, Mr. NAACP, first as field secretary and then as executive secretary. He came as close as anyone to getting an anti-lynching bill passed by Congress in 1921 to 1922.

When he became poet emeritus at Hampton Institute, where a special chair had been created for him, that was to be his last career. He was born in Jacksonville, Florida, in 1871 and died in a car crash in 1938, and in between what he accomplished earned him the title Renaissance man. His was a remarkable life, brilliantly lived. It was said that the one thing that was exasperating about Johnson was that he never got angry. Being levelheaded, showing restraint, remaining calm in times of crisis, these were his strengths and they served him well throughout his life.

Johnson wrote *Along This Way,* as he tells it, because his novel, *The Autobiography of an Ex-Colored Man* (published anonymously in 1912) was so convincing that many thought he had written it about himself. But the work was fiction, loosely based on the life of a friend who had passed for white, and Johnson kept his friend's secret. Johnson faced no such dilemma since he was much too dark to ever think of solving the race problem thusly, even if he had wanted to. But because the novel was so heartfelt, speculation arose that it was his own story, and the word "autobiography" simply added to the confusion. He decided to clear up the matter by writing his real autobiography, which he published in 1933.

Johnson's first job after graduating from Atlanta University was as principal of the grammar school that was his alma mater. To help pay for college, he taught in the summer in rural Georgia, and walked seven miles to get to the nearest town on weekends. Because so much of the walk had to be done in the sun, Johnson sauntered along the back roads of Georgia in a suit, shirt, and tie, with an open umbrella posing as a parasol.

As successful as Johnson was as a songwriter and diplomat, that aspect of his life was overshadowed by the more imposing accomplishments of his poetry and prose, and his work for the National Association for the Advancement of Colored People (NAACP). "Lift Every Voice and Sing" was set to music by his brother Rosamond, and it became so popular that it has been dubbed the Negro National Anthem. When Johnson started at the NAACP, the organization was just beginning, and its Southern roots were still tenuous. As field secretary, he did the pioneering work that made the organization a truly national one. It was backbreaking, dangerous work that took him into the small towns as well as the major cities of the South, which were then in the process of becoming their most racist.

In 1916 the NAACP had sixty-eight branches in the North and West and only three in the South, with a total membership of

348. Johnson's insistence on organizing the South was opposed by some of the board of directors, who feared that the threat of violence made it too risky to try. Johnson disagreed. If the organization did not become truly national, he argued, it would never be truly effective. Attacking white racism from the North would mean nothing if blacks in the South did not fight for themselves.

He began the task of organizing the South in 1917 and within two years he had proved his point. By 1919 the NAACP had 310 ranches, 131 of them in the South. But these were the hell years for black America. Nell Persons was burned alive in Memphis. Six thousand black people were driven from their homes in East St. Louis, Illinois, and hundreds killed, some of them burned alive in their homes. Thirteen black soldiers were taken out of their barracks in Texas at predawn and hanged. In Estill Springs, Tennessee, a black man was tortured then burned alive. James Weldon Johnson was the man on the firing line throughout this period, the man who was expected to provide a voice, to cry out, to create a dialogue, to find a solution that was effective on some level, any level. As much as he despised Woodrow Wilson's bigotry, Johnson managed to see him and to make a desperate plea for intervention, hoping that the chief executive would act to stem the hate-filled violence—violence that was as American as cherry pie, as H. Rap Brown was to say forty-five years later. Wilson hadn't even heard of the Estill Springs torture death. (He said it was hard for him to believe that such a thing could happen in America!) He promised to do something and stopped some of the hangings of black soldiers on the home front, but nothing much beyond that.

In 1919 Texas asked for all the records of the NAACP, not only to harass them but to compile a hit list. The executive secretary of the NAACP at the time was a white man, John R. Shillady. He rushed to Austin to comply with the request and was beaten badly in public by the men with whom he had just met. Among them was a constable and a judge. The governor was ecstatic with praise for the hooligans. Johnson says Shillady never recovered psychologically from the beating. "I don't think he was ever able to realize how such a thing could happen to [him], [after all he was] free, white and twenty-one." Shillady resigned soon after and that's when Johnson got the job. All of Johnson's work made him a national figure, and there were several occasions where he was heckled because of his importance.

Johnson's other careers, were just as filled with drama. He joined the foreign service after Teddy Roosevelt let it be known that he would appoint him once he qualified. (Johnson had helped get Roosevelt elected when he ran for president in 1904, following the death of McKinley.) Johnson passed the exam and was eventually posted in Nicaragua in 1905, where he spent four years. Nicaragua offered a shorter route to the Pacific than Panama, which was what made it so important to America. While Johnson was first consul in the port city of Corinto, a rebellion broke out that had its roots in the filibustering of the period. A Nicaraguan general killed two Americans charged with invading the country. During the rebellion, the American ambassador was cut off in Managua and all the action centered in Corinto, since America was able to land marines there. James Weldon Johnson was the *55 Days to Peking* hero of the hour, the diplomat who guarded American interests against a foreign enemy a la Charlton Heston, since he was the civilian authority with whom the captains and admirals of American naval vessels conferred and to whom they often deferred. He was the man who decided whom to give refuge to in the consulate, which meant diplomatic immunity. In one instance he "detained" the president of Nicaragua; on another he gave asylum to *another* Nicaraguan president and helped him to flee the country.

In his Broadway period (from 1901 to 1904) Johnson worked with Florenz Ziegfeld and, along with his brother and their partner Bob Cole, was under contract to Klaw and Erlanger, the leading Broadway producers of the day. They received a king's salary for being the best show doctors of the period, coming up with songs to give an ailing show what it needed to survive.

It's all part of the story of this amazing American hero—African-American hero—JWJ.

23

THE NEGRO PRESS IN THE UNITED STATES

by Frederick Detweiler

CHICAGO: UNIVERSITY OF CHICAGO PRESS, 1922

Detweiler's book stops with the first year or two of the twenties. By the time the Negro press became the black press, it had seen the best of its pioneering days, when reading a black newspaper in a Southern town could be a life or death affair. Detweiler is often contemptuous of his subject. He calls them "avowed" newspapers, and says of white hostility to the *Chicago Defender*, "Naturally one expects [it]." But no black writer that I've come across has done the yeoman's work of digging up a record of the heroic days when black correspondents were lynched in the South for working for black newspapers, when domestics were fired from their jobs because they were found reading a Negro newspaper, when the attorney general of the United States made it difficult for black newspapers to use the mails. This is the record that needs to be remembered, or certainly retold, not the becalmed period when black journalists were given the same courtesies in press conferences that the rest of the Fourth Estate enjoyed, whether they were native to the country or not, and whether they could speak English or not. If we have to endure the patronizing tone of a thinly disguised racist to resurrect the heroism of these men and women, then so be it.

Detweiler writes about the *Chicago Defender* more than any other black newspaper because it was the most prominent during that period, but one does not get the sense that the other publications are just throw-ins. There is a comprehensiveness to this history of the early decades of black journalism which make the valiant attempt of these men and women to create an independent voice for their race very appealing. It was black America doing the things it always does, fighting mightily for uplift of its own, only to be bullied and muzzled and mocked and expunged from the official record of the times. And generations later, with that record forgotten, a lone black man or woman is looked at and castigated for being "violence prone" for being "lazy," for being "shif'less" and "unreliable." Not that Detweiler doesn't subscribe to these sentiments. He does, though not too aggressively. In trying to present the early days of black journalism as an impoverished attempt at a modern discipline of communication, he has told a tale of valor instead.

He begins his history with the following report:

SOMMERVILLE, TENN., Feb. 7, 1919—White people of this city have issued an order that no "colored newspaper" must be circulated in this town, but that every "darkey," must read the *Falcon*, a local white paper edited by a Confederate veteran. . . . Since the invasion made . . . by black newspapers . . . people have been leaving by the wholesale, seeking better opportunity and development in northern cities. The edict was issued against the newspaper when white men were forced, because of the lack of help, to plow the fields.

As the above suggests, the black newspaper was a serious weapon against racism at one time. But the attitude toward controlling blacks in the South was always schizophrenic. Richard Wright writes in *Black Boy* about not being able to get a library card so he could read H. L. Mencken because blacks weren't allowed to use the public library in most Southern cities. So when blacks started their own newspapers and it had an impact on blacks that was inconvenient for the white South, blacks were told that if they must read, they could only read the slave master's paper. One can therefore assume there were no black authors in those libraries.

Crisis magazine, *Challenge,* and the *Chicago Defender,* all black publications, were singled out for special attention by the South. An article in the *Defender* was credited as the cause of a riot in Longview, Texas. The governor of Arkansas claimed *Crisis* and the *Defender* were responsible for riots in his state, and he would ask the postmaster-general to exclude them from the mails.

Again, in 1919, the attorney general of the United States investigated black newspapers and magazines. He said in a report to the Senate, "The influence of the Negro press in general [is not] to be reckoned with lightly." In 1921 John Lee Eberhardt of Athens, Georgia, a black man who was a staff member of the *Philadelphia American,* was jailed as a suspect in the murder of a white woman. He was taken from the jail by a white mob and burned at the stake. Said the *American:* "It is believed by many [in Athens] that [his killers wanted to] 'get' Eberhardt for circulating the [newspaper]. More than five thousand took part in the lynching."

The Messenger, edited by A. Philip Randolph and Chandler Owen, ran articles with headlines such as "Lynching: Capitalism Its Cause; Socialism Its Cure." It published Claude McKay's poem, "If We Must Die," which ends with the lines [We'll die] Like men. . . . Pressed to the wall, dying, but—fighting back! In 1919 when a prominent black man said he was an American and proud of it, the *Messenger* replied: "Think of a Negro being proud to be an American!" A year earlier, it had published an article entitled "Pro-Germanism Among Negroes." The editors, at an open meeting, said the article was satirical and sarcastic, but the Department of Justice confiscated copies, arrested and jailed the editors, and drafted Chandler Owen. Their second-class mailing privileges were also taken away.

In 1916 one white observer was amazed "that there are more than 450 newspapers and other publications . . . devoted exclusively to the interests of colored people, nearly all edited by

Negroes," which seemed to alarm Detweiler as well. He called black newspapers that dealt with life and death issues "race" papers, and what they wrote he dubbed "propaganda." However, Detweiler qualified the second conclusion with "If we claim the Negroes as a minority group . . . it must be pointed out that the Negro press is not all propaganda: it has a substantial basis in the everyday sort of news and advertising business on which the normal newspaper depends."

That may be, but it was the so-called propaganda that caused all the trouble. Detweiler quotes a sixteen-year-old Jamaican girl from Panama, Rebecca Hall. She had been imported by a white woman for domestic service in Key West, in 1920. When the white woman ordered her to throw away her copy of *Negro World*, her reply was "You make me laugh. This paper is worth more to me than all the jobs you can give me. If I am to go I shall go with this paper, and if I am to stay I'll stay with it."

Of course, with integration came "opportunities" for black journalists to work for white newspapers. Some of these journalists spent their entire professional life without ever writing one article about the problem of racism in America. They had press privileges wherever they went. They joined the union and ended up retiring with a pension. And throughout their lifetimes, they were held up as an example of someone the race should be proud of, limited though they were in what they could say about race issues. There is still the lingering feeling in many quarters that if it's political and an opinion and it's in a white newspaper, it's an editorial or a column. If it's political and an opinion and in a black newspaper, it's propaganda.

24

THE GUARDIAN OF BOSTON: MONROE TROTTER

by Stephen J. Fox

NEW YORK: ATHENEUM, 1970

Along with Booker T. Washington and W. E. B. Du Bois, Monroe Trotter was considered one of the three most influential black men in America in the first two decades of the twentieth century. From 1898 until his death in 1934, at the age of sixty-two, he fought an uncompromising battle against racism in the most modern terms. He was considered a radical, who was as far to the left as anyone could get and still work within the system. His manner of attacking all and sundry, from presidents down—and not always in print—gave him the reputation of being *mad* or *crazy* or something worse. His manner of protest was too extreme even for Du Bois. And the contempt bordering on hatred that he and Booker T. Washington had for each other amounted to nothing less than a blood feud.

Born into the black aristocracy of Boston and its environs, in the white suburb of Hyde Park, he came by his militancy naturally enough. His father had been recorder of deeds in Washington, D.C., the highest post a black had held in government to that time. Before that he had been an officer in the Union army. After the war he resigned from a position in the post office rather than put up with its racism.

Educated at Harvard, where he graduated magna cum laude five years after Du Bois, Trotter had an inheritance of twenty thousand dollars to get him started. He was a fairly successful real estate agent with a mostly white clientele before he embarked on his career as a crusading journalist. In 1899 he married Geraldine Pindell, also of the black elite: she had attended grammar school in Everett and business college after that, and her uncle had led the fight to integrate Boston schools in 1850. Life was as full of promise and bourgeois ease as life could be for black newlyweds in America at the time. They had a lovely house on a hill in the suburb of Dorchester, a wide circle of friends, which included Du Bois and his first wife and daughter, who stayed with them one summer. The Trotters themselves never had children.

Trotter got into the newspaper business almost as an avocation, but with one purpose in mind, once the printer's ink got into his veins. The *Guardian,* he said, "would be an organ which is to voice intelligently the needs and aspirations of the colored American." The first issue appeared in November 1901. By the time it was all over, thirty-three years later, he would be overwrought and unkempt—an old man whose best years, as Fox continually points out, were at least a decade behind him. The several houses he had owned, the twenty-thousand-dollar inheritance, and the money from his real-estate business had all been spent to support his great passion.

What separated the *Guardian* from other black newspapers of the day was Trotter's almost contemporary stand on the major issues of race, issues that black Americans are still confronted with. He insisted that black people have the franchise when most of white America was hailing Booker T. Washington's emphasis on labor and industrial education. Washington's position was that full citizenship, which would mean complete participation in the political process, was something black America could and should wait for since black America had made a terrible mess of Reconstruction. To Trotter that was blasphemy, and he took the first chance he got to challenge Washington in public on his fawning at the feet of a white establishment that had little or no regard for African Americans or their problems.

The meeting was to be a Washington foray into Trotter territory, arranged by Washington's many friends (Andrew Carnegie led the list). Trotter had drafted nine questions to put to the wizard of Tuskegee. The fourth one asked, "When you said: 'It was not so important whether the Negro was in the inferior car as whether there was in that car a superior man not a beast,' did you not minimize the outrage of the insulting Jim-Crow car discrimination and justify it by the 'bestiality' of the Negro?"

Trotter never got to ask the next question. A fight broke out, and he was arrested for disturbing a public meeting, even though he was not involved in the fisticuffs. Washington was so well connected that he was able to make sure the charges stuck and Trotter spent thirty days in jail. Although his abrasive manner and modern style of plain speaking horrified the likes of Du Bois and James Weldon Johnson, and most of the white liberals who founded the National Association for the Advancement of Colored People (NAACP), Trotter's jailing was considered outrageous and illegal, and brought him much support, especially from Du Bois. It was Trotter who lit the fire that helped Du Bois create the Niagara Movement, which Du Bois later took, whole cloth, into the NAACP.

Fox has written a workman-like biography of the standard scholarly genre, heavily footnoted. His was probably the last book to be written about blacks that used the word *Negro* indiscriminately throughout the text, a word that Trotter never liked. Trotter was using the term *Afro American* as early as the teens, along with *colored*. The obvious racism of the label *Negro* was one that he understood sixty years before the advent of Black Power. Since there is no Negro land and no Negro race and people are identified by the color of their skin, their place of birth and their ethnicity, the only purpose that the word Negro served was to put black people in an implied place of further inferiority—almost as if they had an asterisk beside their designation as an American citizen. Not that Fox can be blamed for following the fashion of the time.

Fox cavils over what he calls Trotter's long decline, by which he means the last fourteen years of his life, a time when many new currents often made it seem that time had passed him by. But this criticism is absurd, not only because Trotter started so early that to be as effective as he was for close to a generation meant that he had a long run indeed; but more to the point, nothing that Trotter was fighting to solve was solved while he was fighting to his dying day to solve—nothing!

What Trotter did achieve by his example, his point of departure, and his analysis of the problem in its many manifestations, was to insist on the only solutions that would give black America actual equality before yet another century passed them by while they were still trying to be equal! Most blacks, however, didn't take themselves seriously enough to believe that they could get anything but partial equality or they didn't have the backbone to put up the kind of fight that was needed if their aim was to get real equality, since doing so would have meant making the kinds of sacrifices Trotter and his wife made throughout their adult lives. When she realized that the man she married had become a leader of men, Deenie, as she was affectionately called, abandoned her quiet vale in Dorchester, rolled up her sleeves, and went to work running the business end of the newspaper. She never rebuked her husband or thought of deserting him for forcing her to give up the comfortable life, selling the house and furniture and finally being reduced to what Fox calls "genteel poverty." She died prematurely at the age of forty-five, a victim of the flu epidemic of 1918.

What were the stands that Trotter took, what were the things that he wrote in his editorials that were so alarming to blacks and made even the liberal whites of the NAACP shudder? To begin with, he refused to participate in any organization that was white dominated, as was the NAACP in the early years. He didn't see his newspaper as a business enterprise, but as a public service, so he never made any money from it. He would take no ads for hair straighteners or skin lighteners, and because he was a teetotaler, he wouldn't take liquor ads (or ones for tobacco), either. His constant insistence that black America should have the vote and have it now, not later, was considered militant. As basic as that right might seem now, it was fought bitterly in both the North and South for the next fifty years, and like busing, sent up a red flag to most of white America when they heard it being demanded by anyone black.

In addition to the Booker T. episode, there was Trotter's nose-to-nose confrontation with Woodrow Wilson, who was instituting segregated working conditions for black clerks in the federal government. The two men "slugged it out" for forty-five minutes. It was not so much the substance of Trotter's demands that irked Wilson as his manner, notes Fox. Trotter seemed to treat the president as just a man as opposed to a massuh. Wilson refused to see Trotter again and always called him Tucker thereafter.

Trotter's attempt to get to the Peace Conference in Versailles in 1919, where the Allies were parceling out the spoils of World War I, to present demands "for full democracy for Colored Americans" reads like a novel. He had to use an alias and hire on a steamer as a cook who spoke French—he could do neither—and enter France illegally since the State Department wouldn't issue him a passport.

Fox raises a question as to how he died. Did he fall from a roof because he had become disoriented, something that had been happening to him in his last years, or did he jump? However it happened, he carried the loving memory of his wife with him. Fox quotes from the *Guardian* one of Trotter's last dedications to her that he published over the years:

> To my Fallen Comrade, Geraldine L. Trotter, My Loyal Wife, who is no more. To honoring her memory, who helped me so loyally, faithfully, conscientiously, unselfishly, I shall devote my remaining days; and to perpetuating the *Guardian* and the Equal Rights cause and work for which she made such noble, and total sacrifice, I dedicate the best that is in me till I die.

25

THE MIS-EDUCATION OF THE NEGRO

by Carter G. Woodson

WASHINGTON, D.C.: ASSOCIATED PUBLISHERS, 1933

Carter G. Woodson, more than anyone, helped make Black History a respectable discipline, long before black America had the clout to force its general acceptance on the academic establishment. Never a supplicant at the foot of white learning, Woodson said it took him thirty years to *get over* his Ph.D. from Harvard. That thought is a fitting introduction to *The Mis-Education of the Negro*.

The author's thesis, simply stated, is that blacks have no business allowing themselves to be educated by white America. He has particular scorn for educated blacks, those whom W. E. B. Du Bois called the Talented Tenth. He says that they have lapped up their Plato and their Nietzsche and the literary canon of the West by the bucketful and then gone on to try to fit into a world that neither wants them, nor is willing to treat them as the equals of whites of similar or lesser accomplishments. These people, writes Woodson, have been educated away from their race.

A decade ago, I was teaching at Medgar Evers College in New York City. One of my colleagues (he had been in prison and that gave him a manly aura, and he had been befriended by Norman Mailer and that gave him legitimacy) was the leading exponent of teaching the non-European tradition. I applauded the effort and taught Jean Toomer's *Cane*. I asked what he was using in the course, and he looked at me without a hint of self-reproach and said William Faulkner's *Light in August*. I once asked an educator, a black woman at a more prestigious university, why there was such an emphasis on the western tradition, the European one. Why did minority students have to take Conversations of the West courses to the utter exclusion of any other types of conversations? She asked "What do you mean by *Western tradition?*"

What's to be confused about? If you're going to teach a version of history that tells the story from someone else's perspective, then you have to teach books that include that perspective. Faulkner patronized blacks throughout his life, especially the black mammy in *The Sound and the Fury*. Some believe that black Africa has no tradition worth studying. For anyone who doesn't know what a non-European tradition is, or why Eurocentrism is a skewed view of the history of the world, I recommend Du Bois's *World and Africa*. You'll be amazed at how much tradition there is in the world that is non-European.

But in the *Mis-Education of the Negro*, Woodson goes beyond choosing one book over another. He condemns the race as a whole for allowing itself to be reduced to such docile and acquiescent acceptance of inferiority that it is willing, even by implication, to believe that it has contributed very little to the nation's history, to its culture in particular (and even less to the culture of the world), and knows only what the master who made it a race of slaves in the first place has told it that it should know. He adds that from this sense of subservience has come the willingness to succumb to racist police, to vote for a major political party's candidates only to be scorned soon after until the next election, to allow charlatans to pose as leaders of the race only to sell it out and pocket the profits, to allow foreigners to provide the goods and services that any self-respecting group would provide for itself, especially in its own neighborhood.

In one of the most telling quotes in a book filled with truly inspired ones, he writes: "When you determine what a man shall think you do not have to concern yourself about what he will do. If you make a man feel that he is inferior, you do not have to compel him to accept an inferior status, for he will seek it himself. If you make a man think that he is justly an outcast, you do not have to order him to the back door. He will go without being told; and if there is no back door, his very nature will demand one."

Of course, black people need something beyond the spirit of independence and belief in their ability to build a new utopia. Woodson offers a plethora of ideas. He points out that black America need not be ashamed of its past and need not accept white academia's interpretation of it. He tells us that trial by jury was an African concept originally, and of course the smelting of iron, and that Africans were the first to domesticate the sheep, goat, and cow, and they produced the first stringed instruments. "[R]ecent catalogues of leading Negro colleges [show] that . . . they give courses in ancient, medieval, and modern Europe, but they do not give such courses in ancient, medieval, and modern Africa. Yet Africa, according to recent discoveries, has contributed about as much to the progress of mankind as Europe has, and the early civilization of the Mediterranean world was decidedly influenced by Africa." But the basis for a black independence of mind based on history goes deeper than black African contribution to the development of the world. If Christ was black, then the whole basis for Christian ethics and the Christian religion as practiced today is the gift of a man who was black—not white.

Woodson discusses the world of literature and the arts to make a point closer to home about the potential vitality of what the black cultural contribution could and should be:

Some one has said that the music of Poland was inspired by incidents of a struggle against the despots invading . . . their . . . land. The Greeks never had an art until the country was overrun by hostile Orientals. Some one . . . immortalized in song the sons who went forth to fight. . . . Another carved in marble the . . . youth who blocked the mountain pass with his body . . . to defend the liberty of his country. These things we call art. In our own country [whites], being secure in their position, have never faced such a crisis; and . . . Europeans, after whose pattern American life is fashioned, have not recently had such experience. White Americans, then, have produced no art at all, and that of Europe has reached the point of stagnation. Negroes who are imitating whites, then, are engaged in a most unprofitable performance. Why not interpret themselves anew to the world. . . . Some Negro with unusual insight would write an epic of bondage and freedom which would take its place with those of Homer and Virgil.

He then goes on to say: "The Negro in his present plight . . . does not see possibilities until it is too late. He exercises much 'hindsight,' and for that reason he loses ground in the hotly contested battles of life. [A]s a rule [he] waits until the thing happens before he tries to avert it. He is too much like a man . . . knocked down in physical combat. Instead of dodging the blow when it is being dealt he [arises] from his prostration dodging it."

It's an idea whose time may never come, this fighting spirit and sense of real independence that Carter G. Woodson espouses. But if it ever does, look out. There will be no need to fire one shot, to stage one sit-in, to call one meeting, or sing one song. The revolution to give blacks complete equality will have come without those who would hold on to the past even knowing that it has happened. It will all be over. Racist policemen will no longer be able to keep their jobs, racist congressmen will be ridiculed out of existence, and Hollywood will have to make black men and women romantic leads, no stupid wigs, no second-man status under the guise of equal billing, no use of comedy to keep the nigger on his ass in the fight and after.

Books 26 through 32:

INFANTS OF THE SPRING—
A LITERATURE ARISES FROM THE
HOLOCAUST

Y THE 1920s black America had been out of slavery for two generations, which meant a solid
middle class had had time to establish itself on a
large scale. As W. E. B. Du Bois wrote in a suggested
plank to Teddy Roosevelt's Bull Moose Party platform
in 1912: "The Progressive Party recognizes.... That a
group of 10,000,000 people who have in a generation
changed from a slave to a free labor system, reestab-
lished family life, accumulated $1,000,000,000 of real
property, including 20,000,000 acres of land, and reduced their illiteracy from 80 to 30 percent, deserve
and must have justice, opportunity and a voice in their
own government." Teddy, predictably, didn't think his
Progressive Party should be that *progressive* and said no.

A middle class also means a leisure class, one that
has the time to participate in the arts, and create a literature of its own, all of which black America had done
before the century was two decades old. That this period, which came to be known as the Harlem
Renaissance, happened as quickly as it did is a testament to the vibrancy of the black artistic spirit, a spirit
that can be traced back to African roots, where tribal

life was almost exclusively defined by dance, song, and oral history as both entertainment and documentation.

The man who called the period a new awakening for black America was Alain Locke, a leading professor of philosophy at Howard University. He announced the arrival of a New Negro in an anthology by that name that attempted to define the epiphany. First published in 1925, *The New Negro* has remained a seminal volume that includes works by Jean Toomer, Zora Neale Hurston, Langston Hughes, W. E. B. Du Bois, Claude McKay, and a host of others. As the poet Robert Hayden explains in the 1969 Atheneum edition: "The New Negro writers rejected the 'minstrel tradition' in American literature, with its caricatures and southern dialect, and they likewise rejected overt propaganda and 'racial rhetoric' for the most part as obstacles to literary excellence and universal acceptance."

But as Nathan Huggins says (in Must-Read No. 27), the proclamation of a New Negro was more a statement of intent than it was a well defined version of what the modern "Negro" was becoming. Certainly black America had changed by 1925—and the change was reflected in what black America wrote. The black American was not so much a new Negro as he was an evolved one—and he may not have been as "old," as Locke had thought.

Before the Jazz Age could get out of the twenties, the Depression was upon black and white, old and new alike. By 1935 Harlem had rioted, in part because of Mayor Fiorella La Guardia's refusal to give the community any of the relief money that the rest of the city was getting. Atrocities abounded that added to black America's sense of frustration. In 1934 three black youths were arrested in Harlem and beaten for allegedly stealing thirty-eight cents. They were convicted and sentenced to the penitentiary for a total of ninety years.

However, under Roosevelt's New Deal, the Works Progress Administration (WPA) gave black artists, writers, painters, and choreographers the chance to develop in their respective fields as never before. It enabled Orson Welles to put on his legendary production of *Macbeth* at the Lafayette Theatre in Harlem, perhaps the most illustrious example. But the WPA was short-lived, killed in 1939 by Martin Dies of Texas and his House Un-American Activities Committee. As Hallie Flanagan writes in *Arena,* her history of the Federal Theatre, one congressman, who voted to disband the WPA had been so happy with its impact on his state that he called her to discuss plans for the coming year, at which point she informed him that, thanks to his vote, there would be no coming year.

But there would be World War II.

26

CANE

by Jean Toomer, with a foreword by Waldo Frank

NEW YORK: BONI AND LIVERIGHT, 1923

Jean Toomer wrote *Cane* in 1923, and it became a classic of the black renaissance, influencing the likes of Langston Hughes, Zora Neale Hurston, and Wallace Thurman, if not in style, then certainly in content. In his excellent introduction, Arna Bontemps makes a compelling argument for the work's continuing reputation as a classic of American literature as well. *Cane* is a supreme example of an experimental work that creates a unique statement that enriches the spirit and extends the syntax of literature.

Through a combination of short stories, poems, prose poems, and a novelette that forms most of the second half of the book, Toomer depicts the rural black generation that followed the end of slavery in completely authentic and convincing terms, even though he does so from the point of view of an urban, literate, semi-northern mind. The women he depicts touch every facet of feminine emotion. Some love with an open passion that is unrestrained. Some allow themselves to be loved, enveloping their paramour in their ardor. Others fight for love, sometimes victoriously and sometimes disastrously. Their lives are often lived in an

interior world that makes the world around them seem extrane-
ous, but Toomer has found a truth in each one of these exquisite
creations that makes them memorable. He has not avoided the
horror of racism in the process.

The men depicted in *Cane* fuse into a whole also, and, like
Richard Wright's Bigger Thomas (see "How 'Bigger' Was Born,"
found as an introductory essay to some editions of *Native Son*),
remain indelible in our minds as much by their insistence on
being men, despite the Southern bigotry that they face, as by their
Southern charm. These rural Southern types are juxtaposed
against the owner of property, best represented by Rhobert, and
the other burgher types who inhabit the cities where blacks are allowed to live in large numbers. The women in the North are
shown as more shallow than those of the rural South, less interested in how or what they feel than they are in what they can get
in the marketplace for what they have to offer.

As Bontemps points out, Toomer's groundbreaking work preceded Faulkner's experimental *Sound and the Fury* by nine years.
Tennessee Williams was just nine when *Cane* was published. The
Lost Generation of Ernest Hemingway and his ilk hadn't really
begun. Thus Toomer's innovations should have garnered him
some acclaim, just as nonuse of punctuation marks garnered Faulkner some of his literary recognition. But for all of his precocity
(Toomer was in his twenties when he wrote *Cane*), the man disappeared from the world of his contemporaries almost without trace.

As was discovered later, he had become a member of a well-to-
do Quaker commune and actually hid his racial identity from the
people around him. When it was suggested that his daughter by
his first marriage was black and that he was himself black, his response was so oblique that the matter was allowed to drop.
Because of this ambiguity, Toomer has a mixed reputation in
most quarters. Some blacks see him as a rat who deserted his ship
of race, others see him as a brilliant writer who should be judged
on the basis of that talent and that talent alone.

Among many whites, Toomer simply isn't known, which is not
an uncommon problem for black artists of any level of achievement. Or if he is known, he's certainly not understood because he

does not write in a Southern dialect, as this selection from Kabnis
indicates:

> Kabnis: Near me. Now. Whoever you are, my warm glowing sweet-
> heart, do not think that the face that rests beside you is the real
> Kabnis. Ralph Kabnis is a dream. And dreams are faces with large
> eyes and weak chins and broad brows that get smashed by the fists
> of square faces. The body of the world is bullnecked. A dream is a
> soft face that sits uncertainly upon it. . . . God, if I could develop
> that in words. Give what I know a bull-neck and a heaving body,
> all would go well with me, wouldn't it, sweetheart? If I could feel
> that I came to the South to face it. If I, the dream (not what is
> weak and afraid in me) could become the face of the South. How
> my lips would sing for it, my songs being the lips of its soul.

Toomer was not drowning in the poverty and ignorance that
was the lot of so many black Americans—the condition of black
America that white America continues to be comfortable with. But
the brilliance of the one light Toomer left us still shines lumi-
nously for all to read. In his introduction Bontemps quotes Toomer
on the duality of his racial heritage:

> I seem to have seven blood mixtures. . . . Because of these, my po-
> sition in America has been a curious one. I have lived equally amid
> the two race groups. Now white, now colored. . . . Within the last
> two or three years, however, my growing need for artistic expres-
> sion has pulled my deeper and deeper into the Negro group. And
> as my powers of receptivity increased, I found myself loving it in a
> way that I could never love the other. It has stimulated and fertil-
> ized whatever creative talent I may contain within me. . . . The
> mould is cast, and I cannot turn back even if I would.

The troubled young poet who travels through Cane was a genius—even if his flame, so brightly lit, burned but briefly. There
are very few writers who have written more passionately and
more poetically or with more vision about their people.

Toomer went South after the "breakup of Pinchback," his
mother's father, and within two years saw what he saw: the last
glimpse of a sunlit race soon gone. After them would come a new
Negro and a new South and the generation that followed Booker

T. Washington—social uplift and the organized religion of the towns and institutions like the NAACP. The pagan purity, the canebrake freedom, the freedom to openly love and lose and love again would never come again. But it will never be lost to us, either, because Toomer captured it for all time.

27

HARLEM RENAISSANCE

by Nathan Irvin Huggins

NEW YORK: OXFORD UNIVERSITY PRESS, 1971

Aside from being an excellent history of a very complex period, Nathan Huggins's study of the Harlem Renaissance, from its advent in the 1920s until the depression killed the enthusiasm, raises many provocative and even confrontational issues about black culture. That Renaissance—everyone, including Huggins, calls it the "so-called Renaissance"—saw the first real flowering of the arts by black Americans: the poetry, prose, and drama, the essay, painting, and sculpture of contemporary black artists caught the imagination of literary cognoscenti everywhere, at home and abroad. The fact that it seemed so compatible with the Jazz Age that men like F. Scott Fitzgerald had posited, made it that much more attractive and gave it much more staying power. It was a movement that had something different to say and so many voices—primarily black ones for the first time—to do the saying. But in the rush to create a first flowering, this movement, quite expectedly, left a lot unsaid. After all, the Harlem Renaissance was operating in a hostile environment. The Ku Klux Klan was the hit organization of the decade; its ranks swelled to over four million members (according to the *Encyclopedia Britannica)* and its parades in the nation's capital drew one hundred thousand— as robust an exercise in racist hatred as the freedom of assembly allows.

As Huggins observes, neither the politics of Marcus Garvey nor anyone else on the black side who wasn't a conservative (such as George Schuyler) could succeed during this era for two simple reasons. Blacks had no real voting power, therefore no serious political base. In addition, fear-mongers, division, and subversion were everywhere. He quotes Du Bois to make his point: "If we organize separately for anything—'Jim Crow!' scream the Disconsolate; if we organize with white people—'Traitors! . . . They're betraying us!' yell all the Suspicious. If, unable to get a whole loaf we seize half . . . 'Compromise!' yell all the Scared. If we let the half go and starve—'Why don't you do something?' yell those same critics."

In addition to these political divisions, the Harlem Renaissance had to fight long-standing beliefs of inferiority. Even writers like Countee Cullen (although Huggins mentions Langston Hughes in this context as well) were still unsure about how equal they were. Cullen's "Yet Do I Marvel" ends with the lines "Yet do I marvel at this curious thing: / To make a poet black, and bid him sing!"

Black literary models left over from the nineteenth century still included the plantation-grinning, banjo-on-his-knee Uncle and the happy Mammy taking care of the chilluns. In contrast to them were conservative prototypes of the Gilded Age: the rigid middle class (black Babbitts) doing everything possible to deny the existence of the other brother (or sister). They were equally sterile, opposite ends of the same spectrum—the one because it had no control over its own image, the other because, in its attempt to deny its past, it had created a vacuous antiseptic present. In spite of their lingering sense of inferiority and the adverse climate they faced, writers such as Hughes and Cullen were a literary revolution. Hughes especially, with his rivers that carried the soul of the race ("The Negro Speaks of Rivers") and his downtrodden women of the night and their pimps singing the "weary blues."

Looking to Africa as she "sate in state" the way so many have looked to Albion or Venice for inspiration might have been evidence of a new pride in being black, still, says Huggins, the appeal to the motherland was not as symbolic of a black assertion of cultural equality as it might seem to suggest.

> It was easier to use the African tradition as a means of giving racial quality to art than it was to discuss the significance of Africa to the Negro. Alain Locke had found it difficult and was reduced to a simple assertion of faith in a valuable African legacy. Other Negro intellectuals were equally perplexed by the African heritage. All seemed to know, or sense, that Africa should mean something to the race; there should be some race memory that tied black men together; ambiguity and doubt always left the question unresolved, however. Countee Cullen's poem *Heritage* did little more than show that poet's quandary.

And, of course, the white imprint on the Harlem Renaissance is crucial to any discussion. Carol Van Vechten's *Nigger Heaven* was the preeminent contribution in that regard. Van Vechten was not only there, but he put himself at the center of it all. He knew everyone, took anyone who was anyone on a tour of *his* Harlem, had something to say about every and anything having to do with all of it, artistic, social, political, and whatever else was left over. *Nigger Heaven* was lambasted by D. H. Lawrence. Writes Huggins: "Lawrence failed to see reality or honesty in the book. . . . He saw here a 'nigger book' which feebly copied the luridness of Cocteau. . . . The respectable characters were indistinguishable from white, and the love affair [between the two main characters] a 'rather palish brown.' " Everyone either hated the title or was forced to defend it.

Huggins brings up many other intriguing issues. He points out that both blacks and whites needed the Renaissance—black Americans for obvious reasons, and white Americans because "White . . . men who sensed that they were slaves to moral codes, that they were cramped, found Harlem a tonic and a release. Harlem Negroes' lives appeared immediate and honest. Everything they did—their music, their art, their dance—uncoiled deep inner tensions. Harlem seemed a cultural enclave that had magically survived the psychic fetters of Puritanism." That achievement alone should have made the Renaissance, so-called or not, a major chapter in American literature.

Militancy as a literary theme came to the fore for the first time during this period. Claude McKay's poem "If We Must Die" so alarmed Henry Cabot Lodge that he had it read into the Congressional Record as evidence of the "unsettling currents among black Americans." Not so Winston Churchill. He recited it during World War II as a rallying cry. It was the same old double hex. If a white man lets out a yell, it's "yahoo" time. If a black man does it, they send in the FBI to make sure the niggers don't get too restless.

Beyond expressions of militancy lay the urgent need to find an authentic black voice in *all* the arts. Huggins's descussion of visual art and sculpture is as arresting as his discussion of literature. But it is to literature that we look for the Renaissance's ultimate definition of what it accomplished. In discussing Jean Toomer, Huggins says: "Toomer's answer is to find one's roots in the homeland, the South, and to claim it as one's own. It is to look into the fullness of the past without shame or fear. To be, and to relive the slave and the peasant and never be separated from that reality. . . . Of all these efforts to define a Negro identity, Jean Toomer's seems the most profound and provocative."

Before the Harlem Renaissance, black culture and black artistic expression was a callow, unformed child, despite all its pretty clothes and its happy-go-lucky, buck-and-wing manner. After the Renaissance, both black culture and black artistic expression had come of age. The angry Young Turks of the 1960s not only picked up where the Renaissance writers and thinkers left off, but indeed used the earlier models as their literary and artistic point of departure. No matter how great or small black achievement in literature, drama, and art has become, the renaissance of the twenties, in Harlem, was and will always be the fountainhead.

28

THEIR EYES WERE WATCHING GOD: A NOVEL

by Zora Neale Hurston

PHILADELPHIA: LIPPENCOTT, 1937

It is clear from the opening lines that *Their Eyes Were Watching God* deserves its heralded reputation. The brilliant poetic metaphor of the prose is the primary reason for the arresting quality of the work. But the story is there from the beginning as well.

Zora Neale Hurston's reputation as one of America's truly gifted black writers rests primarily on this novel. But to say that she was also a controversial figure throughout her lifetime would be to understate the case. She voted for Robert Taft. She thought the *Brown* decision of 1954 was an insult to black people. For over five years, she was supported financially by a white, domineering would-be patroness of the arts, Mrs. R. Osgood Mason of Park Avenue, and often had to demean herself to get the handouts. Everything that Hurston wrote belonged to Mrs. Mason, and Hurston had to account for the money she received, over fifteen thousand dollars, in minute detail.

In an introduction to a Hurston reader, *I Love Myself When I'm Laughing* (The Feminist Press), Mary Helen Washington quotes a letter from Hurston to Mason begging for money to buy a pair of shoes. It said in part, "[W]e . . . agreed that I should only own one pair [of shoes] at a time. I bought a pair in mid December. . . . [But] my big toe is about to burst out of my right shoe." She also had to list personal items she purchased, such as Kotex.

Washington defends Hurston against her many critics, and rightly so, by pointing out that, during her lifetime, she was often judged harshly because she was being judged by men. Washington quotes the black critic Darwin turner from his book *In a Minor Chord:* "[Hurston was a] quick-tempered woman, arrogant toward her peers, obsequious toward her supposed superiors, desperate for recognition and reassurance to assuage her feelings of inferiority. . . . It is in reference to this image that one must examine her novels, her folklore, and her view of the Southern scene."

Washington then points out that Turner does not evaluate Jean Toomer's work on the basis of "his marriage to a white woman or his refusal to be identified with blacks after the publication of *Cane.*" Instead, Turner defends Toomer's "vehement insistence that he was neither 'Negro' nor 'Caucasian'—but a member of the 'American' race—as 'philosophically viable and utterly sincere.' "

Part of Hurston's problem, in addition to always being evaluated by men and ending up an archconservative herself, was that she failed to conform to what was de rigueur for black writers of the Harlem Renaissance and into the forties: taking a militant stand when it came to a discussion of America on any level—cultural, political, sociological, or artistic. She wanted to write about the human heart without encasing the black spirit from which it springs in a body ground down by racism. Because she was a Southerner (she was from a small town in Florida), she found it possible to overlook the evils of the South, particularly since the North was just as racist as far as she was concerned.

In spite of the controversies and her questionable politics, Hurston was a major figure of the Renaissance, so important that Wallace Thurman, another Renaissance light, wrote her into *Infants of Spring* as Sweet Mae Carr, "a Negro opportunist cut-ting the fool for white folks in order to get her tuition paid and her stories sold," according to Washington. Langston Hughes and Hurston collaborated on a play, *Mule Bone*, but they had a falling out over the project when he tried to include a third writer, another woman. In summing up the incident, Hughes remarked, "Girls are funny creatures." She aroused the ire of Roy Wilkins of the National Association for the Advancement of Colored People when she was quoted in a newspaper interview as saying that Jim Crow worked because blacks in the South had everything that whites had even though there was no social mixing. She said she was misquoted.

Hurston left home at age fourteen. Her mother had died when she was ten and she didn't get along with either her father or the her stepmother. Her first job was as a maid and a wardrobe assistant in a Gilbert & Sullivan traveling show. Over the years she was a schoolteacher, a maid again, and a librarian. She published three other novels, two books of folklore, and several articles.

Their Eyes Were Watching God was written in seven weeks, after the breakup of her marriage. She modeled Tea Cake, her only real love in the novel, after her former husband, and the depth of her feeling for the real-life Tea Cake is given full rein in the passion of the novel. Although Washington claims in her introduction that the novel is one of ideas, surely this is not the case. Trying to find sociological substructs for feminist work in this book is as much cant as damning Zora Neale for not being militant. It is its representation of the power of love and its trials and tribulations, and the heartaches and the suffering that her heroine Janie goes through that makes the work memorable. Janie's journey from child to woman, her refusal to compromise her search for the romantic ideal and accept the cold reality that the real world offers, and even the selfish domination of her first two husbands—these are the heart and soul of *Eyes*, and what has made it an icon of feminist literature for the last thirty years.

The lovers, who find a way to watch God and find each other at the same time, are almost irresistible characters. If in the great scheme of things God, in his wisdom, allowed tragedy to overtake them, leaving Janie alone with only the memory of her love for Tea Cake to console her, then so be it.

Richard Wright was less than enthused by the degree to which Hurston wrote in the argot of the backwoods black of the early part of the century. But that was her strong suit. Hurston's ear is unerring in recapturing the speech of the Old South that still very much existed at the time the Renaissance was in full flower. In one sense the work is two novels in one. The dialogue fills much of the action and is used to introduce dozens of characters who form part of the backdrop to the three sections that the work divides itself into naturally. Janie is an adolescent being forced by her grandmother to marry an older man she doesn't care for in part one. He is cold and removed and holds her impoverished background against her. The second marriage, without benefit of divorce, to a bold, forceful, accomplished man, who literally creates a town out of a crossroads, and her last and only love, the younger, romantic, tender, loving Tea Cake, make up parts two and three.

Janie's second husband wants to make her a poor version of Caesar's wife. She has to work hard in the store, but she's too important to engage in anything that goes on around her. She has to be, as his wife, above the common folk and their common pleasures, at all times be above reproach. The husband, however, can enjoy the laughter of "the world' as it suits him. When she stands her ground against him in public after he has ridiculed her in front of the crowd, he further humiliates her by striking her in the face and driving her from the store. Then he moves out of the bedroom. Just when it seems as if he's going to destroy her and her heart that he feels is "too easily made glad," Hurston has him die of kidney failure, leaving Janie a woman of substantial wealth. She literally lets her hair down (the husband had forbidden it while he was alive) and falls in love with a much younger man, scandalizing the community.

Hurston's style at times echoes Emily Dickinson's. She presents the human heart as a thing of beauty and a joy, even after death. When Janie was forced into her first marriage because her grandmother saw her kiss a young man over the fence, even though it was her first and only kiss, Hurston describes how she made the rite of passage from adolescent innocence to forced womanhood.

> So Janie waited a bloom time, and a green time and an orange time. But when the pollen again gilded the sun and sifted down on the world she began to stand around the gate and expect things. What things? She didn't know exactly. Her breath was gusty and short. She knew things that nobody had ever told her. For instance, the words of the trees and the wind. She often spoke to falling seeds and said, "Ah hope you fall on soft ground," because she had heard seeds saying that to each other as they passed. . . . The familiar people and things had failed her so she hung over the gate and looked up the road towards way off. She knew now that marriage did not make love. Janie's first dream was dead, so she became a woman.

Hurston's definition of love, which we get from Janie's account of what happened when she left with Tea Cake, is as good as Frost's definition of poetry—that it's what's lost in translation. She writes: "[T]ell 'em dat love ain't somethn' lak uh grindstone dat's de same thing everywhere and do de same ting tuh everything it touch. Love is lak de sea. It's uh movin' thing, but still and all, it takes its shape from de shore it meets, and it's different with every shore."

And finally, the end of the novel itself:

> The day of the gun, and the bloody body, and the courthouse came and commenced to sing a sobbing sigh out of every corner in the room; out of each and every chair and thing. Commenced to sing, commenced to sob and sigh, singing and sobbing. Then Tea Cake came prancing around her where she was and the song of the sigh flew out of the window and lit in the top of the pine trees. Tea Cake, with the sun for a shawl. Of course he wasn't dead. He could never be dead until she herself had finished feeling and thinking. The kiss of his memory made pictures of love and light against the wall. Here was peace. She pulled in her horizon like a great fishnet. Pulled it from around the waist of the world and draped it over her shoulder. So much of life in its meshes! She called in her soul to come and see.

29

Marcus Garvey and the Vision of Africa

edited by John Henrik Clarke

New York: Random House, 1974

The bibliographic text on Garvey is voluminous, and he deserves the attention. Garvey was born in Jamaica and he formed the basis for his ideas of black independence while in exile in Costa Rica. His perfectly legal approach to solving the problem of racism that black Americans faced following World War I should have been welcomed by the authorities as a rapprochement instead of viewed as an act of subversion. Black men in America were being lynched because they still had their uniforms on after coming back from the war. It was a uniform that had been issued to them legally and that they had not dishonored while wearing it. Garvey comes along and says to black America: Don't lynch in return. Learn to create your own organizations, your own ways and means of self-help. Start your own institutions and be proud of who you are—Black! And for that Herbert Hoover and the rest ran him out of the country.

John Henrik Clarke organized this text around various periods of Garvey's life. He begins each section with commentary, includes the work of one or two other writers who discuss the major themes of the period, and finally adds a healthy dose of Garvey by Garvey. In part I, "The Early Years," Garvey's widow, Amy Jacques Garvey, writes about blacks who came North to escape the lynching and peonage of the South:

> The preachers and ward politicians were designated as leaders for these new Northerners. There was no all-Negro organization; the National Association for the Advancement of Colored People was, and is, an interracial organization. At that time its officers were mainly whites and mulattos, like Dr. Du Bois, and later Walter White, who looked white. . . . [Garvey] opposed integration of the races as racial suicide and an easy solution put forward by persons who did not have the courage and determination to keep on fighting for their rights to live and work as other racial groups did.

Garvey's movement had its greatest impact between 1920 and 1925. Officially called the United Negro Improvement Association, it attracted support not only in America, but in the Caribbean and Central America. Garvey wanted Africa for the Africans and tried to establish a settlement in Liberia. He sent engineers and equipment to make the dream a reality. The Liberian government was pressured by America and England to renege on the agreement, however, and fifty thousand dollars' worth of equipment was seized before the colony was built. The European powers feared any spread of real nationalism on the continent at the time, since most countries in Africa were still European colonies.

Garvey was prosecuted for mail fraud in 1923. Clarke's book describes the trial, which was a joke. An empty envelope was put in evidence that was supposed to have contained a letter or circular inducing a man named Dancy to buy shares in the Black Star Line, the shipping company Garvey had formed. And that was the basis for the charge. The district attorney, in addressing the all-white jury, began with "Gentlemen, will you let the Tiger loose!" When Garvey was convicted, the prosecutor was congratulated for "bagging the Tiger." Garvey couldn't get bail because all the bondsmen said they would be blacklisted if they carried the bond. Fifteen thousand dollars in cash was raised to get him out. But he was sentenced to five years and was sent to federal prison in Atlanta. The golden age of Garvey's movement was over.

What had created this witch-hunt? Was it simply the sight of black men and women parading in the streets of Harlem, smartly dressed in uniforms and following a black man who rose from soap-box orator to a man of power and influence among his own people? Garvey's United Negro Improvement Association gave the poor black man on the street, the one without much education, the one who still had a touch of the Southern plantation on him, a huge step up in self-esteem and self-confidence. However, because no one white had organized it, and no one white had approved it, it couldn't be allowed to exist, no matter how legal, how well-intentioned, or how much it would have been applauded if it had been an exercise in white power. When the Garvey movement is taught in a history course, the professor must be hard put to explain what happened to Garvey and why he was considered such an ominous "Tiger."

A. F. Elms's article from *Opportunity* (1925) is included in part II, "Years of Triumph and Tragedy." He writes: "[B]efore Garvey there has not been a man who stirred into expression the consciousness of the Negro peoples to the extent that he succeeded in doing. . . . Negroes all over the world have come to think of themselves as a Race . . . as never before." So perhaps Garvey was a tiger after all. He demonstrated that you cannot lynch a people, make it illegal for them to vote when the law says they can, depict them as buffoons and servants with borderline intelligence in film and on the stage, keep them out of the marketplace and the workforce and allow others (who aren't even citizens) into both areas. They won't stand for it—unless they are black and in America and have no choice.

In a letter outlining his main ideas, Garvey wrote the following;

- Do you believe the Negro to be a human being?
- Do you believe that the Negro should be taught not to aspire to be the best imitation of the white man, but the best product of himself?
- Do you believe that the Negro should have a Government of his own in Africa?

• Do you believe that the Negro should be encouraged to regard
and respect the rights of all other races in the same manner as
other races would respect the rights of the Negro?

Yes, Garvey did preach separation of the races. Yes, he was
against intermarriage. Yes, he did meet the head of the Ku Klux
Klan before he went to prison. But none of that explains why he
was destroyed. Lunatic white fringe groups arm themselves, kill
federal agents, and threaten local police, and they get treated like
grandma on a binge. But then they're not black.

30

100 YEARS OF LYNCHINGS

edited by Ralph Ginzburg

NEW YORK: LANCER BOOKS, 1962

Ginzburg lists five thousand lynchings of black men from 1859 to 1969 in his *100 Years of Lynchings*. Some of the thirty states included are: Alabama, with two pages of lynchings (about 220 men killed); Arkansas, with one and a half pages; California, with three men lynched; Georgia, represented by three pages; Iowa, with three men killed, one of them of unknown identity; Kentucky, with two and a half pages; Maryland, with one person listed; Nebraska, two men killed; New York State and Washington State, with one man each; Texas, represented by one page; and Wyoming, five men killed. But, as he acknowledges, this is only a partial list. There are thousands more that we will never know about.

When we read the accounts of these atrocities from newspapers and magazines of the period, it becomes almost impossible to explain the tens of thousands of people who participated in these lynchings for an entire century. Neither a national crisis nor a natural disaster made these men lose their sense of perspective.

Their behavior makes cannibalism seem civilized since the canni-
bal at least has a practical reason for what he does.

The lynchings became carnivals. Candy and whiskey were
brought to the event. Children watched along with mother and
father. Often there were complaints that the "nigger was killed
too fast." Burning men alive and then scrambling for a finger or
an ear to keep as a souvenir must take us *beyond the pale*. However, the burying of this history of horror does not seem to be due
to the psychological need to deny something that is too horrible
to contemplate. History has simply been indifferent to this American holocaust, as Ginzburg's book attests. But the savagery cannot be gainsaid.

THE SPRINGFIELD (MASS) WEEKLY REPUBLICAN,
April 28, 1889.
Sam Holt, the murderer of Alfred Cranford and the ravisher of the
latter's wife, was burned at the stake, near Newman, Ga., this af-
ternoon, in the presence of 2,000 people. The black man was first
tortured before being covered with oil and burned. . . . Before the
torch was applied to the pyre, the Negro was deprived of his ears,
fingers and genital parts of his body. . . . Before the body was cool,
it was cut into pieces, the bones were crushed into small bits, and
even the tree upon which the wretch met his fate was torn up and
disposed of as "souvenirs." The negro's heart was cut into several
pieces as was his liver. Those unable to obtain the ghastly relics direct paid their more fortunate possessors extravagant sums for
them. Small pieces of bones went for 25 cents, and a bit of liver
crisply cooked sold for 10 cents.

NEW YORK HERALD, December 30, 1900.
Professor Albert Bushnell Hart, of Harvard College, speaking here
before the American Historical Association, said that if the people
of certain States are determined to burn colored men at the stake,
those States would better legalize the practice.

CHICAGO RECORD-HERALD, May 23, 1902.
Dudley Morgan, a negro accused of assailing [a] Mrs. McKay . . .
was burned to death at an iron stake here today. . . . [He was tied]
to the stake until he could only move his head. The crowd had
swelled to 5,000 when the husband of the woman applied the
match and the pyre was soon ablaze. Burning pieces of pine were

thrust into [Morgan's] eyes. . . . He was tortured in a horrible manner. The crowd clamored continuously for a slow death. . . . The negro's head finally dropped, and in thirty minutes only the trunk of the body remained. Parts of the skull and body were carried away. The men who captured Morgan were then held above the heads of the mob while their pictures were taken. The last words of the doomed man other than the incoherent mutterings made in prayer were: "Tell my wife good-by."

VICKSBURG (MISS.) EVENING POST, February 8, 1904.
An eyewitness to the lynching of Luther Holbert and his wife, Negroes, which took place in Doddsville yesterday, said: "[T]hey were tied to trees and forced to hold out their hands while one finger at a time was chopped off. The fingers were distributed as souvenirs. The ears of the murderers were cut off. Holbert's skull was fractured and one of his eyes, knocked out with a stick, hung by a shred from the socket. Some of the mob used a large corkscrew to bore into the flesh of the man and woman . . . to their arms and legs and body, and then pulled out, the spirals tearing out big pieces of raw, quivering flesh every time it was withdrawn."

WASHINGTON POST-TIMES-HERALD, September 1, 1955.
DATELINE—GREENWOOD, MISS.
The body of a 15 year old Chicago Negro, Emmett Till, who had disappeared after he allegedly made "fresh" remarks to a white woman was found floating in the Tallahatchie River today. He had been shot through the head. Two white men, one of them the husband of the woman allegedly insulted by the boy, have been charged with kidnapping the victim from the home of his relatives here: Roy Bryant, and his half-brother W. J. Milan. Both men were found innocent by an all-white jury before the month was out.

There's nothing more to be said. The victims were from "a degraded race." The ones who killed them were "civilized" because they were white.

31

THE WAYS OF WHITE FOLKS

by Langston Hughes

NEW YORK: A. A. KNOPF, 1934

The short stories in this collection (there are fourteen in all) range from Deep South plantation tragedy to tales of Midwestern lynching to Northern flimflam. Some of the stories are searing in their depiction of an unrelenting destruction of black people—their humanity and their lives—and some are wickedly sardonic.

Poetry was Hughes's first discipline, and it is as a poet that he is best known. Beginning in 1926, his volumes include *The Weary Blues, Fine Clothes to the Jew* (published a year later), *Shakespeare in Harlem* (1942), *Montage of a Dream Deferred* (1951), and *Ask Your Mama: 12 Moods for Jazz* (1961). But these titles just head the list, which runs to twenty-one titles. A complete bibliography of Hughes's life's work has hundreds of items, including seventeen books of fiction; two autobiographies, *The Big Sea* and *I Wonder as I Wander;* operas and dramas, including a collection of five of his plays; works he edited alone and in collaboration with others; works translated by him, and juvenile fiction.

So why have I chosen to discuss a collection of his short stories? For one, Hughes has been almost completely overlooked as a prose stylist. His collaboration with Milton Meltzer on *A Pictorial History of the Negro* and a pictorial history of black entertainers, *Black Magic,* are well-known, as are his *Simple* stories, and, of course, there is his poetry, especially *The Weary Blues* and *Fine Clothes to the Jew.* But Hughes is at his best, both in poetry and prose, when he's a minimalist. The short story form allows him to be just that as no other genre does save poetry.

I chose to open the door to this somewhat unheralded gift of an acknowledged master to add even more luster to an already illustrious name. The uncluttered deftness, the beauteous ease of the writing in these stories is pure poetry in prose. Here's the melodious beginning of "Cora Unashamed":

> Melton was one of those miserable in-between little places, not large enough to be a town, nor small enough to be a village—that is a village in the rural, charming sense of the word. Melton had no charm about it. It was merely a nondescript collection of houses and buildings in a region of farms—one of those sad American places with sidewalks, but no paved streets; electric lights, but no sewage; a station, but no trains that stopped, save a jerky local, morning and evening.

Cora is a maid for a white family from the time she starts the eighth grade. When she gets pregnant by a young white man, he leaves town and she has to raise the child, a girl, by herself. She does so, loving it dearly, but the child dies of whooping cough. Subsequently, the daughter of the white family, the same age as Cora, has a daughter also, but that child is somewhat retarded and the family treats it poorly. Cora adopts the child, unofficially, and gives it the only real love it ever knows. When the girl grows up, she too gets pregnant, and the family forces her to have an abortion. She does but doesn't recover from the operation. At her funeral, Cora calls out to all assembled that they killed her, then she packs up and leaves the family forever.

Cora stays in town, however, living with her parents and earning what she can from gardening. The fact that Cora is unashamed of her life, in spite of an illegitimate child and her second-class citizenship, which she must endure till the end of her days, gives her a dignity that the white family, for all their money and social position and freedom, will never have.

The story called "Home" is a brilliant surprise, with its serene beginning and violent ending. Roy Williams is a violinist who has been in Europe for several years making a good living playing in jazz bands, although he's a classical musician by training. But he's not well: something tells him he's going to die and he should go home to do it. Little does Roy know how ignominious will be his end. When he arrives in the small Missouri town, all the local whites gawk at this well-dressed (spats and gloves) nigger. He's hailed and well met by a white fellow who knew him in school. His mother shows him off at the local church, and everyone thinks it's grand. The local music teacher (a middle-aged white woman) invites him to play at the school and accompanies him on the piano. That's even grander.

One evening he goes out for a walk. In the center of town the local cinema is just letting out. Williams runs into the music teacher and they greet each other. He tips his hat, and as she is about to take a step down, he instinctively holds out his hand to help her. She almost slips and lets out a cry, glad nevertheless for the assistance. In that instant, everyone in town who sees the familiarity descends like a hungry wolf pack on Roy Williams. He is killed, and the word is that he tried to rape her right there in public. She was struggling to get away from him—that's when she cried out.

"Slave on the Block" is a delicious send-up of a white couple, Ann and Michael—artists who live in Greenwich Village. She paints and he plays the piano. They have discovered what used to be called Negritude. "[T]hey were blessed with a wonderful colored cook and maid—until she took sick and died in her room in their basement. And then the most marvelous ebony boy walked into their life, a boy as black as all the Negroes they'd even known put together." They hire him to take care of their garden, which consists of one small box, so the wife can paint him and the husband can recompose the songs he sings and put his own name to them. The wife gets tired of painting him in clothes and has him strip to the waist because, as she says, "He is the jungle." Finally, she decides to paint him as a pure primitive, calling the work "Slave on the Block."

The new maid shows him where Harlem is, and they end up in the basement together, which interferes with the wife's painting and the husband's composing. By this time "the slave" has the run of the house, so when the husband's mother shows up, unused to seeing "Negro servants" walking about smoking and doing as they please, she lays down an ultimatum. Either "the slave" goes or she does. But by this time the "slave" has been emancipated and takes not only the maid, but his body and his songs with him. Poor Ann and Michael are left inspirationless and distraught.

In the last story, "Father and Son," Bert, the son of a white plantation owner and the owner's black housemaid, kills his father because he tries to get Bert to work in the fields after allowing him to go to school for two years up North. Bert takes his own life before the mob can get to him. They hang him in the public square anyway, pretending that they caught him alive, yet the suspicion that he cheated them was whispered too loudly. Bert's brother Willie (also the slaveholder's son), is captured and lynched as well. Willie had been compliant, willing to obey his white father in everything and anything. He even berated his brother Bert for bringing his Northern ways back South where they didn't belong. But such are "the ways of white folks"—loyalty didn't protect poor Willie from the mob's need to "set things right."

32

THE LAST OF THE SCOTTSBORO BOYS

by Clarence Norris and Sybil Washington

NEW YORK: PUTNAM, 1979

The case of the Scottsboro Boys was notorious. If you lived in America in the thirties, it was as familiar to you as the O. J. Simpson trial or the attempt to impeach Bill Clinton. Benjamin Quarles, in *The Negro in the Making of America,* gives us this description of the case:

> On March 25, 1931, nine [black] adolescents were charged with the rape of two white women while on a freight train in Alabama, and two weeks later eight of the boys were sentenced to the electric chair. The NAACP hastened to furnish legal counsel, but the Communists cried out that [their] International Labor Defense was better equipped to represent the boys, since legal procedures alone would not be successful. Mass meetings and international propaganda must also be used, ran their argument, and in these techniques they had developed special skills. The ILD persuaded the parents of the boys to let them handle the case.

The Last of the Scottsboro Boys is Clarence Norris's autobiography. It is also his life as a Scottsboro Boy since the two are indistinguishable—he had no life other than as a Scottsboro Boy. It is also an eloquent indictment of the depth and all-pervasiveness of the racism in the South during the Depression. However, throughout the book, in the midst of describing the worst horrors, Norris's tone remains calm and understated. He writes that everyone had to stand on line to get the flour and beans the government was handing out to keep the country from starving. But as Norris states, "Negroes risked their lives to try and get the relief because white folks thought *they* should have it all."

When a freight car filled with hobos, all breaking the law by riding the rails without paying, filled up with almost as many blacks as whites, the white hobos decided that there were too many black ones in *their* car. They told Norris and the rest they had to jump or they'd be thrown off, even though they were in the middle of nowhere and the train was moving at a good pace. A fight ensued and the blacks did the throwing off. They let one fellow stay on because by the time they got to him, the train was going too fast.

Not willing to take their beating like men, the white hobos went to the law and lied about what had happened. They claimed the men had raped two white prostitutes who weren't even in the car. When the train was stopped, half of Alabama was waiting for the nine men. They were almost lynched then and there, but they were taken to the nearest jail instead, which happened to be in Scottsboro. That's how the Scottsboro Boys got their name. As a result of that fair fight and that alone, Alabama spent hundreds of thousands of dollars and more than seven years trying to put the nine black men in the electric chair. One of the prostitutes they allegedly raped recanted her story almost from the beginning. Of the nine, one was so racked with syphilis that he was hardly a rape suspect: his genitalia were swollen and he had sores all over him. Another was almost blind and walked with a cane.

The lawyer most responsible for their defense, Samuel Leibowitz of New York, challenged the convictions on the grounds that there were no blacks on juries in Alabama. The state forged ten

names and insisted that they were black. Leibowitz got a hand-
writing expert to state that the names were forged, so Alabama
convened a special grand jury and put a black man on it, and
the nine were indicted all over again. One judge, not courageous enough to throw out the charges completely and free the
nine then and there, did, however, order a new trial because he
said the evidence wasn't strong enough for a conviction. He
was never reelected and eventually left the state, but he had set
the stage for a new trial. Alabama really got serious then. It as-
signed a hanging judge to the case who overruled everything
Leibowitz said or did and let the prosecution say or do anything
it wanted.

Once the outside world got wind of this attempt at legal lynching, money and food and letters of support poured in from all
over the globe. This just made Alabama angrier. Norris and four
others would spend twelve years in jail before their sentences
were commuted and they were given parole. Jailers refused to let
anyone see "the Boys." Wherever they went, their reputation followed them. Prison guards attacked Norris and white inmates attacked him; one even tried to poison him. But he and the others
fought back. One of them, Ozie Powell, even cut the throat of a
deputy sheriff while they were being transported from one jail to
another. Norris describes what happened:

> [W]e were loaded into three cars. . . . I was in the back handcuffed
> to Ozie. . . . The sheriff was driving and his deputy, Blalock, was
> sitting beside him. Blalock started cussing our "Communist, Jew,
> Northern lawyers." He said we'd be a damn sight better off with
> Southern lawyers. Ozie told him, "I wouldn't give up the help I
> have for no damn Southern lawyer that I've seen." Blalock slapped
> him. He didn't know that everyone of us had knives. We'd cut the
> lining in the fly of our pants and put the knives in there.
>
> Ozie pulled out his knife, yanked Blalock's head back and slit
> his throat. Blood shot everywhere. . . . The sheriff got out and
> [yelled], "one of the black bastards cut the deputy. I am going to
> get rid of all these sons of bitches right now!" He fired into the car
> and shot Ozie. The bullet went into him above the right ear and
> came out the corner of the automobile.

The governor of Alabama visited one of the prisons where Norris was being kept and told the entire prison population that "The lowest white man is better than the highest-class Negro who ever lived." As Norris points out, that was an open invitation to commit murder. One white guard committed suicide after requesting that the Boys sing hymns for him. No one knows why he did it, but perhaps the injustice was more than his conscience could take.

Charles Bickford and James Cagney were two of the many celebrities who fought for release of the Scottsboro Boys. Cagney's career was almost ruined after a check he'd written to help pay their legal fees showed up at the headquarters of a communist organization. That's why he made *Yankee Doodle Dandy*: he had to prove that, his support for the unjustly accused men notwithstanding, he really loved America. Playwright John Wexley wrote *They Shall Not Die*, based on the case. It was produced in New York.

When Alabama finally paroled Norris, it was only on the condition that he be paroled in Alabama, where he would continue to be hounded, forced to work for thirty-five cents an hour and submit to being called every "nigger" epithet known to man. So he jumped bail and ended up in New York. For the next twenty-three years, he was a good citizen for the most part. He got married and raised a family.

In 1970 he tried to clear his name. The head of the Parole and Pardons Board in Alabama said that if he came back and served the three years left on his commuted sentence, they could make a deal. They just wouldn't let go of the bone. Norris said, "Hell, no!" and Alabama was eventually persuaded to give him a full and unconditional pardon. By 1976 Norris was finally able to travel freely using his own name. He looked up all his relatives who were still living. That, unfortunately, didn't include his mother.

What happened to the other Scottsboro Boys? One died of lung cancer, one committed suicide after stabbing his wife to death, one choked to death in the middle of an asthma attack. But the last of the Boys, the one they tried the hardest to kill (he was sentenced to die in the chair three times), not only lived to tell about it, but became a published author and celebrity who appeared on television and gave a speech at, of all places, the University of Alabama! Norris died in 1989 at the age of seventy-six.

Books 33 through 40:

MAKING THE WORLD SAFE FOR

DEMOCRACY—AGAIN!

W HEN THE Second World War began, black America found itself rigidly segregated with little hope of dismantling the system of apartheid under which it was suffering. World War II presented another chance for social and political uplift, if only the nation would be grateful that the black man was willing to fight and die for the Republic for which it stands. When Joe Louis beat Max Schmeling in their second bout in 1934, Harlem went wild with glee. Harlem and Black America at large had little else to celebrate. But no matter how much Joe Louis contributed to making the world safe for democracy, he had to do so in a segregated army. Lena Horne was asked to do an armed forces tour to entertain the troops. At one of the bases, as she sang, she moved smoothly away from the white troops, past the German officers who were POWs (they even had better seats than Joe Louis) until she was in front of the "colored" section, whereupon she stopped, turned her back on the rest of the soldiers, and sang only to her own. The rest of her tour was canceled, and she never sang for the American armed forces again.

America was not ashamed of its racism and certainly not interested in apologizing for it. Ten years after the war was over, however, the Jim Crow laws of the South were finally assaulted by the Supreme Court's decision in *Brown v. the Board of Education;* which banned segregation in public schools. A team of lawyers from the NAACP led by Thurgood Marshall, argued the case before the court. Martin Luther King, Jr. was emerging as the great leader of the next decade; the success of the Montgomery Bus Boycott was his entry into the national stage

By the time the sixties rolled around, America could no longer refuse to apologize for its system of apartheid. But the death of apartheid didn't come easily. The cold war politics that made Joe McCarthy a power in the U.S. Senate played havoc with Paul Robeson's career. His challenge to racism and his mildly worded compliments of the Soviet Union for its courteous treatment of blacks saw his earnings plummet from seventy-five thousand dollars a year to seven thousand dollars.

Richard Wright was in Paris writing *The Outsider. Time* magazine, among others, claimed he was no longer relevant as a voice of protest in America: he had abandoned the fight by running away. In fact, Wright was able to criticize America in much plainer terms from abroad than he could have if he had stayed home. But for this man of conscience, there was a price to pay. When he wanted to criticize France for its handling of the Algerian War, he had to remain silent. He would have been expelled from France if he hadn't, and there was no place else to go.

Ralph Ellison's *Invisible Man* did not run afoul of the powers that be, so it was received with open arms by white liberals and the black intelligentsia alike. That gave black America something other than Joe Louis to cheer about.

33

THE AFRICAN-AMERICAN SOLDIER

by Michael Lee Lanning

NEW YORK: CITADEL PRESS, KENSINGTON PUBLISHING, 1997

Black America has been used unashamedly by the nation in times of war and then abandoned in times of peace. White racists North and South have choked on the idea of black men in uniform, consequently what they've accomplished in the battlefield has been lied about, vilified, or ignored. The same degraded personality that allowed blacks to be reduced to the level of beasts of the field for the whole period of chattel slavery is the one that viciously attacked him while he was still in uniform and after he had done his heroic part and had to take it off. Blacks, of course, joined the ranks to prove their manhood, their patriotism, in hopes that such valor and rallying round the flag would help get them some of the rights at home that they so sorely lacked. They needn't have bothered.

In *The African-American Soldier,* Lanning begins his overview with Crispus Attucks and ends with Colin Powell. He gives Attucks full credit for the famous massacre of Boston and describes in detail the bravery of that hero, who for fifty years after his death was honored with a public holiday in Massachusetts.

Powell, who is secretary of state as of this writing, could find no decent housing in North Carolina when he was stationed at Fort Bragg in 1962 and had to send his pregnant wife back to her parents in Alabama to give birth.

In between his descriptions of these two men and their achievements, Lanning tells about the persecution, fear, dread and loathing faced by black men fighting for their country's honor, from presidents (Teddy Roosevelt was especially insidious) to generals to sheriffs to "ordinary" citizens. In chapter one he writes about this contradiction as it applied to Crispus Attucks: "The irony of his heroism was that as a black man, [he] would not have enjoyed the benefits of American independence had he lived. Although he knew this, he was willing to give his life for the good of the country. In so doing, he joined a long line of other African Americans who would also sacrifice themselves for freedoms and benefits they as individuals could not enjoy."

An Ohio regiment used a TWO-YEAR-OLD [my caps] black boy for target practice at an embarkation depot in Florida on their way to fight in the Spanish-American War. They wanted to see how close they could get to him *before* hitting him. Sheriffs in Atlanta and Nashville pistol-whipped unarmed black soldiers returning in railroad cars from that war and then bragged about it publicly. "The Atlanta police force met the Third North Carolina . . . and went from car to car clubbing the unarmed soldiers. In Nashville . . . seventy-five policemen and two hundred citizens beat the soldiers with pistols and clubs" for no other reason than to keep them in their place now that they were back in the land of the free and the home of the brave.

During World War II, Pvt. Felix Hall was lynched in his barracks in Fort Benning, Georgia, while he was alone and on leave. Why was he in his barracks if he was on leave? Because he couldn't go into town, leave or no leave, since they didn't like "niggers" in town any more than they liked them in the military. He stayed in camp because he thought he'd be safe there.

The War College made studies of the possible effects of integration "on the overall effect of military efficiency" several times over the years. In 1912 it recommended that blacks be kept out of artillery regiments "because of the technical skills required to . . . operate guns and produce accurate, safe fire." In summary the report declared that "Blacks . . . were . . . inferior to the white race in intelligence and mental abilities." The War College struck again in 1939 when it declared that African Americans were "far below the white in capacity to absorb instruction." The college then included a "nigger" joke to make its point, which Lanning includes on page 163 of his book. And, mind you, this was published in an official document.

Lanning also describes how Black Jack Pershing—he had commanded black troops early on, thus the sobriquet—was forced to accept black soldiers as fighting men, rather than cooks and busboys, in the American Expeditionary Force in World War I. He had no weapons for them, no support services, and no plans to deploy them. They were, of course, a completely segregated unit. When the French, who were desperate for manpower, said they would take the black troops, Pershing made the transfer so quickly that one of his colonels wrote a friend, "Our great American general simply put the black orphan in a basket, set it on the doorstep of the French, pulled the bell, and went away." Under the French they excelled. Writes Lanning, "All four regiments performed well. . . . The 369th earning the French Croix de Guerre. [They] became known as the 'Men of Bronze' to the French and 'Hell Fighters' to the Germans. . . . 171 officers and men of the regiment received individual awards of the Croix de Guerre or the Legion of Merit." *They* called themselves the Black Rattlers. "[They] spent 191 days on the front line, longer than any other American regiment, black or white. During that time, the 369th never had a single soldier taken prisoner by the Germans, and the regiments never surrendered a single foot of ground to the enemy."

Before the armistice could be signed, the American command wanted its Black Rattlers released *immediatement,* so they could be sent home before they made any French women pregnant. Marshal Ferdinand Foch, the French commander, refused the request and they were allowed to stay until after the surrender, whether they miscegenated or not!

During World War II, five-star general "Hap" Arnold was forced to accept the black flyers from the Tuskegee squadron in his command in North Africa. Lanning writes that he did his best to defame the unit as a prelude to disbanding it. In secret memos to his senior officers in Morocco, he asked for confirmation that black pilots "tire quickly." When aides pointed out the counterproductive effect of such attempts, Old Hap lost his customary smile and gave it up. Dorie Miller was a messman, second class, on the battleship USS *West Virginia* when it was hit in 1941. Miller rushed on deck, dragged his captain to safety, then manned a gun that he had not been trained to use and proceeded to shoot down two Japanese planes, and may have shot down two more. He was rewarded by being promoted to mess attendant, first class!

Douglas MacArthur was displeased, according to Lanning, at the fast rate of segregation during the Korean War, so he put a halt to it. When a black infantry unit, the Twenty-fourth, performed poorly, word spread through the ranks like wildfire and a soldier's ballad quickly sprang up in honor of the event. Lanning makes it clear that several all-white units failed as miserably as the Twenty-fourth, but no one sang any songs abut them. He then details the heroism of individual men in the Twenty-fourth and lists the many reasons why the unit failed—the same reasons blacks fail in society—no education, no employment opportunities, being falsely accused of crimes and even more falsely convicted, so that incarceration puts an end to any gains made.

If black men are the equal of white men when given half a chance, then the violent, unhinged pathology that they endure whenever they are about to put the lie to their inferiority, is, it would seem, based on more than custom. Obviously a fear of the black man's abilities as a man regenerates the racism in the white man and makes him manifest that racism, often uncontrollably. The excuse given most often between the World Wars for not giving blacks command was that white men simply would not serve under them. The netherworld that black men inhabit is one that not only denies them any real recognition for their exploits after the fact, but also finds reasons to deny them the opportunity to be heroes, whether they can be or not.

Lanning's last chapters tell a happiness tale of black men and women being fully integrated into the services. He stresses that the number of blacks in command positions has risen to four times what it had been before Korea, but still the number is only half of what it should be based on population figures. The fact is, Americans are unable to ridicule black pretensions to bravery any longer and have to allow blacks full access to all opportunities for advancement in a peacetime, volunteer army. It can't maintain itself at sufficient strength otherwise because there aren't enough middle-class white men and women interested in "serving their country." Consequently, society has had to acquiesce to black equality of sorts in the armed forces.

Proof that America is neither thrilled with the idea of that equality, nor ready to celebrate yet another emancipation, can be found in Hollywood's silence on the matter. No black heroes have been portrayed in any of the films about Vietnam, even though the black casualty rate there had reached 23 percent by 1967 and stayed that way for another two years. The Academy Award-winning film *Saving Private Ryan*, hailed the all-conquering white hero in a manner that is simply a continuation of the John Wayne days.

So blacks have almost reached some sort of parity in the armed forces, even the women, who were treated worse than the men, but let's keep that a secret. We, the aggregate American, don't want to disturb our psychosis by really trying to solve the problem of racism. It's much easier to just look at the face in the mirror, dribble at the mouth, and admit to ourselves, "I'm a racist because I'm an American, so there!"

34

INVISIBLE MAN

by Ralph Ellison

NEW YORK: RANDOM HOUSE, 1952

Invisible Man is probably one of the most widely read novels in America and beyond in the last fifty years. For those who don't know its story, a nameless man spends most of his life assuming that playing by white America's rules is the fitting and proper way to proceed in the world. When he finds out that he will never have a life worth living with that approach, he makes his separate peace and descends into the underground where he won't have to be used by the world above. But in the end, he decides to come out into the light and face whatever gods there may be.

By placing his protagonist in a self-made hermetic seal, where the contradictions of the world cannot obtrude, Ellison creates brilliant literary ramifications. The fluid range of his central character's experiences—from rural backwoods southland, to Harlem, to downtown New York radicalism and back to Harlem again—create a broad canvas on which the individual response to the problems of emotional self-awakening can be examined to the fullest extent imaginable in a book of fiction.

In addition to his mastery of style and the dramatic intensity that he creates throughout, Ellison has so personalized the masks of our culture that the literary experience also becomes a sociological one. As a consequence, he gives us a look into the hypocrisies of our national character that alone makes this work an enduring classic.

Ellison is the third member of the golden triumvirate that began with Jean Toomer and has Richard Wright at its apex. Ellison's incandescent use of language, coupled with his sense of human displacement, is not so much disparate in its picaresque effect as it is a modern representation of the cracked mirror filled that yields many splendid prisms. His work exists the way life does: it's simply there forever. There are people who reread it year after year, much the same way people go back to *Hamlet* or *Lear* for spiritual sustenance. No greater tribute can be paid to any writer.

Invisible Man is not just a novel filled with rich visual imagery and abundant personal experiences, but a novel of ideas. The reader is drawn into the world of Harlem in the 1930s, when race riots erupted because Mayor Fiorella La Guardia refused to share whatever relief the federal government was giving New York City with the black unemployed. When the Triboro Bridge was being built right at Harlem's doorstep, and upward of 40 percent of the black population in Harlem was on the breadline, not one black worker was hired to work on the project. It was also a time when the Communist Party, Ellison's brotherhood, was the only real force blacks could join to fight the monolithic racism that surrounded them. Ellison's ability to immerse us completely in that world is another testament to his skill as a stylist.

But the primary theme of the novel is the idea of invisibility— the invisibility of black America when black America is being looked at by white America. Someone white may look at a black person and ask, "What invisibility?" They see violence, hostility, ethnic difference, attitude, hip-hop rap, basketball, whatever the clichés—everything but the invisibility they suffer. But, of course, the invisibility is what's inside: the pain, the gullibility, the insatiable need to be wanted, to belong or at least be allowed to survive, the willingness to still believe in the goodness of things, in the hope eternal, the lamb of God on this side of Jordan.

Invisible Man (we never learn either of his two names, which in a five-hundred page novel is quite a trick) begins by playing by the rules and believing in them passionately. He's almost willing to die for them and certainly willing to pin all his hopes for success on the rewards that will come from obeying them. They are the rules of Booker T. Washington, the separate-but-equal world of the clenched fist in economics and the separate fingers in the world of social intercourse. They are also the rules of W. E. B. Du Bois and the Talented Tenth: the idea that an educated black elite could beat America at its own game by playing within the rules, but doing it so superbly, that merit would destroy race hatred.

Ellison's protagonist never comes close to any real flesh-and-blood relationship with anyone. His family in the South is referred to here and there, also namelessly. He has sex with one white woman, which he does not enjoy, and does not give much detail about. He pretends with another white woman, Sybil, for whom he does not feel any warmth, that they committed the act, even though they didn't. (She got drunk and passed out.) She's glad to hear it and makes him promise to do it again. He promises. And he fears for her life in a way that he fears for no one else's when he realizes that she might be caught in the race riot that leads up to the novel's end. There are no other women in his life from his college days or before whom he thinks about or wants to see again or even remembers, whether fondly or not. He's dissociated even before he realizes that the world has played a trick on him—the trick of passing him from one would-be benefactor to another with the secret directive, "Keep this nigger running." When he's mistaken for Rinehart (the pimp, hustler, jackleg preacher, tough-guy gangster), the emotional reality of the mistake as Ellison presents it is to wonder about what is the *rind*—the man's outer self—and what is the *heart*—the man's inner self.

The novel is most satisfying when Ellison is essaying the hypocrisy of the communists or the futility of black resistance in the face of overpowering odds. The political analysis and writing are both impeccable. For the rest, the human drama is strongest in its nonexistence as much as it is in creating a character who can't find a place—a context in which to exist—and whose story is made so compelling, so effective by that failed effort endlessly attempted.

Ellison ends *Invisible Man* by reaching out to the principle that the country was founded on, suggesting that since the founders had betrayed the principle that all men are created equal by allowing slavery to exist from the very beginning, maybe it is up to the disfranchised, the hated, and the unwashed to reaffirm it, and in so doing become the saviors of us all, black and white alike. Looked at from the vantage point of half a century later, Ellison's suggestion to pass the burden to the bottom of the sociological heap might seem like a vain hope. Trying to save the integrity of the nation by holding on to the principle on which it was founded is a risky mandate at best for black America, if black America accepts the racist reality of what is and what has been, even in the very recent past.

Ellison is still regarded as having written one of the great American novels sixty years after it was published. While he never matched that achievement, it was enough, he didn't have to any more than Herman Melville had to match *Moby Dick*.

35

THE OUTSIDER

by Richard Wright

NEW YORK: HARPER BROTHERS, 1953

The Outsider picks up where *Native Son* leaves off. In *Native Son,* the alienation of Wright's antihero Bigger Thomas is clearly established. Bigger is trapped in hopeless impoverishment of both body and soul, and since the black persona has been trapped in this way throughout the history of the country, the black character in general has had to live an underground existence in the real world and in the world of his inner life.

In a long short story, *The Man Who Lived Underground,* Wright takes a different approach to the problem of the Outsider by removing him from the diurnal round—the same approach Ellison employs at the end of *Invisible Man.* Bigger, in an existentialist reach that is the thematic prelude to *The Outsider,* kills in order to find some meaning to his inner void. The act is not done consciously, but it's clearly the impulse that was driving his id. Doomed to live in an underground world above ground, he has no other answers that help him cope with his emptiness and at the same time keep him alive. He can't even put into words the awful torment of being adrift in a reality that has no place for him, because beyond being a servant doing a servant's work, for a servant's wage, he has no existence, no occupation. Like Othello's, his occupation's gone! Unlike Othello, it's gone because it never existed, and can never exist in the land in which he's a native son.

Bigger's lawyer, Max, is frightened by the emotional freedom that finally comes to Bigger once he understands what he's done and why he did it. When he tells Max, in an almost rejuvenated moment, that he's all right, even with the death sentence hanging over him, Max recoils from fright and can never look Bigger in the face again. He even says his final adieu with his back turned. Wright has his antihero create the basis for his heroism through the profane act of killing not one, but two women, not for money or sex or revenge, but as an act of the will—to free himself from the stinking Jim Crow world that's drowning him.

In *The Outsider*, Wright goes beyond killing as an attempt to create meaning for a life that has none. Instead he tries to answer that most fundamental question: who are we really, once we've stripped away the protective devices we hide behind to keep our myths as reality, our hatreds as rational, our desires camouflaged as comforting, domesticated ambition—instead of seen for the raw, naked urges that they are.

Cross Damon, the protagonist of *The Outsider*, unlike Bigger Thomas, comes to the early realization that he has played society's game because he's been too unaware of his inner self to do otherwise. He's estranged from his wife, sees very little of his three sons, and has only a superficial emotional attachment to his mother. Also, he has just found out that his girlfriend (who's pregnant) is underage. Because he's black in Chicago in the forties, he's raw meat for the powers that be once his women decide to turn against him. He's not a willing victim and he's not innocent, but neither can he fight back.

His wife, Gladys, gets a lawyer, goes to the postal authorities (he's a clerk), and tells them about the underage girlfriend. (It's a rape, of course.) Then she tells Cross he has to take out a loan and give her the money, and if he's a good boy he can keep his job, but he has to sign both the house and the car over to her. With Dot, the pregnant girlfriend, joining forces with Gladys,

Cross has no choice. He gets the money in cash, endures the insults of his white supervisors, and calls his wife to tell her he's on his way to give her the money. The subway he takes crashes, and the mangled body of another black man is mistaken for his.

He's officially dead, so he decides to leave it all behind and start anew, but not as a good citizen taking advantage of a second chance. His new beginning will be as a man emancipated from society's rules—all of them. And his disaffection is not primarily the result of race. Later, when Cross is thinking of the woman he comes to love, he asks himself, "How could he allow her to love him for his Negritude when being a Negro was the least important thing in his life?"

The idea is not new. A man can deny everything that society considers holy: another human being's life, love of family. And the only thing that has meaning is that to which he, the man, gives meaning. In *The Stranger,* Camus confronted that idea at least ten years before Wright did. Meursault (Camus's antihero) simply withdrew, dissociating himself from his actions so that the gun that he's holding that kills the Arab simply goes off (the trigger "gave way"), but this is not the case with Cross Damon. He kills four men and he intended to kill each and every one of them: Joe, a fellow postal worker, also black, who runs into Damon in a whorehouse after he's been declared dead. (Damon clubs Joe to death with a bottle.) Gil Blount, a communist who recruits Damon for the party and wants him to live in his home to provoke a confrontation with the landlord who's a fascist. (Damon clubs both of them to death while they are fighting over his right to live there.) Jack Hilton, another communist who suspects that Damon killed the other two men. (Damon kills Jack with Jack's own gun.)

The question of why we should listen to a man willing to play God with other men's lives never gets asked because the novel is so riveting, so articulate, so sure of its ground intellectually, so compelling in its narrative flow—its characters so vivid, so fully drawn. Nothing is wasted, no element is unnecessary to the emotional success of the work. In its grasp of the conflicts in man that make him grapple with his nature, for good or for evil—and his will to assert himself in the end—*The Outsider* is easily the twentieth-century equal of *Moby Dick*.

Damon is not a reformist who wants to substitute one religion for another. He does want to obliterate one type of evil—the reason for three of the killings—on moral grounds. The basis for his morality is his own credo, his own idea of right and wrong. While Camus's antihero assumes no responsibility, has no sense of a morality that can compel action, Wright has his man plunge ahead because he is seeking answers to questions of good and evil, right and wrong.

As in *Native Son*, Wright includes a white lawyer (this time a district attorney) who is, to a degree, a kindred spirit of the protagonist. This lawyer, Ely Houston, witnesses Cross's capacity to withstand all the pressures of society—the cries of his children; the agony of his wife, who wants to deny and accuse him at the same time; and the news that his mother died from shock when she found out that it wasn't her son that she buried—and he, himself, against the demands of familial love demonstrates that he was capable of committing the murders.

Houston doesn't lock the black man up and throw away the key. There is no abuse of power, no stretching of the law to make Damon a victim. Houston tells Cross that since he can't prove that he killed the men, he's not going to hold him and try to manufacture evidence. He is going to let Damon go. Damon has played God, lived by his own rules, and that will be his punishment.

Since Damon is not psychotic, he feels the weight of his actions, realizes that in his attempt to reorder his world he has simply stepped into the feces of the world itself. However, Damon feels innocent even though he acknowledges what he has done because he's done it to find himself, to be able to live life with a sense of morality, of the rightness of things.

But Damon's new order doesn't work. It can't work. That's the tragedy of life: we can't really reorder it. Once we realize this we are defeated, because the only other option is to live by the duplicity that everyone else lives by: obeying when we have to; violating people, principles, and things when we can get away with it;

accepting our successes as the only rewards; and trying not to let our failures corrode us.

If the novel had stopped there, Wright would still have written a masterpiece. But there's a part of the equation that can never be ignored—the emotion of the human heart, those feelings we call love. We have not truly tested the human condition if we ignore the role love plays in determining who and what we are. Damon loves the wife of one of the men he has killed, although that's not why he killed him. The woman, Eva—young, white, frail, sensitive, an artist—loves him in return. But she sees a black man who she thinks is a victim and whom she wants to help protect from the world—the racists and the communists who just want to use him. Damon desperately tries to make a life with this sensitive spirit. Finally he tells her about the murders and explains that he committed them because he was trying to find out how to live by his own rules. Since all three men were racist tyrants in their own right, expunging them was part of the process. This revelation is too much for Eva and she kills herself by jumping from a sixth-story window.

How does a person find a clean place for the inner self, one that allows for integrity on one's own terms? In the end, Wright seems to say, it can't be done. Man can't be reformed. We can't rebuild our lives by our own lights, we can only trade and barter and compromise and come to some accommodation with the world as it is, hopefully without paying the price of madness.

But Wright doesn't end there. He leaves us with a supreme irony. After being shot down in the street by hit men from the Communist Party who figure out that he had killed two of their own, Damon is taken to a hospital where Houston tries desperately to find out what he learned about it all playing by his rules. Houston asks him, "How was it with you?"

"It was horrible," Damon replies.

"All of it . . ."

"But why? *Why?* Try and tell me . . ."

"Because in my heart I'm innocent. That's what made the horror . . ." Then he dies.

36

HERE I STAND

by Paul Robeson

NEW YORK: OTHELLO ASSOCIATES, 1958

In the foreword to *Here I Stand,* written in 1957, Robeson had this to say: "For more than ten years they [what he calls the Big White Folks] have persecuted me in every way they could—by slander and mob violence, by denying me the right to practice my profession as an artist, by withholding my right to travel abroad. To these, the real Un-Americans, I merely say: 'All right—I don't like you either!' "

Since his death in 1976, at age seventy-seven, Robeson has gone through a renascence of monumental proportions. Books proclaiming him a maligned American giant have shown up in every quarter. Retrospectives of his films proliferate, and television biographies and displays in libraries (in universities and out) appear almost annually. This phenomenon is similar to America's post mortem gratitude to Abraham Lincoln for saving us all—North and South—by successfully prosecuting the Civil War. In part, we are expressing our guilt that he was so unappreciated while he was alive.

As early as 1933, Robeson was trying to find "an Art that is purely Negro, that is not dependent on Western and European influence." And by the following year he was an outspoken critic of the Nazi persecution of the Jews. Not that that brought him any significant goodwill in the end. In 1935 Robeson had his first taste of what if felt like to be treated as a whole man. Touring Russia that year he said, "Here, for the first time in my life, I walk in full human dignity."

In 1942, while performing in Kansas City, he stopped in the middle of the concert and pointed out the segregated seating of the audience. He continued the concert, but said he did so in protest. Hundreds of whites walked out of the audience in response. That same year he received his first listing as a presumed communist by the House Committee on Un-American Activities (HUAC). Just prior to that, he had been cited by the secretary of the treasury for "distinguished and patriotic service to our Country."

In 1943, when he was opening on Broadway in *Othello*, the Federal Bureau of Investigation was already listing him as a leading communist and issued a detention card that allowed for his immediate arrest in a national emergency. His *Othello* became a huge hit and the longest-running Shakespearean play on Broadway. After the Broadway run, it toured forty-five cities in seven months.

Robeson appealed to President Truman for federal anti-lynching legislation in 1946, but Harry said it wasn't time for him to act. When Robeson suggested that America could not logically take the lead in punishing Nazis at the Nuremberg trials (then in progress) and allow the lynching of black citizens in America to go unpunished, Truman became angry. Loyal Americans should not, according to Harry, mix domestic problems like lynching with foreign policy. (See *Paul Robeson Speaks*, edited by Philip S. Foner, Citadel Press.)

In 1947 HUAC included Robeson in a list of a thousand communists. The wheel of his car was tampered with and flew off on a St. Louis highway. His response was to stop giving concerts in order to work against racial injustice. Said he, "I must raise my voice, but not by singing pretty songs." In Peoria, Illinois, the city council refused to let him sing, anyway. The Albany, New York, Board of Education did the same, and the New York State Supreme Court said he might sing if he confined himself to a musical program.

In 1949 the Associated Press quoted him as saying that blacks would not fight in a foreign war. That set the stage for the riot in Peekskill, New York, in August. Rampaging whites smashed the stage, torched the chairs, and attacked concertgoers. Robeson and his supporters returned in September and he finished the concert, but an even more serious riot ensued, injuring at least 150 people.

After that it was all downhill. NBC banned him in 1950 and the State Department withdrew his passport. The next year, Walter White of the National Association for the advancement of Colored People criticized him vehemently in an article in *Ebony* magazine. Roy Wilkins, White's successor, followed suit by calling him a "Kremlin stooge." Before it was all over, Robeson would be blacklisted by record companies, and his car would be tampered with again. When he was summoned by HUAC in 1956, he was defiant, saying that the committee members were "the true un-Americans, and you should be ashamed of yourselves." By 1958 the U.S. Supreme Court forced the State Department to return Robeson's passport. It was his sixtieth year, and he capped the celebrations with a sold-out appearance at Carnegie Hall. It's also the year that *Here I Stand* was published.

Not an autobiography, although it is rich in biographical detail, *Here I Stand* is a statement of Robeson's principles, which describes where he stood in his fight for a true American democracy, for his people as well as other "minorities," such as underpaid factory workers of whatever ethnicity. Robeson insists on imbuing this book with a sense of celebration, even though he intones an age-old cry of pain and suffering at the hands of the unjust.

Whatever Robeson took on, he accomplished with spectacular success. He was All-American at Rutgers University, graduated from law school, became a great baritone and an actor who was known internationally. He did not protect himself by playing by the rules, however. Instead he played "outside the lines," which made him fair game for the likes of Walter Winchell, congressional bigots, and the mob. Because of the cold war hatred rampant in the McCarthy era, good, law-abiding American citizens felt licensed to attempt to kill Robeson, with the collusion of the police, during the Peekskill riot. It was not an instantaneous eruption but a well-planned attack on the part of the lunatic right.

Robeson is one of those Americans who had more right than most to call into question American racism. His father had escaped from slavery on the Underground Railroad in 1860, became a successful minister, and raised a family that never broke the law but always defied the rich and the racist. On his mother's side, the family could be traced all the way back to a patriarch who baked bread for George Washington's troops and was a leader in Philadelphia's black community.

Robeson explains that one of the primary objections to his criticism of American racism was that "Paul Robeson . . . was ungrateful to the good white folks who had given him wealth and fame and that he had nothing to complain about." Of course, what happened to Robeson's career still hangs like a pall over actors in film and television. Surely, with so many black superstars in show business today (more than twenty at the top), there must be one who is political. But the destruction of a man of Robeson's caliber tells them that they too had better beware, for if it could happen to him, it can certainly happen to them. Consequently, black actors don't have the constitutional rights of a Charlton Heston or a John Wayne. Those rights are the preserve of the ultra-conservative—as distinguished from the racist.

There was a lot for Robeson to criticize. He appeared in a Shakespearean play in London with an interracial cast fifteen long years before he was allowed to do so in America. And his American appearance in Othello, as successful as it was, was an anomaly. Indeed, interracial casting was one of the things that killed the Federal Theater Project during the Depression. Robeson didn't grin and bear it. Why should he? He was a man, not a house servant pretending to be an artist.

He attended the Paris Peace conference in1949, and seven years later, he had to appear before HUAC to explain what he had said there. When he did so all too eloquently, Francis Walter (coauthor of the McCarran-Walter Immigration Act) started banging the gavel to shut him up. Robeson was supposed to be apologetic, not act as if he were convinced of the rightness of his position. But because he wouldn't be browbeaten by the congressional bullies, he was considered un-American!

James Eastland, senator from Mississippi, was one of the bullies. He was a rabid racist who had blacks working for him in peonage conditions. Robeson called his number when he said that most of the world did not want to go to war against the Soviet Union, adding, "It was inconceivable that anyone would go to war for an Eastland."

"Let me make this clear, the South will retain segregation," Eastland had said. Paul Robeson and the world saw one hundred congressmen from both the House and the Senate sign a manifesto denouncing the *Brown* decision and declaring they would fight it with every means at their disposal. Instead of backing men like Robeson who stood ready to defy the racists, America turned its back on them and left them to fight alone. Be black, be American, but don't exercise any American rights, unless everyone white says it's all right. Otherwise you get lynched one way or another.

"Whites hate and fear [Robeson] simply because he is the conscience of the U.S. in the field of color relations," a San Francisco newspaper noted. Another in Virginia wrote:

"Paul Robeson is a great artist and a deeply sympathetic human being. His own success did not blind him to the wrongs suffered by his race. . . . To deny him the right to travel [the government wouldn't even let him travel to Canada, and you don't need a passport for that] to sing and to speak as he pleases; to put him in the pillory of a Congressional Committee and let lesser men bait him, is more hurtful to American prestige abroad than any intemperate statement he ever made."

When Robeson wrote the following, he was declaring his belief in the American democracy and should have been speaking for all Americans:

> In all the terms in which power is reckoned in America . . . we are in a weak position; and from this the conclusion is drawn that the Negro can do little or nothing to compel a change. . . . It must be seen, however, that this is not a case of a minority pitting itself against a majority. . . . If we wanted to gain something for ourselves by taking it away from the . . . majority, the effort would plainly be hopeless. . . . We seek the equal rights to which we are entitled under the law. The granting of our demand would not lessen the democratic rights of the white people: on the contrary, it would enormously strengthen the base of democracy for all Americans.
>
> The granting of our demand for first-class citizenship . . . would not in itself put us in a position of equality. . . . But the equal place to which we aspire cannot be reached without the equal rights we demand, and so the winning of those rights is not a maximum fulfillment but a minimum necessity and we cannot settle for less.

Sad to say, he wasn't.

Here I Stand has been made into a film in which Robeson plays himself. It's also available on DVD.

37

The Autobiography of W. E. B. Du Bois

New York: International Publishers, 1968

His was a voice crying out in the wilderness for most of an entire century, and in all that time he cried out most often in vain because most often he cried out alone—unheeded, denied of men, deserted by his own, both the ones he had sired intellectually and spiritually and the ones who stood side by side with him until the going got too rough. He was hounded by the Federal Bureau of Investigation (who wasn't, who had anything of consequence to say for the more than half century that J. Edgar Hoover was in charge of our most prestigious law enforcement agency?), defamed by Dean Acheson, persecuted by the State Department, indicted as a criminal, denied a passport for seven years so as to muzzle him internationally, excoriated by the Catholic church, made *persona non grata* by Walter White and the National Association for the Advancement of Colored People, and after all that he was the last man standing until his death in Ghana in 1963 at the age of ninety-five.

Du Bois was not without his faults. My stepfather, who knew him, said he was condescending even to men of his own stature.

He called Thurgood Marshall a man of "narrow cultural background." And he was unable in writing more than four hundred pages on his life, to give his first wife of over fifty years more than a few scant passages. He talks of her tenderly when they first meet and marry, and of one Christmas spent joyfully in what can only be described as genteel poverty. He's then candid about how sexual issues and his constant travel estranged them. And that's it until we hear cryptically of her death and burial, followed by his second marriage to Shirley Graham a year later.

What he can write about and does voluminously, and even repetitiously, are the Pan African conferences (not that they weren't important) and communism. And many speeches and essays that he's included in their entirety could have been omitted since they often covered ground that he had already essayed more than adequately elsewhere in the volume. This does not mean that the work is a difficult read by any means. It's an epic chronicle of what we were as a nation and what we still are. And it is a completely engrossing story of how a New England youth, growing up in an environment that would make him suspicious of politics, reticent to the point of abstinence in matters of sex, and completely abstemious when it came to the more popular indulgences (he did come to enjoy a good bottle of wine, but could never bring himself to sit at a bar comfortably) became a well-traveled sophisticate who knew Europe (Germany especially) as well as he knew his native land.

Du Bois started out as a dutiful son of an infirm, withdrawn, impoverished mother, who spent most of her life alone. When her husband went off to make a life for his family and sent for her, she refused to go because *her* family was against it. She died, propitiously as Du Bois admits, when he was deciding whether to go off to college or stay in Great Barrington, Massachusetts, and take care of her.

Because he had a brilliant mind and was rigorously self-disciplined all his life, school was Du Bois's natural métier. By the time he went to Fisk he already had an excellent education. There he learned about his own people in their natural habitat, as it were, and taught in the most rural and desolate areas of the

South in the prehistory days of the penultimate decade of the nineteenth century. He was even raped by the mother of one of his pupils whose house he boarded in as part of his financial arrangement. Harvard wouldn't accept his degree from Fisk, so he entered as a junior *and* did two more years in graduate study after getting his Bachelor's Degree. From there he went to Berlin to round out his graduate work. As he ironically remarked, Harvard may not have recognized Fisk, but the University of Berlin didn't recognize Harvard! When he returned to America at the age of twenty-five he was the most educated of men, and his Harvard doctorate was still ahead of him.

His goal early on was to bring his people *in toto* into the new dawn as equals through the ivory tower of scientific investigation and research, with sociology and history as the basis for his assault on what he saw as the main barrier to black equality—ignorance; ignorance on the part of America to what black people had accomplished and what they were capable of, given half a chance, and ignorance on the part of his own people about what their forebears had accomplished in the motherland over the centuries.

It was from this idea that his much maligned concept of a Talented Tenth arose (10 percent of the black population, which was 10 percent of the entire population). This Talented Tenth would not form an exclusive elite, but would lead the other 90 percent into emancipation. In Du Bois's mind, the truths that he would uncover through research and study would gain a wide reading and change not only men's minds, but influence their actions as well, for the better.

Finally, he realized that the enormous success of capitalism by the beginning of the nineteenth century made it imperative to justify slavery and the slave trade in moral terms, since that was where the money came from that made capitalism possible. When slavery was played out, imperial colonialism took its place. In both cases, black and brown people were exploited, as chattel slaves in the former system and reduced to peonage in the latter, the natural resources of their lands expropriated when their bodies were no longer the resource of choice.

This was an evil that Du Bois could not get out of his mind. As academic and as scientist, he saw the consanguinity between the basis for Europe's (and eventually the world's) wealth and the need to make racism respectable by making black (and brown) people less than human. The result: he became a firm believer in the "God That Failed"—communism. He was unable, as many other writers and thinkers were, to give up the dream that, as practiced in Russia and China, communism was the system that would save us all—black and white alike. Richard Wright, John Steinbeck, and many other writers had all seen communism's flaws and confessed their apostasy in *The God That Failed,* but not Du Bois. Time and again he hails China and Russia and hopes for a partnership between them and Africa. Du Bois never mentions or tries to find an accommodation for the six million people in Russia who starved to death in the thirties because of Stalin's brutal experiments in agrarian cooperatives, and the three quarter of a million that he killed outright in the purges.

His legacy, for which we should be forever grateful, is his uncompromising and unerring analysis of American racism at home and abroad. Du Bois had ample opportunity to experience that racism firsthand. Because he always fought it, he was its constant target, not just as a black man, but as *the* black man who most embodied black America's will, often indomitable, to stand against racism and sacrifice whatever had to be sacrificed in the bargain.

He was always brilliant. One of five graduates to give speeches at his commencement in 1890, he chose Jefferson Davis as his topic. Afterward, a faculty member observed that he treated his subject with "contemptuous fairness." He said in part:

> "I wish to consider not the man, but the type of civilization which his life represented: its foundation is the idea of the strong man. . . . Individualism coupled with the rule of might. . . . It made a naturally brave and generous man now advancing civilization by murdering Indians, now hero of a national disgrace, called by courtesy the Mexican War; and finally as the crowning absurdity, the peculiar champion of a people fighting to be free in order that another people should not be free."

Later in Du Bois's career, what the National Association for the Advancement of Colored People said after it acquiesced to Walter White's demand that Du Bois be sacked is a fitting if incomplete bow to his greatness:

> He created, what never existed before, a Negro intelligentsia, and many who have never read a word of his writings are his spiritual disciples and descendants. Without him the Association could never have been what it was and is . . . A mere yes-man could not have attracted the attention of the world. . . . We shall be the poorer for his loss. . . . [N]o one in the Association can fill his place with the same intellectual grasp. We therefore offer him our sincere thanks for the services he has rendered, and we wish him all happiness in all that he may now undertake.

When the State Department got around to getting a grand jury in Washington, D.C., to indict him for refusing to register as a foreign agent during the hysteria of the McCarthy era, his friends fell away like flies. Essex House in Manhattan had been reserved days before the celebration of his eighty-third birthday. As soon as the indictment was handed down they canceled the contract and returned the deposit. Men like Mordecai Johnson, venerable president of Howard University, to his undying shame, shunned him. Both of his graduate and undergraduate fraternities (one of which he helped found) rebuked and or avoided him. As he wrote, "The intelligentsia . . . the successful business and professional men . . . [were] either silent or actually antagonistic." The charges were so absurd that the judge, a conservative Catholic, threw the case out without even allowing it to be presented to a trial jury.

But Du Bois's greatness is not in "here" or "there," in "this" or "that." "Though up and down without he could define and in and out with rule and line," as Omar Khayyam wrote. He, in all he cared to know, was never deep in anything but the wine of human truth. That truth lay in not bowing to the gods of racism, no matter how mighty their armies, how overflowing their coffers with the gold wrung out of the bodies and very souls of black Africa at home and abroad, no matter how relentless the enforcement of their unjust laws, even with the connivance of black men. As Du Bois says at the end of his Autobiography, "Teach us, Forever Dead, there is no Dream but Deed, there is no Deed but Memory." And if black America forgets or refuses to remember, it will always be unworthy to rule itself, to be men and women equal in everything. What made him so dangerous? The fact that when the lion roared the whole world heard it.

38

STRIDE TOWARD FREEDOM: THE MONTGOMERY STORY

by Martin Luther King Jr.

NEW YORK: HARPER & ROW, 1958

Martin Luther King, Jr. was born in Atlanta, Georgia, on April 10, 1929, into the black elite on both sides. It was an insulated world that was set apart from the vast majority of southern blacks. At twenty-four, King had finished his graduate work at Boston University, had been married to Coretta Scott for a year and was a year away from earning his Ph.D. He had his first job as pastor of the Dexter Avenue Baptist Church in Montgomery, Alabama, which in one of the supreme ironies of history, stands—as it stood then—directly across from the Montgomery State-house in Capitol Square, where Jefferson Davis was sworn in as president of the Confederacy.

From all the evidence, it seems clear that King went to Montgomery with no other motive than to become a good pastor to his flock. At the beginning of the Montgomery bus boycott, when he met with the city council to make his first set of modest demands, he was still leading a very discreet group of middle-class lawyers, preachers, teachers, and undertakers. But the press seemed to love him from the start. When the attention descended on him and the Montgomery Improvement Association or MIA (the official name of the boycott), he soon realized that the stakes were nothing less than the preservation or destruction of the Southern way of life.

King didn't jump ship when that realization hit him; instead he grew as large as the challenge. Not even his father, who had been a legendary fighter against racism in his time, could comprehend what his son was taking on. He thought Martin had started something he couldn't finish and wanted him to come home to Atlanta, where he would be out of harm's way. Probably no one really understood the historical significance of King's battle until the man had been dead for many years.

Montgomery, self-proclaimed Cradle of the Confederacy, had one of the most rigidly segregated bus systems in the country in 1954. The first four rows of seats were for whites only. Even if the rest of the bus were filled to capacity, a black person would have to stand over those empty seats in the first four rows. He or she could not, under any circumstances, sit in any one of them. One man was killed; another, who was blind, was dragged for some yards when he was caught in the bus door; and a teenage girl was thrown in jail after being roughly treated by the police, all because they either sat in those seats or disobeyed the bus system's policy of segregation in some way.

The rules on Montgomery's buses were taken very seriously and rigorously enforced. If the first four rows were full and a black person took a seat behind those four rows, when a white person boarded the bus, the black passenger would have to get up anyway and give his or her seat to the white passenger. If the bus got so crowded that blacks couldn't get to the back, even to stand, they had to pay their fare, then *get off the bus* and reenter at the rear. Once they had put their ten cents in the box and gotten off, however, the driver would often drive away before they had a chance to get back on, leaving them standing in the street. In addition, the drivers used every racial epithet known to Montgomery and the world in addressing blacks. Calling an old woman "girl," or a grandfather "boy" was the least of it. *Cow, bitch, monkey,* and black ape headed the list of the nonprurient expletives.

This was the situation in December 1955 when Rosa Parks boarded a Montgomery city bus on her way home from work. She took a seat behind the first four rows, which was legal. At the next stop several white passengers got on. Since all the seats were taken by this time, Mrs. Parks and three other black passengers were ordered by the driver to get up and relinquish their seats to the whites. The other three obeyed; Mrs. Parks didn't. She was arrested, fingerprinted, and locked up for violation of the city ordinance.

As King points out in this excellent account of the boycott, Montgomery's black middle class was as divided and as obsequious as a professional class could become in a modern city in the mid-fifties. Whatever power existed was hopelessly divided among the various religious denominations and one or two professional organizations, so Montgomery seemed like the last place on earth where the first volley in the civil rights revolt would be fired. At the first meeting called by blacks after Mrs. Parks's arrest, it was agreed that the buses should be boycotted until the segregated system was abolished.

They decided to begin the boycott the following Monday, which gave them only two days to get the word out to the rest of the black community. A flyer was run off and distributed. A maid, who was not too well read, gave her flyer to her employer, who immediately got it into the hands of the city's leading newspaper, the *Montgomery Advertiser*. The *Advertiser* reported the story in the most ominous tones possible, running it on the front page. The organizers of the boycott could not have, in their wildest dreams, done a better job of informing black citizens of their intentions. Everyone quickly learned about the boycott, even in outlying districts.

King, at whose church the first meeting was held, was unanimously chosen as president of the MIA. As he writes in *Stride Toward Freedom*: "The action had caught me unawares. It had happened so quickly that I did not have time to think it through. It is probable that if I had, I would have declined the nomination. . . . My wife and I had just agreed [a few weeks before] that I should not take on any heavy community responsibilities since I had so recently finished my thesis and needed to give more attention to my church work."

The city council rejected the first compromise plan that the MIA offered, which was a mild accommodation that did not even violate the segregation law. Instead, the mayor went on television to announce that he was going to get tough. He and his two commissioners immediately joined the White Citizens Council. They had blacks arrested for minor traffic violations, or no violations at all. King was arrested for driving thirty miles an hour in a twenty-five mile an hour zone. But the boycott was a success from the beginning; 99 percent of Montgomery's blacks refused to ride the buses.

A bomb was thrown onto the front porch of the King residence while Mrs. King was in the house. The sound of the explosion was so loud that it was heard blocks away. Two nights later the home of E. D. Nixon (one of the original organizers) was bombed, and both Ralph Abernathy's church and his home were destroyed by bombs. The MIA struck back by filing a suit in federal district court asking for an end to bus segregation on the grounds that it violated the Fourteenth Amendment. The city's attorneys argued that if bus segregation ended, Montgomery would become a battleground of violence and bloodshed. One of the three judges asked, "Is it fair to command one man to then surrender his constitutional rights, if they are his constitutional rights, in order to prevent another man from committing a crime?"

The judges decided in favor of the MIA, and the city appealed to the U.S. Supreme Court, the same court that had decided the *Brown* case. The Supreme Court acted without listening to any argument; it simply said, "The motion to affirm is granted and the judgment is affirmed."

That night the Ku Klux Klan rode.

King got a letter of warning: "If you allow the niggers to go back on the buses and sit in the front seats, we're going to burn down fifty houses in one night, including yours." The city commissioners also refused to comply with the judgment. They issued a statement: "We will not yield one inch, but will do all in [our] power to oppose the integration of the Negro race with the white race in Montgomery, and will forever stand like a rock against social equality, intermarriage, and mixing of the races."

A teenage girl was beaten by four or five white men as she got off a bus. A pregnant woman was shot in the leg. As the violence increased, it became obvious that, at the same time that the city was trying to force blacks to submit to its racism, it was also plunging itself into anarchy. Montgomery had a choice: It could either go under or it could obey the law.

In a few weeks, peace prevailed, and the people of Montgomery rode their buses undisturbed—eighty-six years after the Fourteenth Amendment became the law of the land and fourteen months after Rosa Parks was arrested. Of course what King and the others accomplished in Montgomery in 1955 went way beyond a bus boycott. By getting the Supreme Court to "reaffirm," it was forcing law enforcement throughout America to enforce *Brown* in ways that counted. The South of James Eastland and the rest had simply ignored the decision and continued on their merry Confederate ways. Martin Luther King, Jr. stopped them from doing that in Montgomery. And because of Montgomery and what the boycott's success meant to black America, he went on to become the great leader that the world knows.

The best homage to so great a man is to quote his own words. Understanding him might not be possible. His courage, viewed from the distance of the thirty-three years since his death, seems almost too immense. He was, in his place and time, standing alone. Not that he didn't have many men and women standing with him. But he was alone in their midst since he was not only the head, but the heart and soul of the movement. He, more than most, came to symbolize it. He was the only man whose death was needed to bring the era to an end. If those who loved and followed him could have died with him, many of them would have. But that was his destiny and he couldn't share it.

The leadership that he and a few others provided had all but disappeared when the millennium drew to its close. Now we have many eminent survivors of that period of accomplishment who saw so many walls that were legal barriers to equality come tumbling down. They all have their reminiscences, their stories to tell of the day "Martin" did this or said that. But none of them can continue his work. They can only talk about it. True, the times have changed, and it takes more than *one* man to create a movement. Yet we cannot give the civil rights movement any credence, unless we place King at its epicenter. The living memory of his achievements will outlast almost every other memory of our time and his. But he lived those times and his speeches, sermons, and other writings come as close as we can get to comprehending it all.

From "Letter From Birmingham City Jail," in response to an open letter from eight white "liberal" clergymen calling on King to let the local and federal courts decide the battle for integration:

> Birmingham is probably the most thoroughly segregated city in the United States. Its ugly record of police brutality is known in every section of this country. Its unjust treatment of Negroes in the courts is a notorious reality. There have been more unsolved bombings of Negro homes and churches in Birmingham than any city in this nation. . . . We know through painful experience that freedom is never voluntarily given by the oppressor; it must be demanded by the oppressed. . . . I have never yet engaged in a direct action movement that was "well-timed." . . . For years now I have heard the words "Wait!" It rings in the ear of every Negro with a piercing familiarity. [It] has always meant "never. . . ." We have waited for more than 340 years for our constitutional and God-given rights . . . [to getting] a cup of coffee at a lunch counter.

From an interview in *Playboy:*

> *Playboy:* Dr. King, are your children old enough to [understand] the issues at stake in the civil rights movement?
> *King:* Yes . . . my oldest child, Yolanda. . . . asked me, "Daddy, why do you have to go to jail so much?" . . . I tried to make her understand that someone had to do this to make the world better—for all children. She was only six . . . but she was already aware of segregation. . . . We always passed Funtown, a miniature Disneyland, on our way to the airport. Yolanda would inevitable say, "I want to go to Funtown. . . ." I really didn't know how to [tell] her

why she couldn't go. [Eventually] my wife and I [sat] down with her and [tried] to explain it. . . . [Tears rolled down her face] when [we] told her that Funtown was closed to colored children.

The quotations are from *A Testament of Hope: The Essential Writings of Martin Luther King, Jr.,* edited by James Melvin Washington and are not to be found in *Stride Toward Freedom.*

39

SEX AND RACISM IN AMERICA

by Calvin Hernton

NEW YORK: DOUBLEDAY, 1965

Racism has perverted us psychosexually, Calvin Hernton tells us
in *Sex and Racism in America,* and he shows how much of the
awful, twisted history of sex between the races, black and white,
has been buried in parts of our subconscious where it will never
be found. A *New York Times* obituary, published upon Hernton's
death on October 27, 2001, said in part:

> In *Sex and Racism* Mr. Hernton, a sociologist by training, exam-
> ined the ways in which racism operates in concert with relations
> between the sexes. The result, a complex, uneasy and sometimes
> violent pas de deux was, he argued, the historical legacy of a social
> dynamic begun during slavery.

In his book, Hernton begins with the perversion of the southern white woman's identity:

> [Even though] the scantily clad white woman is irresistibly entic-
> ing as the ubiquitous sex symbol of our times . . . the southern
> white woman, reared and nurtured in the tradition of "sacred

white womanhood," has had to deny and purge herself of every honest and authentic female emotion that is vital to being a healthy woman. . . . [Instead] she's become the "chaste" white woman [that all black men try to rape].

This myth, Hernton maintains, was not created by the southern white woman, but by the southern white man. He argues that because the southern white man found it impossible to stay away from the "animal attraction of black women," he assumed that his women would have the same irresistible "animal" attraction for the "black 'bucks.' " As a consequence of exacting a terrible price for a sexual indulgence between a black man and a white woman at the very same time that he was indulging in the act itself with the black woman, unhindered and uninhibited, the southern white man was consumed with not a little guilt, which was expeditiously dealt with by killing black men and in so doing getting rid of their penises, the one obstacle to his, the southern white man's psychosexual peace of mind.

Hernton quotes from *The Mind of the South,* by W. J. Cash: "In the mind of the Southerner the word *rape* is not only applied to sexual assaults on white women by Negroes, but to any attempt at changing what the Southerner called 'our way of life.' The actual danger of the southern woman being violated by the Negro has always been comparatively small . . . much less, for instance, than the chance that she would be struck by lightning." Concerning this preoccupation with rape, Hernton says:

> While [the white woman] did not actually lynch and castrate Negroes herself, she permitted her men to do so in her name. And she enjoyed, as certainly as white men did, the perverse sexual ecstasy of hearing and knowing about lynching and castration. . . . The white woman accepts this image as a means of proving to herself that she was *sexually* attractive, if not to white men, at least to black "savages."

He then states that open knowledge of sex between a white woman and a black man would be a "blatant challenge to the most neurotic facet of the white mans' ego," and would be an assault on a southern way of life that has been maintained for 350 years.

Hernton underscores this point by relating an incident in Mississippi in which a white woman accused a black man of rape even though he was across the street from her when she said it happened. Her explanation was that he did it with his eyes. He was summarily charged, convicted, and sentenced. Hernton also gives several examples of white women forcing black men to have sex with them by threatening to cry rape if the men refused. One of these men was so trapped by a white woman in Florida for what seemed like forever. He finally got his brother to write him a letter saying their father was dying, and that's how he escaped. But Hernton also records successful marriages between white women and black men.

Hernton discusses the plight of the black woman in chapter 5. He says of her:

> [I]t has been the Negro woman, more than anyone else, who has borne the constant agonies of racial barbarity in America, from the very first day she was brought in chains to this soil. . . . Through the years [she] has suffered (and endured) every sexual outrage that a "democratic" society can possibly inflict upon a human being. . . . What these atrocities have done to her personality as a female creature, is a tale more bloody and brutal than most of us can imagine.
>
> [In the antebellum South] black people were not considered to be human beings. They were wild savage creatures "without souls." Negro women were forced to give up their bodies like animals to white men at random! [The ones] who tried to maintain a measure of dignity in regard to their sex were beaten, burned, lynched, and treated worse than dogs.

As a consequence of such an assault on the psyche, Hernton argues, it becomes almost impossible for black women to think of themselves as ladies and to express themselves sexually the way a lady would, especially since during the years of degrading sexual exploitation, they had to stand in public naked on the auction block to be fondled or supposedly "inspected" in the most intimate of places. With the failure of Reconstruction, the black man was made a virtual vagrant in the South. His home, his livelihood, his means to acquire an education, to compete, to even succeed were all stripped from him. With no man to protect her, the black woman was once more "on the auction block," if not literally, then certainly in the form of being without any defense against any white man who wanted her and could take her without any fear of reprisal or legal interdiction. Once more she was "raped." But not even being a sex object saved her from the atrocities of the pyre.

Hernton quotes from an article in *Freedomways*, which also discusses the sexual violence faced by black women:

> From 1891 to 1921 the South lynched forty-five Negro women, several of whom were young girls from fourteen to sixteen years old. . . . One victim was in her eighth month of pregnancy. . . . she was suspended from a tree by her ankles. Gasoline poured on her clothes and ignited. [Her] abdomen was cut open. The unborn child fell to the ground. A member of the mob crushed its head with his heel. And, this didn't happen in Nazi Germany [or] thirteenth century Europe [but] in the South . . . in the nineteenth and twentieth centuries. . . . Even today [1966], throughout the South, white men are able to extort sexual pleasures from Negro women in the course of the women's employment, or in the course of their seeking employment.

Hernton also discusses the legend of the black man as a Minotaur whose sexual prowess even the gods are unable to explain:

> [T]here are Negroes who are afflicted with the white man's mythological concept of Negro sexhood. Their behavior around white women is strictly sexual . . . It is not simply a matter of trying to exploit the white man's sex image of the Negro. . . . These Negroes are diseased by the racist's grotesque sex image of them, which, after all, is nothing more than a myth.

He begins his chapter about white men with an incident that took place in Atlanta when he was fifteen. A white man came up to him, called him "Boy," and asked where he could get some

"Negra p———y." Several years later, when he was a grown man in Harlem, a well-dressed white man came up to him and asked where he could find a colored woman, "a nice one!" At another point he states: "Because his concept of the sex act made him think of it as something dirty, sinful, and savage, the white Southerner found it difficult to relate to his own women. He was inhibited by the Calvinist interpretation of sex as befouling the dignity of man."

Sex and Racism in America is a book that needs to be read because it explains a great deal about the horrible legacy of bigotry and its impact on one of the most fragile and at the same time most important aspects of our lives: our sexual identity. Of course, much has changed since 1966, when the book was first published. The last miscegenation law on the books, in Hawaii, wasn't repealed until the sixties. Yet, in a *New York Times* poll taken in the late nineties, 25 percent of all whites in the South said they still favored a law banning marriage between the races. But that view has not blighted the white-black landscape. In any city, be it Phoenix, Arizona, or New York City, you can find interracial couples in plain view, unselfconsciously holding hands and being close.

How much of the racist syndromes that resulted from the traumas of the past still haunt our sexuality, even if only in our dreams, is anybody's guess. But Hernton has done us all a service, whether we're interested in significant others of another race or not, by helping us to face the awful truths of the past in order to free ourselves to feel our sexual desires without shame. He has also helped us to look at others without confusion or fear if their preference for a life mate happens to be of a different color.

40

ADAM BY ADAM:
THE AUTOBIOGRAPHY OF
ADAM CLAYTON POWELL, JR.

New York: Dial Press, 1971

Told with humor and style and a fair share of *j'accuse*, *Adam by Adam*, the autobiography of Adam Clayton Powell, Jr., is an excellent reprise of the turbulent and challenging life of one of the most important men in American politics in the second half of the twentieth century. Powell was the son of a relatively privileged Baptist minister in New York City. In 1930 he was sitting in his father's Pierce Arrow limousine waiting at a traffic light in the Bronx when he saw hundreds of black women "huddled against the wall in the rain . . . unemployed domestics . . . selling themselves to whoever comes by for ten cents an hour." In that moment, he was only twenty-two, the problems of his people became his problem—his burning passion—and would remain so for the rest of his life.

Powell got his first real chance to join the fight when five of the most prominent doctors in New York City came to him for help. As the heir presumptive to his father's powerful Abyssinian Baptist Church, in Harlem on 137th Street, he was already a power in his own right. The doctors had been banned from Harlem

Hospital because they were black. The superintendent of the hospital refused to see Powell and the commissioner of hospitals for the city laughed when he tried to discuss the situation. So he called a rally at City Hall, and six thousand people showed up. The acting mayor wouldn't talk to him, and the police wouldn't let him into the meeting of the Board of Estimate, a city organ, a sort of senate that divided the spoils. When he finally did get to address the Board of Estimate, the doctors were not only reinstated in short order, but the entire hospital staff was integrated as well.

From then on, Powell had one major victory after another. He forced the department stores in Harlem to hire black salespeople by organizing and manning the picket lines with the slogan "Don't Buy Where You Can't Work." To keep poor people from being evicted from their homes in the height of the Depression, he organized rent strikes, telling "the owner of the building [to] 'Put that family back in their home or we will have every family . . . refuse to pay rent.' " The threat was effective: the costs of the city marshal's services alone would have been prohibitive if the landlord tried to evict the entire building. Once the tenants withheld their rents, the game was over.

Powell and the committee he formed (originally the Committee on Harlem Hospitals) to coordinate his efforts in fighting racism were quite inventive. They gave Consolidated Edison an ultimatum: either hire blacks or they would declare Tuesday of each week a lightless night. Merchants kept their lights on for security reasons, but if they didn't want their windows smashed, they would have to turn off the lights, which was the committee's objective. So, in the end, it was the merchants who forced Con Ed to integrate.

When the telephone company stood fast on its policy of segregated employment, Powell said his people would start dialing the operator by the thousands all at once, clogging switchboards and preventing any call from going through. The telephone company caved in. Next came the pharmacists. Powell got a job for every black pharmacist in Harlem in four months. And then came the World's Fair of 1939, over which Grover Whalen reigned as chairman. He didn't see why "you cannot have a World of Tomorrow [the Fair's slogan] from which you have excluded colored people." By the time Powell get through with him Whalen knew why, and close to six hundred jobs went to blacks in all areas of the fair.

By supporting Mike Quill (the granddaddy of Irish labor in New York) in his fight to organize the bus company in 1941, Powell got Quill's support in a campaign to get black bus drivers hired. Black people stayed off the buses in Harlem for twelve days in support of Quill. Once Quill won, he honored the bargain. White drivers refused to drive through Harlem so that the bus company would have to employ black drivers or lose that segment of its revenue, and the white drivers abandoned their buses in the streets. Because the bus company was on the verge of going bankrupt, they capitulated to Powell's demand that for every white man employed, two blacks would be employed until things leveled off.

When Powell was elected to Congress in 1944, the first thing he did was to integrate the Washington press corps in the gallery of the House. Next he opened up the cafeterias to all the employees of Congress. He used a tactic called the Powell amendment to fight racism by forbidding federal funds "to those who sought to preserve segregation."

On the other hand, at the Bandung Conference in Indonesia in 1955, he stood up to Russia when it attempted to use the conference to attack racism in America. The State Department was too stupid to realize that 1.4 billion people represented at one conference should not be ignored, so when his plane landed, no one from the U.S. embassy was at the airport to greet him. The ambassador didn't go near him, that is, not until after he'd struck the blow for American "democracy" against the Russians.

This was the usual state of affairs: Powell brilliantly, often single-handedly, led and won many fights for the right cause (e.g., against racism or exposing police corruption) and at the same time, he was vilified by the forces of reason and liberalism that should have been on his side from the beginning. Eleanor Roosevelt, the *New York Times*, and Northern Democrats in general, all turned against him at one time or another. When Adlai Stevenson flip-flopped on civil rights in 1956, Powell backed Eisenhower, who became instrumental in getting the first civil rights bill passed in Congress in eighty-two years. Mrs. Roosevelt never forgave him for supporting the Republican ticket, no matter how much he had won for his people from the deal.

With each success, opposition to Powell grew. In his six years as chairman of the House Committee on Education and Labor, "it produced more laws without a single defeat than any other committee in the history of the Republic." In spite of this superlative legislative record, in 1966 three members of Congress spearheaded an assault to strip him of his power and all three were from the North: Frank Thompson of New Jersey, John Brademas of Indiana, and Jim O'Hara of Michigan. Powell writes: "These three men knew that I had too much power because I controlled most of the domestic legislation of the United States of America." And he wasn't afraid to use it.

Powell used that power to integrate the veterans hospitals and to give the residents of the District of Columbia the vote in presidential elections. When he blew the whistle on police corruption in New York City, the government spent a half million dollars trying to prove that he had defrauded them of three thousand dollars in unpaid income taxes. That was one of the times that the *New York Times* took umbrage. (The other time they said he was a racist.) Because Powell had proven that New York policemen were on the take, the newspaper accused him of trying to "push" the police commissioner "around."

He might not have roused so many enemies to join forces against him if he hadn't had the audacity, the chutzpa to support Stokely Carmichael's (Kwame Ture) cry for Black Power. Powell spends the last chapter of his book defining in detail what Black Power meant and means. Of course, the phrase doesn't send the blood pressure of anyone afraid of "those people" skyrocketing today as it did then. Powell's three congressional foes were moved to rage when he dared to embrace the Black Power movement while he was a congressman and the head of an all-powerful committee.

It was the old racism rearing its ugly head. A white man can do or say anything and he's protected by constitutional guarantees, or lauded for being the tough, red-blooded All-American hero. A black man shows a rifle in public (which is legal in some states if it isn't loaded) and he gets arrested. Racist, white Southerners used the most rabid, filthy language in the *Congressional Record* to describe blacks as apes and monkeys who just came out of the trees (Rankin, Bilbo, et al.) and they were protected legally to so indulge. Powell just wanted to give black Americans the same freedom of speech, which allows any citizen to espouse any doctrine they wish short of treason. Black Power declared that black people deserved the same kind of power that white people have: economic, political, police, judicial, legislative, and sociological. But in the hands of Powell's congressional adversaries that was taking the constitutional ideal too far.

By the mid-1960s there were so many congressmen who were *really* guilty of breaking the House Rules (beginning with the man who chaired the committee to investigate Powell, Wayne Hays of Ohio) that—in light of their crimes—the feeding frenzy to get Powell was simply a case of unabashed racism. Of course, the Supreme Court ruled that Powell's expulsion was unconstitutional. But during the two years it took for the verdict to be handed down, Powell's constituents in Harlem were without congressional representation. When the House finally let Powell back in, they demeaned him by forcing him to pay a twenty-five thousand dollar fine and stripped him of his twenty-two years of seniority. He accepted the humbling so the people he represented wouldn't be without a congressman for *another* two years.

It was the same old war cry. When the black voice in the wilderness tries to follow the American system of standing tall and fighting for justice, the response is: Get that nigger at all costs, and don't waste a heartbeat listening to any argument he has to make or to consider its merits.

Now, nearly forty years later, some may consider Congress's treatment of Powell unjust. But black America still has to show up with hat in hand, a grin on the face, and the mantra "We're not bitter and we don't hate anybody" on the lips if we want to influence any hearts and minds. Maybe we'll get to the promised land if we introduce a retro style in dress and manner: bandannas for the women, stocking caps (they're back already!) for the men, and step aside if someone who really runs the country walks down the street.

Books 41 through 50:
THE EMPEROR'S NEW CLOTHES

---

*F*OX BUTTERFIELD, in a 1998 article in the Sunday *New York Times* "Week in Review" section, reported that "The former slaveholding states of the old Confederacy all rank in the top 20 states for murder, led by Louisiana, with a rate of 17.5 murders per 100,000 people in 1996." The article was titled "Southern Curse: Why America's Murder Rate Is So High." *USA Today* ran a front page story in 1992 that listed some of the many black Americans killed for trying to dismantle Jim Crow in America, with pictures of the slain. In an insert it also listed the 4,709 known lynchings that took place in the country from 1882 to 1968, broken down state by state.

Included on the list is Baxter Bell, who in 1935 was taken from police custody and shot to death for supposedly making "improper advances to a white woman." Baxter Bell was not trying to enforce a constitutional amendment or Supreme Court decision. He probably wasn't even trying to "enforce" himself on the woman, since he was in White Bluff, Tennessee, and most assuredly knew better. But since Southern white lawlessness that was nurtured over the centuries never had any basis for its existence other than hatred for a black face, any racial killing should be listed as a civil rights killing.

In 1965 one of the first black deputies in Washington Parish, Louisiana, was ambushed and shot to death. In

August of the same year, a white seminary student, Jonathan Daniels of Massachusetts, was shot to death after protesting against stores that discriminated against blacks in Hanesville, Alabama. The part-time deputy's sheriff accused of the killing was found innocent by an all-white jury that shook his hand as he left the courtroom. As late as 1968, three black students were killed by highway patrolmen on the campus of South Carolina State College in Orangeburg. The local grand jury didn't even bother to indict the officers. The students were among thirty demonstrating against a whites-only policy at a local bowling alley—that's how ingrained Southern apartheid was. For riding a bus, a black, middle-aged veteran of World War II was almost killed when he and the other riders were trapped inside the bus and it was set on fire. The fury that was unleashed by the innocuous exercise of what should be a citizen's ordinary rights was as unbridled as the fury of the lynch mob.

Black America hunkered down, took the bullets and the bayonets, the nightsticks and the dogs, and managed to both survive and make their point. Major credit for the survival of and gains made by the entire civil rights movement goes to SCLC, CORE, NAACP, SNCC, and the Urban League; A. Philip Randolph, who wanted the march on Washington more than anyone, and to his aide, Bayard Rustin, who did the actual organizing; to the thousands of black people all across America; the Hosea Williamses; the Andrew Youngs; the Jesse Jacksons; the Harry Belafontes; the Fannie Lou Hamers; the Black Panthers; and of course, Malcolm X; and the white Americans who gave their lives to help black America achieve a little more equality, including Viola Liuzzo, the Detroit housewife who was shot down in broad daylight during the march to Selma; to Michael Schwerner and Andrew Goodman, who along with James Chaney died in Mississippi trying to enforce the Fifteenth Amendment to the Constitution. The 1988 film *Mississippi Burning* made heroes out of white men who had little or nothing to do with finding out what happened to these three, while James Farmer, then head of CORE, the man most responsible for seeing to it that the crimes did not go unnoticed or unpunished, was ignored. William Bradford Huie's *Three Lives for Mississippi* is an excellent account of that particular chapter in post-Confederate brutality.

Although water was no longer black or white, waiting rooms were segregated only by gender, and the back of the bus finally became a seat of choice, it took twelve years after the *Brown* decision before the Supreme Court finally insisted on an end to separate-but-equal in the classroom and everywhere else across America. The degree to which American apartheid was a fact of American life before that is attested to by Earl Warren in his *Memoirs*:

Segregation was enforced at all places of public entertainment, including public parks, beaches, playgrounds, libraries, auditoriums, and circuses. States provided for separate telephone booths, school textbooks, elevators, barbershops, and taxicabs. Whites and blacks were prohibited from competing with or against each other in athletic contests, or even from playing with their own color group in close proximity to similar activities by a group of the other color. In some states this principle was extended even . . . to the playing of games such as checkers. There was segregation in the hospitals, prisons, mental institutions, and nursing homes. Even ambulance service was segregated.

The racism even extended beyond death. Writes Warren:

Of all the indignities, I suppose the most macabre one is that blacks could not even lie in peace and at rest in the same cemetery as whites. This was poignantly brought to general attention when cemeteries in the South refused to allow the bodies of black soldiers killed in action . . . to be buried in white cemeteries.

The separate and non-equal brand of racism had become such an absurdity that a black man trying to enter a church in Washington, D.C., on a Sunday was stopped by a church official who told him he couldn't go in. The black man explained that he wasn't there to pray, he was there to do a piece of work for which he'd been hired. The official questioned him closely before satisfying himself that the man was indeed an employee. He let him enter—but *only* after he promised *not to pray* once he got inside.

It was a time of huge social upheaval: opposition to the Vietnam War, the era of the Flower Children, the marijuana age, all of these were expressions of much of the country's dissatisfaction with the lingering bobby sox, Wildroot-cream oil, button-down-collar American fifties mentality. With the advent of black films, albeit cheaply made and artistically questionable, with black men being elected mayor in some of America's major cities (thanks to the *Baker v. Carr* decision, another Warren court triumph, which helped make one man, one vote a reality), black America had taken giant strides to rid itself of the more degrading symbols of its inequality, an inequality that no other minority save the Native American has ever suffered.

Yet black America is still separated from the mainstream of American commerce. In the year 2002, most urban areas boast huge multiethnic businesses—the only minority excluded is the black American one. Black Americans are still excluded from owning or operating businesses in white neighborhoods, and they are scarcely represented in business in their own neighborhoods. This vestige of apartheid is still very much alive and vigorous in its enforcement. Go into town after town and you'll find Asians and Hispanics from every corner of the world owning and operating businesses. There are also many cases of white business owners hiring Asians and Hispanics exclusively. Were it not for jobs in security, the black presence would be almost nonexistent in America's commercial marketplace, except as consumers.

The mighty works of the men and women of this period, from Amiri Braka's plays in the sixties to Randall Robinson's *Defending the Spirit,* published in 1998, the mountain of achievement that saw the end of Jim Crow in the second half of the sixties has given way to a valley of despair that underscores the old Gallic cynicism of *le plus ça change, le plus il reste.* When Congress passed the Civil Rights Bill of 1965, it also changed the immigration laws, throwing out the quotas that had kept immigration to a controlled minimum. Even though the black man could now compete for jobs with the white worker, thanks to the opening up of society that the Civil Rights Bill made possible, he was still out in the cold since someone from Korea, Central or South America, China or Japan or the Philippines could be hired in his stead.

Spanish-speaking immigrants became so numerous in New York and California as a consequence that in the decade of the Clinton years of unparalleled prosperity, both sections saw a decline in average income. In New York 24 percent of the black and Latino population lived below the poverty level, according to a survey taken in 2001 and published in the *Times.* That's uncomfortably close to the Depression figure of a third of a nation. But of course, that was a third of *everyone.* Big difference.

Films are no longer black exploitation; if five black players start in a professional basketball game, the franchise won't go out of business; black quarterbacks are no longer a hotly debated issue in sports bars across the nation; and the African-American sitcoms that do much to trivialize black life have become a staple of TV fare. Oprah Winfrey, Bill Cosby, Michael Jackson, and their ilk are all names that can be included among the mega-rich. In spite of all that, black America is still stuck with the same old problem. It is a minority, the majority of whom are still impoverished in body and spirit because that majority is mired in poverty. It is a poverty that always breeds ignorance, fear, a sense of inferiority, and an inability to find ways and means to climb out of the mire and end the degradation. The black poor know they are not wanted not because they are poor but because they are black.

41

DUTCHMAN AND THE SLAVE

by Amiri Bakara

NEW YORK: GROVE PRESS, 1964

THE BAPTISM AND THE TOILET

by Amiri Bakara

NEW YORK: GROVE PRESS, 1996

These four plays were published separately in the sixties and I know of no subsequent combined edition. *Dutchman* and *The Baptism* are two of the most extraordinary works of modern theater and superior to their companion pieces, so I've addressed both small volumes in this essay. These plays are very early Baraka, but they're his best writing for the theater. The effects of racism on both blacks and whites in America, the hypocrisies that almost everything in the culture stands for when stripped to the skin, especially formalized Christianity, are all brilliantly flayed. The energy and the anger lying in wait in the belly of these two works make them among the best one-act plays in American drama. And that includes Edward Albee's heralded *American Dream, Zoo Story*, and *The Death of Bessie Smith*.

In *Dutchman* Baraka uses the story of the demoness Circe, destroyer of the male of the species, and her predatory search for yet another victim as the basis for his plot. Protagonist is sitting in a subway going somewhere. Femme Fatale comes in (one wag calls her a subway succubus), seduces him, and proceeds to carry out the ritual murder. End of story. Not so *The Baptism*. The Church is the setting, appropriately, for what is essentially the Christ story played out in modern terms. The play is a tidal wave of characters, emotions, and ideas, all thrown together in one mad, impassioned orgy of anger and despair, and a resolution that resolves nothing and mocks everything.

Baraka is a troubled soul in these works, hurt beyond the point of consolation. He had faith, but no more. The world that attempts a rational response to man's existence is behind him. The world ahead is a nightmare of ghouls and dragons and monsters in the form of the man of God, the youth, the sexual deviant, the vestal virgins that were, and the matriarch.

The Slave almost makes a mockery of militant, armed resistance as an answer to racism. But Baraka does more than make this commonsense statement. He seems to be saying that there is no rapprochement between the races. Love, fidelity, progeny, hearth and home, all pale before the monster of race. The black revolutionary, Walker Vessels, his army a day away, shows up at his ex-wife's apartment with a gun. He kills her white husband, has already killed their daughters, and returns to his mythic self after she has been killed by the bombs falling on the house. Walker is driven as much by a need to purge his soul as he is by hate or revenge.

> *Walker*: . . . [I]n spite of the fact that I, Walker Vessels, single-handedly, and with no other adviser except my own ego, promoted a bloody situation where white and black people are killing each other; despite the fact that I know that this is at best a war that will only change, ha, the complexion of tyranny . . . despite, the resistance in the large cities and the small towns, where we have taken, yes, dragged piles of darkies out of their beds and shot them for being in Rheingold ads, despite the fact that all of my officers are ignorant motherfuckers who have never read any book in their lives, despite the fact that I would rather argue politics, or literature, or boxing, or anything, with you dear Easley [the white second husband].

In *Dutchman*, Clay doesn't understand the problem on this level. When he's confronted by Lula, the Circe, he fulminates the way any citizen accosted by a strange woman would. Lula's hidden agenda is something of which he is entirely oblivious. Not understanding the evil of race is unforgivable ignorance to Baraka. So while Walker is tormented by it and self-destructs on some level because of the torment, he at least *knows*. Clay doesn't, so he dies ignominiously.

In *The Toilet*, Baraka once again shows that East is East. The world of the black inner-city ghetto, with its insistence on street-punk violence as the only proof of pubescent manhood, makes the victim of its rage, a white youth, a hero in the end because of his honesty. The gang types who have beaten him up in the toilet of the high school are the villains.

Their leader, Foots, is a little guy with superior intelligence—Baraka in disguise, one would suspect. He is also a physical weakling, not even able to get the better of the white youth, Karolis, after Karolis has been beaten by the gang. Karolis has the added strength that comes from honesty: he's not ashamed of what he feels for Foots. But Foots is ashamed, which makes him the moral coward as well. When the action of the play comes to its close, Foots sneaks back into the toilet and caresses Karolis in his arms and cries over him. Again, the human heart has to be denied because the hatreds of race demand it. And a forbidden love, which might be accommodated in other circumstances, is a double taboo in that context. Both races suffer.

The Baptism almost makes race superfluous. Instead it makes sex the emotional and spiritual bottom line for everything: religious hypocrisy is the monster here. The Minister wants to save the Boy (age fifteen), who has committed the sins of the flesh, both alone and with many. The Minister's reasons seem suspect as they are almost clearly based on that sin itself. The Old Woman is the accuser, almost an archetype of her race. The Homosexual knows the Boy isn't finished sinning yet and wants some of the "action" himself. When the Minister is finally convinced that the Boy has indulged, after the female chorus comes in to attest to that fact, he, the Minister, turns on the Boy to destroy him, aided and abetted by everyone except the Homosexual. The Boy protests that he turned to the man of God for help and understanding, not vengeance. But the Minister and his tribe are unrelenting, so the Boy takes out his silver sword and kills all of them, except the Homosexual, who had tried to save him. The Messenger, in the form of a Hispanic in leather on a motorbike, sent by "The Man," appears to take the Boy back. The Boy protests that he hasn't failed and his work on Earth isn't finished. But the Messenger replies that the Man—his father-god—has ordered him back and is going to blow up "this whole operation." The Boy refuses to go, so the Messenger clubs him, throws him over his shoulder and drives off. The Homosexual wakes up to find the place to himself and goes off to Times Square looking for action.

Clearly, there is no comfort to be found here for the mortal, not in any of the institutions created by man to provide it. The horrors that man has devised to savage his fellow man—race, sexual pathology, moral hypocrisy—are all reasons why Baraka leaves the world to lust and to his Homosexual. It is for the rest of us to contemplate what might have been in another Genesis.

42

THIS LITTLE LIGHT OF MINE: THE LIFE OF FANNIE LOU HAMER

by Kay Mills

NEW YORK: DUTTON, 1993

It was the heart of darkness and Fannie Lou Hamer lived every minute of it. Born in 1917 into the squalor and dirt of Ruleville, in the Mississippi Delta's Sunflower County, Fannie Lou Hamer "was forty-four years old the summer that the movement reached her hometown. [S]he could not vote. She wanted that right, and in her struggle to achieve it, she became a symbolic figure who inspired countless other Americans" to fight for what they wanted, writes Kay Mills in this warm and passionate encomium.

Sunflower County was the home base of the screaming racist James Eastland, the state's senior United States senator. When the *Brown* decision was handed down in 1954, he told his constituents that they shouldn't obey it, and that they had a right not to obey it, Supreme Court decision or no. He also affirmed that blacks were "an inferior race." But Fannie Lou Hamer would drive him to the wall, eventually, and in 1978 he retired from politics rather than run and face certain defeat. She, however, never won an election on either a local or national level.

"In the very end," writes Mills, "her heart failed, the only time it ever did." Like Toussaint L'Ouverture before her, Fannie Lou was not only middle-aged but a servant of postbellum slavery when she joined the revolution. The type of poverty that ground down the Fannie Lou Hamers of this world admitted no escape save death.

In 1904 Eastland's uncle had an argument with one of his black servants and broke into the man's cabin, firing two shots. The servant, Holbert, fired back and killed Eastland on the spot. It took a mob four days to find Holbert, who fled along with his wife. When they were caught, their torture death was so horrible and so infamous that it was reported in newspapers as far away as New York. One thousand people gathered to watch as the couple's fingers were severed one by one and passed around as souvenirs. Next came the ears, then their skulls were fractured, and corkscrews, twisted into their arms and legs and then drawn out, ad civilized, ad Southern nauseum.

So families like Fannie Lou's accepted their fate. As a child, she had no shoes. In the winter, her mother would tie sacks around the children's feet. They had neither hot nor cold running water in the house, no electricity and no heat, so it was as cold in the winter inside as it was outside. When her father managed to scrape together enough money to buy three mules, two cows, a wagon, and some tools and began to "get ahead," a white man, resentful of such American-style ambition by a "nigra" poisoned the well, killing mule and cow. The family never recovered: it was back to sharecropping forever after that.

This was not a sane existence for any man, woman, or child, certainly not in twentieth-century America, nor was it possible anywhere else in the country, except the Deep South. Says Mills, "[T]he Mississippi congressmen's attitude was that their slaves had been taken away from them and they still couldn't forget it." It was what Robert E. Lee had fought to preserve, it was what the well-known silent screen actress Lillian Gish was eulogizing when she rode triumphant with the Ku Klux Klan at the end of *The Birth of a Nation*. It was what the nation at large allowed the South to perpetuate for eighty years, from the end of Reconstruction until the Fannie Lou Hamers rose up and changed the rules in the 1960s.

If all the violations of state and federal law committed by law enforcement officers in the South during the 1960s alone were catalogued, the list would run into the tens of thousands. Maimings, beatings, and killings of black citizens by white officers were almost routine. Add to that the record of the KKK and sundry other whites who were not part of any official *organization* and you have a bloody history indeed. The beating that Fannie Lou Hamer received, ordered by officers of the law in Winona, Mississippi, and administered by black male inmates in their prime, was one such atrocity.

It happened in 1963. By then she was already well-known as a civil rights leader and was on everyone's *get* list. She and a group of followers were on their way home from a training session organized by SNCC, the Student Nonviolent Coordinating Committee (see Must-Read No. 44), in Charleston, South Carolina. When the bus stopped in Winona, some in the group decided to integrate the lunchroom, which was under legal interdiction from the Interstate Commerce Commission not to segregate anyone traveling interstate. Not only were they arrested for trying to exercise that right, but when Hamer got off the bus to find out why her companions had not returned, she too was arrested and taken into a back room of the local jail, where she was placed on a bench on her stomach and first one inmate, then another, beat her with a blackjack until they "[were] exhausted."

In 1964 the Mississippi Freedom Democratic Party (MFDP) was formed to challenge the seating of the all-white Mississippi delegation to the Democratic National Convention in Atlantic City because it was segregated and therefore illegally constituted. Hamer was one of the leaders of the MFDP. When Hubert Humphrey came crawling to their caucus room to beg them not to make the challenge on the floor of the convention, in front of the cameras, Fanny Lou treated him with contemptuous sympathy: "[H]ere sat a little round-eyed man with his eyes full of tears. . . . [I asked him] Mr. Humphrey, do you mean . . . that your position is more important to you than four hundred thousand black people's lives? . . . The trouble is you're afraid to do what you know is right. You just want this job [as vice president]. . . . [B]ut if you take this job you won't be worth anything." In the struggle to gain their rights, the MFDP delegates were facing death every day and would face more deaths when they went back to Mississippi if they compromised.

The question might well be asked, how could this woman leave such an impact if she never held electoral office? She was only one of thousands of others who had suffered beatings and worse in the delta death of forty years ago. The answer is quite simple: In spite of her humble beginnings and complete lack of any formal education (she was picking cotton in the fields at the age of six, which meant she never really went to school), Fannie Lou Hamer was quite simply *sui generis,* that is, one of a kind. Nothing and no one intimidated her, either before or after the beating in Winona. She had eloquence, intelligence, courage, and a powerful presence.

When she died, the mighty and the famous showed up in little Ruleville to pay homage to what she was and what she stood for: Andrew Young, who was U.S. ambassador to the United Nations by then, Hodding Carter III and Charles Evers, both of whom had been there in 1968 when the MFDP and a coalition of liberals got something of what they didn't get in 1964. Carter was Jimmy Carter's assistant secretary of state by then and Evers (Medgar Evers's brother) had been elected mayor of Fayette, Mississippi. They all knew that they had been touched by a giant spirit that left them richer and wiser.

Fanny Lou's husband, "Pap" Hamer, best remembered the ingratitude of the ones she helped the most—her own kind. "My wife loved people but people didn't love her. . . . I would come to [the] house and it would [have] so many people in here I couldn't hardly get in the door. They came to get clothes, food, money— everything. But when she fell sick and was in the hospital . . . the only way I could get people to stay with her was when I paid them. I told her, 'You can't do everything.' They wore her down. She raised lots of money and she [gave it all] to people. And when she died, she didn't have a dime." When she needed money, as little as one hundred dollars for medicine, there wasn't any. Pap was right, she had given it all away.

Hamer had always been vain about her hair (cornrows didn't appeal) and took great care in combing and styling it, no matter the occasion. June Johnson, who was fifteen years old at the time of the Winona incident and was actually shot inside the police station, tells how she showed up in Ruleville one day and there was Fannie Lou sitting in a chair looking out the window, crying. When asked what was the matter, Fannie Lou broke down and confessed that because of arthritis in her hands she couldn't comb her hair, and there was no one to do it now that the handouts and the free food were no more. June proceeded to comb out her hair for her, lovingly, slowly, and carefully. That was what a great woman was reduced to because the plight of poor people in Mississippi meant more to her than taking care of herself.

Hamer walked with a limp for all of her adult life as a result of an injury from a fall as a baby. The bones didn't heal properly because of poor medical care. That limp, coupled with the crippling effects from the beating, made getting around in later years daunting. But she never stayed home when the issue was joined, and she knew she had to be there to make the difference. Her voice, her vast experience, her consummate grasp of the issues, her innate sense of the tactics needed to win all put her in a class by herself. As one lawyer said, "Working for Mrs. Hamer was like having your case 'served to you on a silver platter. . . . In most cases . . . you'd have an organizing meeting and you'd get some names. Then you'd have a few days of seeing who would stick because the bossman would come around, and you'd have someone say "Jim can't do it because his job would be at stake.' When Mrs. Hamer worked on a case, that didn't happen."

Fannie Lou Hamer deserves more honor than history can bestow. She was one of the truly great. In the end, however, even her own people never voted for her overwhelmingly. They seemed envious because she was one of the dirt-poor ignorant who was able to rise dramatically above her lowly beginnings. That lack of support and electoral fraud kept her from winning election to office, although she helped others to win: educated, middle-class, black males. She died in 1977 of heart failure, brought on by cancer, diabetes, and hypertension. The last two, along with kidney problems and a blood clot that affected her sight in one eye, were all direct results of the beating in Winona.

"This Little Light of Mine" was her favorite song and it became her theme song as well. She could always capture the moment whenever she sang it, rekindle the sagging spirits, revive the energy, make the courage strong again. As she herself used to sing:

> If you miss me in the Missus kitchen,
> And you can't find me nowhere
> Come on over to Washington
> I'll be Congresswoman there.
> If you miss me in the Freedom fight
> And you can't find me nowhere,
> Come on over to the graveyard
> I'll be buried there.

43

THE AUTOBIOGRAPHY OF MALCOLM X

with the assistance of Alex Haley

NEW YORK: GROVE PRESS, 1965

He solved nothing in practical terms in his lifetime, neither by living nor by dying. He left no legislative legacy, as did others. Except for a few high schools bearing his name, there probably aren't many monuments to honor the honorable dead, although he gave of his greatness with a generosity and self-sacrifice that makes him worthy of a place in a class all by himself as the true martyr.

He was denied by two of his brothers who abased themselves in public obeisance to his enemies. He was shunned by Muhammad Ali even though he had been the one to champion the then Cassius Clay in the fight against Sonny Liston that made him champion of the world. All the black professionals, what he called the "knee-grows," are still with us, solemnly endorsing the so-called Western tradition in learning, without a thought to the blackness that helped create that tradition. All the Christian ministers are still in their pulpits every Sunday, turning the other cheek and preaching, "Do what I say and not what I do." Malcolm ex-

coriated them all, leaving them skewered on their own lies and
hypocrisies and weaknesses.

When he was Detroit Red, he was the complete thug, the dope
peddler, the hustler, the burglar without sanctimony. He regretted destroying the people he did not intend to destroy. Years later,
he would bemoan the destruction of a young woman named
Laura who ended up on dope and became a prostitute because of
her association with him.

When he was convicted as a first-time offender for burglary, he
got eight years. Some people don't get that much prison time for
murder. The length of the sentence was due primarily to the pedigree of his female accomplice. Like her niece, also an accomplice,
she was not only white but middle-class. As a result, neither she
nor her niece ever spent a day in jail. They were never even indicted.

In jail Malcolm was so antireligious that he was dubbed Satan,
and he became so intransigent that he spent seven of his eight
years in solitary. In jail or out, he was always a purist who, once he
became committed to an ideal, a cause (be it a crime or a new religion), gave it his all with a passion few men are capable of. It
was that character trait that would lead to his dramatic ascen-
dancy and his tragic undoing, which was even more dramatic.

What do we make of a man who gave his all to the black
masses—and had so much to give? Most men who have led black
America have come from the middle class or were allowed to
graduate into it. They took their status as a godsend and suffered
in silence whenever they had to—the price of escaping the
poverty of their fellows.

This was not the case with Malcolm. When he ran afoul of the
law at the age of *seven*, instead of being sent to reform school, he
was allowed to live with an influential white woman of his town,
Lansing, Michigan. He did so well in school that he was elected
class president. But the history teacher told nigger jokes *in class*
and advised him to become a carpenter. He didn't revolt and create a "hate the devil movement" on the spot, but he knew he was
among alien corn. Living a lie to get what he wanted was not possible for Malcolm. One trip to Boston showed him his own kind

in a variety of postures, some resplendent, others decidedly not, and he could no longer grin at the nigger jokes or play the guinea pig making good. The change in Malcolm's behavior was so pronounced that his white caretaker no longer wanted him, and neither did the school. He was so connected to his inner reality that once he was uncomfortable, he made everyone around him uncomfortable.

So he packed up for Boston to live with an aunt as soon as he'd finished the eighth grade. Once there he gravitated to the seedy section of town, where the action was, because he couldn't abide the affectations of the black middle class. When one of his brothers (not one of the Judases) brought him into the Islamic faith in 1952—Elijah Muhammad style (they never called themselves Black Muslims)—he had till that time lived almost completely in a world of crime. When he converted, he converted with a pure heart and practically burned himself up redeeming the black man from mental slavery through the instrumentality that the Black Muslims afforded him.

When he joined the Black Muslims, they weren't more than four hundred by his count. When he left them, twelve years later, they were over forty thousand strong, thanks mostly to his efforts, his dynamism, his magnetism, his brilliance, and his eloquence. As he recalls, his work took him away from his family six months of the year. He never bought a present for any of the four daughters he so dearly loved. He never took out insurance for his family or made a will. He never kept a dime for himself.

When he made the contract with Alex Haley to write his autobiography, he had all the money go to the mosque in New York where he was minister. Mercifully, he changed that part of the contract. Without that money Malcolm X's family would have been destitute once the break with the Black Muslims came, and he would have had to beg for charity from friends if he was going to continue his work. That's how dedicated he was, how driven to repay Elijah Muhammad, the man whom he credited with giving him a new life.

Hustler though he was, he was out-hustled by Elijah Muhammad, who couldn't abide the ability of the younger man. Malcolm

X could more than hold his own with the intellectual elite, amaze college students with his astuteness, and demolish university faculty in open argument. Elijah Muhammad, as a son later confessed to Malcolm, didn't have the intelligence for that kind of fighting.

But the pure heart made another mistake: he criticized the old man in private for having sex with young secretaries in the movement. In so doing Muhammed violated one of his own cardinal rules, rules that he had used to excommunicate others. Now Malcolm was a man who knew every con that was ever run in Harlem, but his need to make black equality a holy quest blinded him from seeing that by mentioning the master's misdeeds, he was destroying the means by which he could bring about his most cherished dream. Malcolm expected the man to whom he thought he owed everything to be as honest as he was. By the time he realized what he had done, he was already dead.

A shortcoming of Alex Haley's *Autobiography* is that it doesn't include a detailed account of Malcolm's rebirth after the break with Elijah Muhammad. Once Malcolm left America, he found a world of white people who didn't automatically hate a black face. Most of this experience, and the degree to which Malcolm became disillusioned with Elijah Muhammad, is not included in the volume. When Malcolm wanted to rewrite the book to include his changed view, Haley dissuaded him. That was a mistake. Not that the early adoration of Elijah Muhammad had to be expunged, but Malcolm's real feelings about the man once those feelings had changed should have been made a part of the official record.

Elijah Muhammad is the only man who could have authorized the attempts on his life, says Malcolm. The first attempt never happened because the man who was asked to kill him not only refused, but told Malcolm. As an ex-Black Muslim, Malcolm was not a threat to America's international prestige and influence initially. But as a player in the international arena, one who pointed repeatedly to America's ongoing racism, he'd stepped up in class. By the time the French refused to let him enter their country, he no longer thought that the Muslims held the lead in wanting him dead. His reasoning: they didn't have the clout to keep him out of France.

So who killed Malcolm? In a way, he killed himself, just as Martin Luther King, Jr. killed himself. He played outside of history, outside of his time and place. But a life that large can't be circumscribed by the logic of common sense. Realizing the implacable forces that were arrayed against him could not have stayed his hand. He was transcendent, no longer living day to day. He was in the future while waking and sleeping in the present. And he knew it. As he himself announced, "I won't live long enough to read my own book."

It's all in his autobiography, as told to Alex Haley, every sad and wonderful heartbeat. As Mark Anthony said of Caesar, over Caesar's corpse, "Here was a man, when cometh such another!"

But what of the matured rhetoric of Malcolm X after he had outgrown the Black Muslims? That is, after all, why he has gained such an exalted position in history as an apostle for black equality by any means necessary. In a companion book, *Malcolm X Speaks* (Grove Press, 1965) most of what he had to say to us is clearly and splendidly laid out. There isn't a page that doesn't have a quotable line and hardly a thought that isn't brilliant. His imaginative use of life and of the times in which he lived make the logic of his arguments unassailable. One theme runs throughout—one thought that drove him obsessively—getting equality, real equality for his people, since without it there's nothing worth talking about.

By Malcolm's time, black America had realized that they had to play for all the marbles or give up the pretense that there was any hope for self-respect, certainly not for respect from the rest of America. As evidenced by the vernacular of the present generation, that need for respect still resonates. A lack of respect is considered the worst of insults: the ubiquitous "Don't *dis* me!" is at once both a plea and a demand, but never just a shibboleth.

Malcolm makes reference to the importance of respect often. His best argument concerns the necessity of owning your own land and the need to acquire it as the driving force behind most revolutions. With land, he argues, you can build a country that's yours. Once you have a country that can't be "dissed," then you will be respected, not for yourself but because of the power of your country.

Black America has no country that stands behind it and gives it that all-important respect among men. To Malcolm, the contempt in which the black American is held as a consequence is the reason why he is essentially a man without a country; the country does not see fit to make him a full member in good standing. Anyone who knows anything knows that he is right about that. Admitting it is another thing.

He used the passage of civil rights legislation to make the point that no one had to pass a law to give an immigrant *his* civil rights. He has them as soon as he walks off the gangplank. The black American has been here for four hundred years and he can't get his civil rights unless *another* law is passed that nobody bothers to enforce for at least ten more years, and then only half-heartedly. Add to that the absurdity of measuring the status of black America by the horrors of the past that are no longer in vogue.

The country has (supposedly) come a long way because blacks aren't lynched anymore (for the most part, anyway) or because black professional women make more money per capita than white professional women with the same education or some other measure of progress. According to Malcolm, who came from the working class, the problems of the vast majority of blacks are not being solved unless they are emancipated from poverty and protected from racism. Anything else is just another civil rights dodge.

Malcolm criticized the nonviolent marches on Selma and Birmingham and the registration drives throughout the South to get votes as another legal sham that gave only a semblance of what it should have given. Black people were trying to register to vote and the nation sat by and allowed law enforcement, under the guise of state's rights, to treat them like criminals, to sic dogs on them and use water hoses so powerful that they ripped the clothes off their bodies. Said Malcolm, "The Second Amendment gives you the right to protect yourself. The law wasn't written just for weekend guerrillas in the backwoods of Pennsylvania with swastikas on their armbands and beer bellies hanging over their silver belt buckles with Indian or nigger heads as insignias."

Take a rifle and shoot the dog was his answer. Of course, the police power would shoot back, since the dog's life is worth more than a black protester's and the dog is an arm of the law in this case. As far as Malcolm was concerned, when the law shoots you for attempting to exercise your rights under the law, you have a right to shoot the law back. You aren't breaking the law—the law is. No one white would ever be attacked anywhere in America for trying to register to vote—not an immigrant whose green card is still wet, nor the poorest of the Appalachian poor.

Ergo, black America is a nation without a country to back it up. When half of the country says you can't vote, and the other half watches while you get beaten in the head for trying, then you aren't a part of that country, you just exist in it at the country's pleasure. Malcolm told his audiences, "You are not American. . . . You don't catch hell because you're a Baptist, and you don't catch hell because you're a Methodist . . . you don't catch hell because you're a Democrat or a Republican . . . you don't catch hell because you're a mason or an Elk and you sure don't catch hell because you're an American; because if you were an American, you wouldn't catch hell. You catch hell because you're a black man."

He left us this quote as a final legacy: "[T]he white man doesn't go along with anybody who's not for him. He doesn't care if you are for right or wrong, he wants to know are you for him. And if you're for him, he doesn't care what else you're for. As long as you're for him, then . . . you become a spokesman."

44

THE MAKING OF BLACK REVOLUTIONARIES

by James Forman,
with a Foreword by Julian Bond

NEW YORK: MACMILLAN, 1972

James Forman begins *The Making of Black Revolutionaries* with: "We are not born revolutionary. . . . This book describes some of the process that molded . . . me into the revolutionary I hope I am, [and] shaped many others into revolutionaries." It is a book that is seminal to a period that was filled with many groups, sometimes competing, sometimes cooperating with each other in the fight to destroy Jim Crow. None of these groups was more pivotal in that fight than the Student Nonviolent Coordinating Committee, or SNCC, as it was more popularly known. And no one was more of a metaphor for the age than James Forman, young man turned revolutionary turned leader. The part he played during his tenure as the head of SNCC was a microcosm of everything the time, the people, and the place stood for.

Early in the 1960s McGeorge Bundy, then head of the Ford Foundation, called a meeting of black civil rights leaders to announce that CORE, the Congress of Racial Equality, would be kept alive through a massive infusion of money while SNCC (Forman's organization) would be destroyed. Forman quotes

Bundy explaining the game plan, but that account of Bundy and the meeting was deleted by a lawyer at Macmillan (which published the book originally). The account was restored in the Open Hand edition. Bundy's thinking was that CORE could be weaned away from the Black Power concept, but not SNCC. Bundy, of course, had been President Kennedy's national security advisor before going to the Ford Foundation.

In the same way that embracing Black Power destroyed Adam Clayton Powell, it destroyed Forman and SNCC. If they couldn't be "weaned" away from it they would get no money and no protection from the establishment. Forman and SNCC were independent, they couldn't be bought, and they wanted a victory for the disfranchised and the powerless, not for themselves.

As a youth, Forman had tried to enlist in the army to get away from a stepfather who took every opportunity to beat him. He had to join the air force because the army, segregated at the time, had a quota for blacks and it was all used up the month he wanted to join. On a clear June night, after he'd finished a four-year tour of duty, he was standing outside a library on the campus of the University of Southern California, taking a breather from his studies, when the hand of fate started him on the road to revolution.

As Forman tells it, he heard someone call out to him in the night:

> "Hey, boy! You there!" A police car pulled up to the curb. Two white cops were in the front seat. . . . I heard them insulting me but I went on looking at the stars."
>
> "Are you talking to me?" I said sharply. . . .
>
> "One of those smart ones, huh!"
>
> I remembered the cops who stopped us as youngsters in Chicago and searched us for nothing. I remembered the cops . . . who stood by silently as I went to them for help.

The policemen took him to the precinct, even though he tried to tell them he was a registered student at USC. They said he looked like a robbery suspect. Filled with a sense of his rights, he fulminated in the station house when no one would let him make a phone call. For his pains, he was beaten so badly that he urinated in his pants:

> I began yelling about my right to use the toilet. . . . "Look, I have to piss. If you don't hurry up and open this cell, I'm going to piss on the floor. . . ." "You better not piss on that floor you sonofabitch," the blond white pig hollered. . . . He opened the door and said, "Follow me. . . ." We reached the corner. He turned and started hitting me hard in the stomach. I doubled up . . . and fell to the floor. "You still got to piss, nigger?" As I barely got to my feet—One-two! One-two! I doubled over once more. "Now shut your goddamn mouth and stop all that shit about your rights. You're a nigger."

Disenchanted with California as a consequence of that incident, Forman moved back to Chicago where he had grown up, and graduated from Roosevelt University in 1957. (After his stint with SNCC, he went on to earn both a master's degree at Cornell and a doctorate from the Union of Experiment Colleges and Universities.) When SNCC asked him to become executive secretary, he was already ten years older than most of their rank and file. He had joined the organization in 1960 after participating in a freedom ride. Before that, he had gone south as a reporter for the *Chicago Defender* to cover the school desegregation fight in Little Rock, Arkansas. That was in 1956.

Even though he had decided that he would not acquiesce to America's brutal racism, the racism that we allow police to continue to indulge in even in the new millennium, he still survived his early manhood without going to prison and achieved the middle-class accomplishment of becoming a schoolteacher, which gave him middle-class respectability. But he would not let that status stop him from risking it all to get into the fight in real terms, which is what he did when he joined SNCC. As executive secretary, Forman brought maturity, wisdom, and organizational skills to an organization that had thrived on being informal and almost leaderless (anything could be put on the agenda by anyone). It lacked the structure, the rigidities, that marked the

National Association for the Advancement of Colored People and the Urban League. He rose to the challenge of leadership and led the students splendidly.

By 1968 the alliance between SNCC and the Black Panthers (which had begun so promisingly four years before) had disintegrated, partly due to the difference in leadership styles between the two organizations and partly due to policy issues. Young Turks like Huey Newton and Bobby Seale didn't take kindly to being told how to proceed by older members such as Forman. Forman tried to tell them that security was vital. But they were from the street, and any brother who was one of them and who was willing to join the fight had to be trusted. That, of course, was an open door through which the FBI could not only infiltrate their organizations, but practically take them over.

There were other differences. Forman insisted that SNCC not become a blacks-only organization, but by 1966 the chairman of SNCC (not to be confused with executive secretary) was Stokely Carmichael (who changed his name to Kwame Ture). Carmichael—Forman never calls him Kwame Ture—decided on a blacks-only policy, which the Panthers opposed, and they made that opposition official in policy statements. H. Rap Brown left the Panthers and took over the leadership of SNCC in 1968, changing the name from Nonviolent to National without losing the well-known acronym. Although Forman doesn't say so, I suspect that his middle-class manner caused resentment among the Panthers, as well as those in SNCC who wanted to adopt an approach that was more "from the street." Forman felt his failure in that regard most keenly because he remained a revolutionary to the very end.

But in the end, he was a revolutionary without an army. He had to leave SNCC after all the years of hard work and dedication because, once Brown took over as chairman, there was really no place for Forman in the organization. In any case, he wanted to write. He had sacrificed his health and welfare (and probably family as well, although he doesn't say so) from the early days to the year Martin Luther King was killed. It was time to move on.

The Black Panther symbiosis would have been a fitting culmination to his work if he could have made it happen. He couldn't, and it didn't.

Consequently, on a Sunday in 1969, alone, but with courage unflagging, Forman invaded Riverside Church, a bastion of liberalism of the cloth in New York City, and read a black manifesto for all the world to hear. Without Panther or SNCC support, he was still revolutionary, albeit in complete control of both his language and himself. By his manner and style, he made it perfectly clear that, if he had chosen to do so, he could have been one of the assembled congregants, who had money, position, and the power that naturally accrues to *those* members of the status quo.

Forman lived (and still lives) for the struggle. The insanities of the sixties, the deaths—all the horrors—are painfully detailed in this book and put into their proper perspective. In the chapter "Moment of Death," Forman tells about not wanting a SNCC demonstration to take place in Monroe, North Carolina, on a Sunday because that was when all the racists were abroad. He's voted down. The demonstration goes ahead as planned in front of the courthouse in Monroe. A mob of three thousand screaming racists converge on them. Young blacks who are not involved in the demonstration gather across the street to watch. Forman knows that these youngsters will be alone and unprotected once the demonstration is over and he and his people have left. He tries to get them to leave, but they refuse.

The cars that had been arranged to get the demonstrators out show up, but Forman has them take the bystanders out first. He's in the process of getting his own people out when one of the deputies stops him from putting a white female demonstrator in a car with black men. Then the deputy takes a shotgun from the car (not concealed, therefore not illegal in North Carolina) and gives the shotgun to one of the mob who looks drunk. The drunk points the shotgun right at Forman's head while the other three thousand scream, "Kill the Nigger!" over and over and over. Forman pushes the woman into the car anyway and the drunk hits him on the head with the barrel of the gun and, as Forman recounts, "separates my hair, splits my skin, opens my skull, deadens my brain, out comes the blood, gushing like a volcano . . . another blow, more blood down my face, into my ear, past my nose, across my chin."

Forman is rushed off to the police station for safety, but before a doctor can be sent for to attend to his wound, he's arrested for inciting a riot!

45

Soul on Ice

by Eldridge Cleaver

New York: McGraw Hill, 1968

No matter what you think of Eldridge Cleaver, you know, when you read *Soul on Ice*, you are in the presence of a first-rate mind and a writing style that is biting, slashing, and awesome to behold. Like so many of the young men who took it upon themselves to lead the assault on racism in the 1960s, Cleaver grew up in an America at its most conservative; the postwar prosperity had made the heartland a heaven on earth for the white majority who saw no reason to help the black minority out of the hell on earth that was America for them. These young men had no way of knowing that the next two decades would give blacks many of the things that they were fighting and dying for at the time.

When Malcolm X came back from his trip to Mecca in 1964 to announce that he had been shown real brotherhood, had been treated as an equal by Muslims who had blond hair and blue eyes and white skin, Cleaver and the rest, rotting away in American prisons for the simplest of offenses (in his case marijuana possession) had only one reaction: Malcolm was a traitor. Whitey had to be the infidel, the enemy who must be destroyed at any and all costs, because a world of complete and rigid segregation was the only one they knew. Their lives had been permanently damaged simply because of the color of their skin.

Many of them died in shootouts, some converted to a new religion, some mindlessly acquiesced to the powers that be, some wrote about it, and some even got elected to Congress. But very few had as wide or incisive a grasp of all the issues as did Cleaver. He had a lot to say, and in *Soul on Ice* he says it, all of it, only too well. His evisceration of James Baldwin alone is worth the price of the book. And his biting wit is ever present. The incident in prison when he thinks of comparing 3-in-1 oil to the mystery of the Holy Trinity is truly hilarious.

But Cleaver was a street fighter first. And in the ideology of the street fighter, the world is a violent place, and getting even is all that counts. How you get even almost doesn't matter. What does matter is that you don't get sidetracked by compromises or rationalizations. In any battle for ideas, whether they end up in blood or not, you are playing to win, and you disdain hypocrisy, weakness, and desertion of principles in the face of the enemy.

Soul on Ice is filled with this passion. Cleaver revels not only in his honesty but in his wisdom. He sees through the twists and turns that we've used to bury race as an issue, to pretend that it no longer exists. He abhors the position that years later allowed Affirmative Action to be done away with because no one was separate and unequal anymore, certainly not because of RACE! We have reached a plateau in the Republic where there are black faces on TV doing almost everything except being the news anchor on network television. In spite of all the progress, democracy has not come to black America. Cleaver knew this two decades before all of the "progress" really set in, and the basis for his argument is an excellent one. He observed:

> By crushing black leaders, while inflating the image of Uncle Toms and celebrities from the apolitical world of sport and play, the mass media were able to channel and control the aspirations and goals of the black masses. The effect was to take the "problem" out of a political and economic and philosophical context and place it on the misty level of "goodwill," "charitable and harmonious race

relations," and "good sportsmanlike conduct." . . . [W]henever a crisis with racial overtones arises, an entertainer or athlete is trotted out and allowed to expound a predictable, conciliatory interpretation of what's happening. . . . [W]hen in reality, all that has happened is that the blacks have been sold out and cooled out again.

His message "To All Black Women, From All Black Men" at the end of the book has become a classic by now.

I have returned from the dead. I speak to you now from the Here And Now. . . . For four hundred years you have been a woman alone, bereft of her man, a manless woman. The white man stood between us, over us, around us. . . . The sound of my woman calling me . . . I heard my woman beg the beast for mercy for me, I heard my woman die, I heard the sound of her death, a snapping sound, a breaking sound, a sound that sounded final, the last sound, the ultimate sound, the sound of death, me, I heard, I hear it every day, I hear her now . . . I hear you now . . . I hear you.

Eldridge (even though, unlike Caesar, you're still with us), when comes such another? Unfortunately for African-American America, never. Not only is his day gone, he's not even properly remembered. Any black American who wants to can throw stones at him now and do so with impunity and without the slightest sense of disloyalty. But in his day, Cleaver was the poet in our midst, notable for his honesty and his searing ability to put into words the hell that blacks were living then and often find themselves living even now.

In spite of today's domestic quietude (not that it's that quiet); in spite of the fact that there are forty black men and women in Congress instead of four; in spite of all the middle-class black families who live in New York City in the borough of Queens; in spite of all the black millionaires and all the rock-and-roll millionaires, all the hip-hop millionaires; all the film stars who are super (and mega) stars; in spite of all these "successes," too much of what has been achieved has been achieved by default. That means all of it can be taken away as soon as the tyranny of the majority (to use Thoreau's phrase) decides it's time for a backlash (or a frontal assault, face first).

Cleaver made it clear that black America owns or controls very little of anything of importance to the nation at large. Black America is still the stepchild that has to stand aside and watch media tycoons from foreign lands, British industrialists, and bankers from every corner of the world in every ethnic variety come to this land of opportunity and prosper, with nothing to hinder them save chance and their own failings. In all seasons, there are still two Americas, one black and one everything else. That was Cleaver's point, and it is his legacy. He didn't tell us anything we don't know. He just said it so well that whenever we read his words, we know that when we stop saying it, we've become the lap dog.

46

SOLEDAD BROTHER: THE PRISON LETTERS OF GEORGE JACKSON

with an Introduction by Jean Genet

NEW YORK: COWARD-MCCANN, 1970

In 1960 George Jackson, then eighteen, was accused of robbing a gas station of seventy dollars. He struck a deal with the prosecution, even though he hadn't taken the seventy dollars. He would confess to the crime and save the county court costs in return for a light sentence. The criminal justice system reneged and sentenced him from one year to life imprisonment instead. He went to jail for that one-year-plus, and that's where he died on August 21, 1971, at the age of twenty-nine, in a shootout in the prison yard of San Quentin. In his book *Who Killed George Jackson?* Jo Durden-Smith suggests that his death was the result of conspiracy. Thus endeth and beginneth the George Jackson lesson.

Earlier, Jackson had substituted himself for another black inmate and simply walked out as the other man, who was scheduled for release. As he himself writes, "All blacks do look alike to certain types of white people." But George Lester Jackson was not hated, kept in prison on trumped-up charges, held in solitary confinement twenty-three and a half hours a day for seven of the eleven years he spent there simply because he had Billy the Kid daring. The black man in America (in prison or out) who decides to fight white racism and does so effectively brings out the beast in white America in a way that is chilling to behold. That genocidal rage cuts across all barriers of class and economic division and white ethnic segmentation. Once you've lived in America, rich or poor, you become infected with the disease that insists that black people can only be equal up to a point. If they stay in their place, they're tolerated; if they try to imitate the American tradition of "live free or die" they become more hated than a child molester.

Why this is so is beyond the scope of this inquiry. Suffice it to say that George Jackson was living proof of this racist hatred. What made him the most hated of the hated was that he was not only a leader of men, but his was a mind that was truly a terrible thing to waste. And his talent as a writer, especially his letters, makes him a rare man among men. In any other culture he would have become a popular hero, a sort of Robin Hood of the proletariat—not so in white America.

Of course one must always add, "Not all Americans who are white are hate mongers or racists." This is obviously so. Even George Jackson attests to this fact in one of his letters. But the problem with absolving the innocent of the broad racist brush is that the innocent do nothing to help rid us of the guilty. In the fight for racial parity, it is too often the guilty who carry the day.

Black inmates in Soledad Prison in California, where Jackson was incarcerated originally, had to endure being called nigger and having food, plates, even human waste thrown at them in their cells by white inmates, Hispanic inmates, and Hawaiian inmates, and they were subjected to this verbal and physical abuse while guards stood by grinning. In the television room, the white and Mexican prisoners sat in the front. If one of them left the room for whatever reason, no black (they were all in the back of the bus) dared move up and take the empty seat. Jackson, however, dared to sit in the front while his fellow black inmates sulked in their rearest of privileges—and he almost got killed for it. Why were they afraid to join him? Because they didn't want to end up in solitary or have their packages from home confiscated, or, worst of all, have a bad conduct sheet follow them to their parole hearing.

Guards gave white prisoners razors or zip guns with which to attack black inmates. One guard even gave a white prisoner a loaded gun. If a white and black prisoner got into a fight in the yard and the black held his own, a guard from the tower would shoot the black prisoner to kill, not to wound. The CBS program *Sixty Minutes* documented this practice (even as sport, with invited guests from outside the prison come to watch) for all the world to see a few years ago. It was a full twenty-minute segment with all the trimmings of follow-up interviews.

Through all this, George Jackson comes down to us from three decades past not primarily as a young man whose manly courage was rare indeed, but as a gifted writer, a man sensitive to the nuances of the human condition, of the wrenchings that family discord create, of the tender ways needed to reach out to loved ones, to build bridges, overcome barriers. As great as his intellectual reach was, it was no greater than his grasp. He would have made a first-rate sociologist in the classical sense, and he would have been no mean practitioner of philosophy, either. But the mix of poverty, being a real man, and his early run-ins with the law (all minor offenses) marked him for death. He had one quality that made him the hated one: he was willing to fight racism tooth and nail and give no quarter, call no truce. He refused to pretend that things were getting better when it was obvious to him that they were getting worse. When he was fifteen, a cop shot him six times, point blank, even though he had his hands up!

Quoting George Jackson is the best way to pay homage to the man as artist and as thinker. This is from a letter to his mother in 1965:

> I am not too manly or sophisticated to say that I love you and all the rest with a devotion and dedication that will continue to grow until I pass from this existence. Anything that will please you, and that falls within human accomplishment, I will carry out. I say this with confidence because of my certainty that you would never ask me to please you by surrendering my mental liberty and self re-

spect; I wouldn't want to live were these, my last two real possessions, to be lost.

In a letter to his father, he writes:

Believe me when I say that I begin to weary of the sun. I am by nature a gentle man, I love the simple things of life, good food, good wine, an expressive book, music, pretty black women. . . . All of this is gone from me, all the gentle, shy characteristics of the black man have been wrung unceremoniously from my soul. . . . I think only of how I live, how well, how nobly. We think if we are to be men again we must stop working for nothing, competing against each other for the little they allow us to possess, stop selling our women or allowing them to be used and handled against their will, stop letting our children be educated by the barbarian, using their language, dress, and customs, and most assuredly stop turning our cheeks.

In another letter to his father, he writes that he's sorry for having ever told a lie or stolen anything or robbed or cheated, not because of the immorality of the act but because in being immoral he's "conforming to Western ways." The privilege for committing such acts, he says, only belongs to white men. This leads him to the question of what "they mean" when they say that blacks should be like them, should adopt their ways of doing things. If blacks adopt capitalism, "Where," he asks, "would we seek our colonies, Europe, the US!? Who would we capitalize on? . . . Who would we kidnap, murder, lynch, enslave, and then neglect!!" In that same letter he addresses the contradiction of Europeans in America in the 1770s, calling their wanting to rid themselves of the Europeans in England a fight for freedom; however, when black men in America attempt to rid themselves of the oppression of the descendants of those same Europeans, it's called "subversion."

Again to his father:

The concept of nonviolence is a false ideal. It presupposes the existence of compassion and a sense of justice on the part of one's adversary. When this adversary has everything to lose and nothing to gain by exercising justice and compassion, his reaction can only be negative.

The symbol of the male here in North America has always been the gun, the knife, the club. Violence is extolled at every exchange: the TV, the motion pictures, the bestseller lists. . . . To die for king and country is to die a hero.

At one point he told his father, "Freedom of the press is for those who own one" (attributed originally to A. J. Liebling). And to his mother he had this to say in another letter: "When the peasant revolts, the student demonstrates, the slum dweller riots, the robber robs, he is reacting to a feeling of insecurity, an atavistic throwback to the territorial imperative, a *reaction* to the fact that he has lost control of the circumstances surrounding his life." Again to his mother: "It is clear that they are not going to give me a chance. . . . Just because I want to be my black self, mentally healthy, and because I look anyone who addresses me in the eye, they feel that I may start a riot anytime. I've stopped more trouble here than any other black in the system."

He wrote passionate love letters to Angela Davis: "Every time I've opened my mouth, assumed my battle stance, I was trying in effect to say I love you . . . African woman. . . . Should we make a lover's vow? It's silly, with all my tomorrows accounted for, but you can humor me." And in another letter to her:

> The lights went out an hour . . . ago. It's 12:45 a.m., June 5, and I love you twice as much as I did yesterday. It redoubles and double redoubles. . . . You may never read this, and I may never touch you, but I feel better than I have for many seasons. You do know that I live, and I hope that by some means you have discovered that I love you deeply, and would touch you tenderly, warmly, fiercely if I could, if my enemies were not *at present* stronger. Love you Woman.

It was Angela Davis who was accused of supplying the guns that Jackson's seventeen-year-old brother Jonathan used to shoot up a California courtroom in 1970, just two weeks before George Jackson's death. The younger Jackson, two inmates whom he sought to set free along with his brother, and a judge were killed in the ensuing shootout. Davis was eventually acquitted of the charges. She had come to know George Jackson through her work for penal reform. After his death she continued that work. In 1971 she published *If They Come in the Morning;* in 1974, *Angela Davis: An Autobiography.* In 1980 she ran for the office of vice president on the Communist Party ticket.

47

AND THE WALLS CAME TUMBLING DOWN: AN AUTOBIOGRAPHY

by Ralph David Abernathy

NEW YORK: HARPER & ROW, 1989

Ralph Abernathy was born in Alabama in 1926, the second youngest of twelve children. His father was a successful farmer who owned five hundred acres of land that produced a cash crop of 150 bales of cotton a year, along with cattle, hogs, and chickens. The Abernathys were well fed even during the dark days of the Depression.

In the fifties, while still an undergraduate, Abernathy decided he would try to register to vote. He shamed a group of classmates into going along with him. The registrar was a little old gray-haired woman who gave them forms to fill out and told each he had failed as soon as she came to a section that had been left blank. Abernathy, seeing this, went back and filled in all his blanks with irrelevant information. Finding no blanks to put an X next to, the woman told him he had "passed" the written portion but had to take an oral examination as well. That consisted of reciting the Thirteenth Amendment verbatim. He realized that the woman probably couldn't really read, given the way she'd reacted to the nonsense he'd put in the blanks, so he recited "My

Country, 'Tis of Thee." When he finished, the woman was more than a little annoyed and said, "And you better had known it or you wouldn't have passed."

Ralph David Abernathy walked side by side with Martin Luther King, Jr., from the Montgomery bus boycott of 1955 until King's death in 1968. In *And the Walls Came Tumbling Down,* written near the end of his life, Abernathy covers not only his years with King but also the quarter century of activism that came after. He also includes some indelicate moments in Dr. King's life that might best have been ignored. For this, Abernathy received much criticism, bordering on calumny, from many quarters. In this writer's personal view, this single act of disloyalty should not mar an otherwise great life, simply and compellingly told.

Walls is Abernathy's autobiography and it provides a rare look at American life, not only because it was lived in the most American of ways—a country boy goes into the army, attends college, and then goes on to try to make the American dream work for him and his kind by staying within the system. In so doing, he was able to renew our faith in America while criticizing it for its monumental failings.

In the major battles to eradicate segregation laws in key cities throughout the country, and by extension all the cities in the country, in its efforts to make Congress, the president, and the courts enforce laws that guaranteed equality to black Americans, Abernathy gives King and the Southern Christian Leadership Conference (SCLC) a .500 batting average. They won in Montgomery, but they lost in Albany, Georgia. They won in Selma, but they lost in St. Augustine, Florida. They won in Birmingham (the biggest victory of them all), but they lost in Chicago.

King and the SCLC were quite effective in the towns of the South. They understood what they were up against there. And as long as they could get police protection, they usually had to face only small groups of racists. In Gage Park, Illinois, however, they faced a howling, screaming mob of thousands that came close to tearing them limb from limb, according to Abernathy's account. They were traumatized there in a way that the Klan had never traumatized them in Dixie.

In one of the finest examples of one man's passion for understanding the human heart overriding a mean-spirited response to the violence that he, himself, has suffered, Abernathy attempts to explain why the white people of Gage Park reacted so violently to black demonstrators in their midst. White people in the South, he explains, were used to seeing blacks wherever they went. The whites of Gage Park never saw blacks in their own neighborhood, and only at a distance in many other instances.

> So the fear of the unknown played a large part in the reaction. . . . The screaming mob that met our fifty demonstrators and drove them out of Gage Park that night were in a state of frenzy born of terror. They thought of themselves as an invaded people. . . . It is the kind of unreasoning fear that has always lain just beneath the surface of racism, a fear nurtured by generations of segregation and all the myths that surround the unknown.

In Birmingham, in the midst of the dogs and the beatings and the jailings, while he was at the pulpit in one of the churches that was being used to hold the rallies, Abernathy realized that the microphone had been bugged. So he talked to the bug, calling it Mr. Doohickey. He said in part: "I want you to know, Mr. Doohickey, that we'll be marching tomorrow by the hundreds. We're going to fill the jail houses, Mr. Doohickey. We won't let anybody turn us around. We won't let the Ku Klux Klan turn us around [and] we won't let Bull Connor [Eugene "Bull" Connor, Birmingham's Public Safety Commissioner who ordered the dogs and hoses on the demonstrators there in 1963] turn us around!" That incident established Ralph Abernathy, not only as a real leader, but also as a man with enough control of himself to find humor in the worst of times and the direst of moments.

St. Augustine, though a defeat in the battle, offered another moment that was not without its humor. After they were arrested and released, King and Abernathy had to find new ways to make an old point: that nothing had been done to rid the city of its segregation laws. Hosea Williams came up with an idea that worked. They would go back to the motel that had refused to serve them food and integrate the swimming pool! Once in the water they caused havoc. Abernathy tells the story:

> In less than a minute the manager came rushing out of the lobby and over to the poolside, waving his hand frantically, screaming, "Get out! Get out or I'll call the police." We laughed and waved at him, and he wheeled around and charged back inside. . . . Five minutes later we heard the distant wail of a siren [and] at least two squad cars arrived and several policemen came rushing into the courtyard, as if they had been called to quell a riot. "OK," one of them yelled. "You niggers are under arrest." "Fine," we said, "come in and put the cuffs on us." "Come out of the water right now," the ranking officer barked and came to the edge, trying to reach out to grab an arm. Instinctively we all swam to the middle and began waving. The water was [soothing] in the Florida sun . . . [and] we were enjoying the frustration of the police, who were trying to arrest us without losing their dignity or getting wet. . . . we floated on our backs or paddled around in small circles . . . [and finally] swam to the side, climbed out, and submitted to arrest.

In a posthumous farewell to Martin Luther King, the man he called his friend, Ralph Abernathy used the pulpit, a place that they had shared so often in life, for his good-bye. He calls it his "Last Letter to Martin." In it he writes that he misses King even though King's been dead just a few days. He goes on to say that he knows King will be busy in heaven, with so much to do and so many people to see. And he's sure God will have a special event to introduce his favorite black activist son to all the others who have gone on before him. He ends with:

> Say thanks to those prophets we quoted all over America [like] Mahatma K. Gandhi. [And] look up Bartholomew. For some strange reason I always liked him.

Ralph David Abernathy, a man of God, never became embittered despite a lifetime of abuse because he followed the highest precepts of his country, the best ideals by which man has lived throughout history. He was honest, he had the quality of mercy, and he was courageous without being ruthless. But his high idealism notwithstanding, he was also a man of such consummate human feelings that he remembered a favorite white saint, in the midst of a letter to the most famous African-American martyr of our time, and was not ashamed to say he really wasn't sure why he liked the saint.

48

THE COINTELPRO PAPERS

by Ward Churchill and Jim Vander Wall

BOSTON: SOUTH END PRESS, 1990

Reading Ward Churchill and Jim Vander Wall's well-documented, authoritative work on one of the sleaziest operations that the U.S. government ever became involved in, the Counter Intelligence Program, or COINTELPRO, one becomes convinced that no one who is black or part of the political left can ever be accused of paranoia if he or she suspects that Big Brother is watching. For anyone politically active in a public way who is even mildly left of center, COINTELPRO proves that there are no freedoms.

Not only black activists, from meticulous observers of the law who preached and practiced nonviolence to those who were ready to use violent means and violent rhetoric to get what they were after, but also Puerto Rican nationalists and socialists were all caught in the web that J. Edgar Hoover carefully wove from the 1920s until his death in 1972 and after. That's more than half a century.

The idea that COINTELPRO was thought up during the sixties in response to the likes of Huey Newton and the Black Panthers is simply a delusion of mainstream middle America. Its methods were the tactics of a police state (the authors call COIN-TELPRO the United States's political police) that went far beyond national security needs. Its everyday, callous violation of the constitutional prohibitions against incursions into the rights of American citizens to political dissent demonstrated that the law is so much chaff when the reactionary forces in government want to go after their opposite number in the private sector.

COINTELPRO's treatment of Martin Luther King, Jr., described in detail in *The COINTELPRO Papers,* is the most egregious example. And what was attempted in his case belongs in television fiction, where shadowy government forces are at work that no one can ever discover. Ironically, conspiracy theory has been used all too often for such drama, but the protagonist, the erstwhile victim has always been white. Now that's absurd. King and his organization, the Southern Christian Leadership Conference (SCLC), were so upright that they refused to work with groups that didn't believe in Jesus Christ.

When the Ku Klux Klan and their ilk began bombing the churches and the homes in Montgomery, Alabama, to keep blacks in the back of the bus, the whole city could have gone up in flames. The blacks were ready to fight fire with fire. The city fathers—the mayor and his council—had miscalculated and lost control of the situation. It was King who stood in front of his bombed-out house, where his wife and child had just escaped death by a hairsbreadth, and told his fellow black Americans to stay calm, no eye for an eye. The mayor and the city fathers were truly grateful, and said so in public.

Yet through some ghoulish, hate-filled megalomania, J. Edgar Hoover spent hundreds of thousands of dollars and man hours to destroy King. King became such an obsession of the Federal Bureau of Investigation and Hoover that even after he was dead, they were still trying to get him! But of course Hoover couldn't do it alone. It was Robert F. Kennedy, serving as attorney general, who approved around-the-clock surveillance and wiretaps on all SCLC offices and King's home. By 1962 King was in Section A of the FBI reserve index, "one step below [the] . . . index [of those] scheduled to be rounded up and 'preventively detained' in concentration camps in the event of a declared national emergency," as Churchill and Vander Wall record.

William Sullivan, Hoover's right-hand man and the head of COINTELPRO, said after King's "I Have a Dream" speech: "We must mark [King] now, if we have not before, as the most dangerous Negro in the future of this Nation from the standpoint of communism, the Negro, and national security . . . it may be unrealistic to limit [our actions against King] to legalistic proofs that would stand up in court or before Congressional Committees." In other words, to hell with the law, get the black commie bastard. Of course King was no communist—he was too much of a fundamentalist Christian. Anyone who doubts that cannot be reasoned with.

When it was announced in 1964 that King would receive the Nobel Peace Prize, Sullivan and his boys put into motion a plan that the authors call "an unvarnished intervention into the domestic political process." They got the Internal Revenue Service to harass him (don't any of these agencies have any integrity?). They tried a smear campaign in the press, and, finally, they put together a composite audiotape that alleged that he was a sex-craved madman who had indulged in orgiastic trysts with prostitutes, proving "the depths of his sexual perversion and depravity." The authors write: "The finished tape was packaged, along with [an] accompanying anonymous letter . . . informing King that the audio material would be released to the media unless he committed suicide prior to bestowal of the Nobel Prize."

King didn't commit suicide, as we all know, and he did accept the Nobel Peace Prize. One of Sullivan's minions, associate director, "Deke" DeLoach, tried to get *Newsweek*'s Washington bureau chief, Benjamin Bradlee, to run a story based on the tapes. Bradlee not only wouldn't cooperate, but spread the word of what the FBI was up to, so they had to back off. By 1969 "[FBI] efforts to 'expose' Martin Luther King, Jr., had not slackened even though King had been dead for a year. [The Bureau] furnished ammunition to conservatives to attack King's memory, and . . . tried to block efforts to honor the slain leader."

Of course, it wasn't just King that COINTELPRO targeted.

The FBI helped kill Malcolm X, Fred Hampton, and other members of the Black Panthers in the Chicago shootout of 1969. According to the authors, they even managed to get Hampton drugged before they shot him. Hoover put together a specious case against Marcus Garvey as far back as 1918, even before there was an FBI. He got Garvey deported five years later and his organization, the UNIA (United Negro Improvement Association), was destroyed in the process. The FBI went after W. E. B. Du Bois. They even tried to destroy the National Association for the Advancement of Colored People, listing it as a communist organization. "Only a series of Supreme Court decisions prevented the entire NAACP membership from being forced to register as 'subversives,' or going to prison for refusing to do so."

We have two Americas. One is innocent, even when it's guilty, and the other is guilty no matter how innocent it is, was, or will be. As Noam Chomsky argues in the introduction to another book on the COINTELPRO papers, by Nelson Blackstock, *CO-INTELPRO, the FBI's Secret War on Political Freedom* (Anchor, 1988), the FBI response to the Socialist Party, the New Left, the Black Panthers, and other political dissenters is blatant violation of the rights of Americans who are doing what they have every legal right to do under the Constitution.

The Republican Party break-in of the Democratic Party headquarters in the Watergate affair represented a mild version of the violations committed by the FBI. Because the offices of the Democratic Party, one of the two major American political parties, was broken into a president of the United States was forced to resign from office. That's as immense a consequence as one can imagine. When the FBI ransacked the offices of the New Left and Socialist Party and killed Black Panthers, the only consequence was that federal judges, who had a low-key, technocrat approach in contrast to Hoover's, were subsequently chosen to head the bureau. The authors note that films such as *Mississippi Burning* were made to burnish the organization's image, so that it could go on undeterred in its onslaught against dissent in public life—the lifeblood of a democracy.

There are still some innocents at home who think that surely all this is behind us, as is the McCarthy era. Not so. The FBI is represented on cable programs weekly as unbiased keepers of the flame, who are going after the bad guys. Not true. The FBI was given the mandate to punish racist police around the nation. The officer in charge of that assignment said on camera that he wouldn't do it because the pensions of those racist police would be threatened and their families would suffer. This conservative mind-set sees the political left as fair game in a hunting season that never ends. Marcus Garvey broke no law. And no one told Hoover to "get him." Hoover gave himself that job, created a file based on nothing substantial, and forced a district attorney to prosecute, and a jury went along with the charade.

America wants its freedoms, but if there are any rumblings of dissent that threaten to get too loud, it wants security more. The perception that the radical right, as represented by the FBI, will protect one and all, no matter how illogical that is, somehow gets accepted. The result is that the freedom to dissent that the political right has, the political left does not have. When a national crisis happens, such as the horror of September 11, 2001, everyone must be superpatriotic or be labeled a traitor.

The Black Panthers hired a white, well-respected forensic expert to prove that the Chicago police's account of the killing of Fred Hampton and the others was a total fiction. When those findings were made public, the man responsible for the calumny, Cook County State's Attorney Edward V. Hanrahan, retired gracefully from the field. His plans for a bigger and better career destroyed was his only punishment. Hampton and the rest were dead, and the police who did the shooting and the FBI who helped, then went about their business. End of story.

49

DEFENDING THE SPIRIT: A BLACK LIFE IN AMERICA

by Randall Robinson

NEW YORK: DUTTON, 1998

Randall Robinson begins his autobiography modestly enough. As a boy growing up in Richmond, Virginia, in the 1950s, he and his family were subjected to more racism than one would expect a middle-class family that studiously avoided any run-ins with the law to be subjected to. He remembers his mother not being able to try on a hat in a downtown department store unless she covered her head first. And he tells us that in 1995, in rural east Virginia, he was still a backwoods redneck's *boy*. "I climb up on the loading platform . . . off Route 13 near Nassawadox . . . looking for the proprietor [of a country store] . . . and [a] young white man . . . leaning on a rusting . . . Ford . . . says to the proprietor, 'A boy just went in theah lookin fuh ya. . . .' It is . . . twenty-five years . . . since I graduated from Harvard Law School. I have conferred with presidents and more than once altered the course of American foreign policy. . . . and I have traveled a long way to nowhere."

Robinson's book is aptly subtitled. Head of TransAfrica, the organization he helped found to fight for human rights in Africa and the Caribbean, Robinson has become an international force in righting some of the wrongs done to black people on both continents. In his book, he proves that keeping blacks in a subservient position, fighting feverishly to ensure that they'll always finish in second place, remains a national obsession. He writes brilliantly and passionately about this large and complex issue, taking us into the seats of power in America in a way that few black Americans could. There've been many black Americans who've been on the inside, but few of them have written about it, and certainly not with the honesty of Randall Robinson.

Bringing down the apartheid government of South Africa was first on TransAfrica's agenda in the 1980s, and its greatest achievement to date. Alexander Haig, who was an arrant racist, as Robinson shows, was Ronald Reagan's secretary of state at the time (no surprise there). Someone from the State Department gave Robinson a copy of a secret agreement between Haig and South African foreign minister Roelof "Pic" Botha. Haig undertook, in the name of the president, to support the apartheid regime hook, line, and sinker.

Robinson was livid. He managed to get the South African ambassador to agree to a meeting in the South African embassy in Washington, D.C. Robinson showed up with Walter Fauntroy, the delegate representing the District of Columbia in Congress, Elinor Holmes Norton, who would succeed Fauntroy as congresswoman for the district, and a member of the U.S. Civil Rights Commission. Robinson and his cohorts in intrigue played the parlor game with the ambassador from Apartheid for half an hour or so, then Ms. Norton excused herself, and got on the phone to every newspaper in town with the story that Robinson, Fauntroy, and the civil rights commissioner were in the South African embassy at that very moment trying to get the ambassador to agree to the dismantling of Apartheid. Well, quicker than you can say Reagan dyed his hair, there was a press mob outside. The ambassador finally realized what was going on and told them to leave or get arrested. Hallelujah, thought Robinson, there is a God. All three, the congressman included, were taken into custody and spent the night in jail.

The groundswell from that coup garnered such support that pickets by the hundreds laid siege to the embassy for two years. When the bill to impose sanctions on South Africa was finally passed, Regan vetoed it, but the veto was overridden and it became law.

When Nelson Mandela became president of South Africa, however, neither he nor his lieutenants repaid TransAfrica by word or deed. They went right over their heads and dealt with State Department officials who had tried to keep them from coming to power in the first place. The idea behind the snub to TransAfrica was that the South African government, now black, could only deal with the real government in America, government to government. Mandela went even further. He was scheduled to attend a fundraiser for TransAfrica. TransAfrica needed the money. Days before the event, after donations had been received and all the arrangements made, Mandela's people called and canceled. Robinson had to give the money back. The African-American fragment was once more, like the novel of the same name, *The Spook Who Sat By the Door*.

Robinson, a man of principle, never blinked. In his next crusade, he almost killed himself in a hunger strike that forced the Clinton administration to stop treating Haitian refugees like animals lost at sea. As he pointed out, "Cubans plucked out of the ocean didn't need to be fleeing in fright from anything. They were all brought to Florida and within a year became eligible for citizenship."

Then came Nigeria and General Sani Abacha, the thug who stole billions (no misprint) of dollars from his people after he had stolen their rights. Robinson's pressure on him was so effective that he offered Robinson a bribe. Robinson could name his price, into the millions. No sooner had he turned down the money than he was asked to help form a coup to get rid of Abacha. He said no to that too. He wasn't the CIA. Robinson doesn't identify the man beyond writing that he was a follower of Muslim minister Louis Farrakhan and "a Nigerian former military officer."

In the book's epigraph Senator Ernest Hollings of South Carolina writes, "Everybody likes to go to Geneva. I used to do it

for the Law of the Sea conferences, and you'd find these poten-
tates from down in Africa, you know, rather than eating each
other they'd just come up and get a good square meal in Geneva."
It is the inescapability of that kind of fundamental racism that has
led to a black America that is adrift at the end of the century in
spite of all the progress we think we've made. Robinson com-
ments:

> Where we had been two Americas, whites and blacks, we were
> soon to become three, the white, the blacks who would now rise
> [thanks to the progress of the sixties], and finally the millions of
> bottom-mired blacks who could not. There would be no serious
> and sustained national compensatory assistance for that last
> group. For the first time African-Americans, class-driven and dis-
> united, were no longer all in the same boat. It was a scantily no-
> ticed watershed leap backward for African-Americans.
>
> Who could have foreseen these problems to come in the heady
> verbose flux of the activist sixties, a time that saw Douglass stud-
> ied, Du Bois read, Fanon revered, King followed, Garvey remem-
> bered, Booker T. decried, Tubman lauded, Malcolm respected?
> Who could have known then that the black community would
> plummet to themelessness, its leadership blunted by the opiate of
> White House invitations—that there would come a time when the
> broader African-American community would have no well-crystal-
> lized idea of what its detailed social and economic objectives
> should be and how these objectives were tactically to be achieved?

He tells us that by the year 2050 the white ethnic majority in
the United States will be a minority. Robinson's warning is well
worth considering: "We are, in America, now sealed off from each
other in well-defined racial camps with negligible intergroup
knowledge or communication. Our nation's white leaders have
elected . . . to ignore the deepening national racial crisis. In so
doing, they have set us all on a course toward disaster." Is his pre-
diction too apocalyptic? Maybe yes, maybe no.

50

HARLEM RENAISSANCE: ART OF BLACK AMERICA

essays by David Driskell, David Levering Lewis, and Deborah Willis Ryan, with an Introduction by Mary Schmidt Campbell

NEW YORK: ABRAMS, 1987

Harlem Renaissance: Art of Black America, originally published as an exhibition catalog in 1987 but reissued in hardcover in 1994, is an excellent exploration of black art of the 1920s and 1930s. Four writers cover the historical background and the art, in separate essays that give us a very lucid view of the Harlem Renaissance.

In her introduction, Mary Schmidt Campbell, dean of the Tisch School of the Arts at New York University, goes over some old historical ground, such as the racism faced by black soldiers returning from World War I. She also found it important to establish credibility for the African-American artist by including numerous allusions to white painters such as Reginald Marsh, Edward Hopper, and Thomas Hart Benton, showing how their approach to modern perspectives in painting was similar. I don't think this choice necessarily helped her case. Nor does she, or any of the other writers, prove that the Harlem Renaissance was the aesthetic matrix of at least three of the four artists discussed in the book in any but the broadest sense. But she's on sure ground when she writes about Palmer Hayden, one of the four:

> [H]is insistence on portraying Blacks with the masks of the minstrels—that is, as performers for a White audience—and his ingratiating references to the benevolence of his liberators, are probably honest, if not particularly ennobling, portrayals of Hayden's very real feeling about his efforts at making art. As such, they are poles apart from Meta Fuller's aristocratic defiance and political sophistication or Aaron Douglas's epic perspective on the history and origins of the African American.

Certainly these artists were not all of one mind, and Campbell has avoided ideology and allowed the artists to represent themselves. The four artists are Meta Vaux Fuller, nee Warrick (b. 1877), Palmer Hayden (b. 1890), Aaron Douglas (b. 1899), and William H. Johnson (b. 1901). Fuller did all of her work outside Harlem: in Paris, Boston, and Framingham. Palmer Hayden took courses at Cooper Union in New York City, but he studied in Maine and in France and painted in a tradition that was almost anti–New Negro, the image that Alain Locke, the spiritual father of the Renaissance, tried to propagate.

Johnson studied in New York, but then went to Europe where he married and found the inspiration for his paintings from 1929 to 1938. Of the four, only Aaron Douglas, who worked and drew his inspiration from the Harlem of the twenties, truly qualifies as a painter of the Harlem Renaissance. This inconsistency is unfortunate, because the book is such a handsome volume and belongs in the private library of anyone with the least interest in American art.

David Driskell's essay, a concise overview of the four artists, is a pleasure to read. In explaining the importance of Meta Vaux Fuller, he writes: "[She] introduced America to the power of Black American and African subjects long before the Harlem Renaissance was underway. Until Fuller, the aesthetics of the Black visual artist seemed inextricably tied to the taste of White America." The examples of her work reproduced here are stunning, particularly "Talking Skull," which depicts a young man kneeling on a dead corpse and looking down at the skull with such feeling that their conversation seems to come to life.

In the case of William K. Johnson, the book combines the lyrical beauty of his early work, the lovely "Still Life" and "Young Pastry Cook" and the haunting "Self Portrait," with the later primitivism of "Jesus and the Three Marys." Looking at these paintings all together, I am simply in awe of his talent.

Palmer Hayden, the curio of the lot, has such power that his work almost jumps off the canvas (or in this case the page). What spoke to him was the black archetypes of cabin and field who eventually found their way to the cities. They are the bucks and sallys and mammies and joes that have been used to caricature the race. But they existed in real life and Hayden used them to crate powerful art.

Aaron Douglas's masterpiece "Aspects of Negro Life" is included here, along with prints of "God's Trombones," "The Crucifixion," "Alta," and so much more. He is the best known of the four and has, fortunately, had a wide following throughout much of his career. The reproductions shown here reconfirm his position as one of the masters of American art, forget the prefixes.

Refreshingly Campbell puts both Wallace Thurman's and Romare Bearden's feet to the fire for their egregiously pernicious—in fact hateful—attacks on the Harlem Renaissance. Thurman, because he was so brilliant, certainly blemished his reputation in this instance. The need to dismiss "all of the principals of the Renaissance—visual artists and literary artists alike—as a 'motley ensemble without cultural bonds' " had to spring from a deep-seated need for self-deprecation.

Bearden, who gained tremendous fame late in life, is harder to understand, since he castigated some of the very things he strove to accomplish in his own work. Perhaps he feared that because of the brilliance of his precursors, he would never have his day in the sun. He need not have worried. Most of them were considered a fad of separatist art and died that way, alas! His work became a fad in a later period when recognition was accorded African-American artists with real talent!

Harlem Renaissance is a beautifully arranged, in-depth look at black genius as alive and timeless as the figures on a Grecian urn. When I look at the work of these four, I can only ache inside at the relative obscurity that at least three of them have suffered. Once it's Negro art or black art or Black Art, then it goes into the separate-but-equal bin, and any serious discussion of its merits waits until the critics have waded through the perennial issues: How valid is it as pure art? How authentic? How good when compared, even without voicing the judgment, to artists descended from a European tradition?

The two other essays are by David Levering Lewis and Deborah Willis Ryan. Lewis, an excellent historian, has written a fact-filled précis of all of the goings-on in Harlem during the 1920s, from political to cultural to social. However, he has included far too much trivia, resurrecting remote figures such as "the first Black club owner to hire waitresses."

Ms. Ryan, a personal friend, has written a workmanlike, unpretentious observation of James Vander Zee, the legendary photographer. I question, however, the amount of space given to the discussion of his work, given the fact that he's amply represented in other volumes.

I would have liked to see this book give more attention to such seminal figures of the Harlem Renaissance who actually worked there and were identified with it in no uncertain terms, such artists as Augusta Savage, Richmond Barthe, and Jacob Lawrence. Still this is a richly illustrated tribute to the African-American artist, among some of the most unsung heroes and heroines that it has ever been America's privilege to discriminate against. There are more comprehensive books on black art and black artists. Cedric Dover's *Negro Art* is one of them. But the fact that this book includes four voices speaking to one broad subject, and represents such a careful look at these superb painters, too often ignored, more than makes up for whatever shortcomings the volume may have.

AFTERWORD

My last editor, Carol Cady, suggested that I provide a brief explanation of why Must-Read No. 50 is out of order chronologically. As a book on art it is meant to represent the timelessness that that world inhabits. Hopefully, there has been some prison reform since the days of George Jackson, and even a black inmate who is militant in his stance against racism will not have to be subjected in the new millennium to having human waste thrown in his face, in a California prison or anywhere else. Mumia Abu-Jamal (an honorable mention since my first editor absolutely refused to have him included) is still fighting for his life, so hope springs eternal somewhere, even if we fail in the end. And Randall Robinson reminds us that nonwhites will be a majority of the U.S. population by 2050. What that will bring in the way of an egalitarian democracy as opposed to one in which the tyranny of the majority keeps blacks in contemporary peonage can only be guessed at.

But the painter is eternal. The present beauty that he offers will, like Keats's Grecian Urn, outlast man's failures, and be a beacon to his perseverance "to strive, to seek to find." Jacob Lawrence will have had a show at the Whitney Museum, in New York City, in 2002. Whatever is alive and vibrant in his art was just as alive and vibrant in it in the twenties when he began to paint. Meta Vaux Fuller, Palmer Hayden, and William Johnson were as good as they can even be when their talent came to full flower seventy years ago. And they will still be as good seventy years from now, whether or not a public whose tastes are dominated by European traditions and European pedigree discovers their genius. So art is a metaphor for the existential urge to be human in the only way that being human really matters.

BIBLIOGRAPHY

1. *World's Great Men of Color,* J. A. Rogers. Vol. 2. Edited by John Henrik Clarke. New York: Macmillan, 1972. Originally published by the author, 1946–47.

2. *Black Cargoes: A History of the Atlantic Slave Trade, 1518–1865.* By Daniel Mannix in collaboration with Malcolm Cowley. New York: Viking, 1962.

3. *The Negro in Virginia.* Compiled by Workers of the Writers Program of the Works Progress Administration in the State of Virginia. New York: Hastings House, 1941. Reprinted by Arno Press, 1969.

4. *David Walker's Appeal, in Four Articles, Together with a Preamble, to the Coloured Citizens of the World, but in Particular, and Very Expressly, to Those of the United States of America.* Edited and with an introduction by Charles M. Wiltse. New York: Hill and Wang, 1965. Originally published by D. Walker, 1829.

5. *William Styron's Nat Turner: Ten Black Writers Respond.* Edited by John Henrik Clarke. Boston: Beacon Press, 1968.

6. *The Travels of William Wells Brown.* Edited by Paul Jefferson. New York: M. Wiener Publishing, 1991.

7. *The Dred Scott Case: Its Significance in American Law and Politics.* Don E. Fehrenbacher. New York: Oxford University Press, 1978. Later published in an abridged edition as *Slavery, Law and Politics: The Dred Scott Case in Historical Perspective.* New York: Oxford University Press, 1981.

8. *Harriet Tubman: Conductor on the Underground Railroad.* Ann Petry. New York: Crowell, 1955.

9. *The Negro in the Civil War.* Benjamin Quarles. Boston: Little, Brown, 1953. Reprinted with an introduction by William S. McFeely. New York: Da Capo Press, 1989.

10. *Captain of the* Planter: *The Story of Robert Smalls.* Dorothy Sterling. New York: Doubleday, 1958.

11. *The Life and Times of Frederick Douglass: His Early Life as a Slave; His Escape From Bondage; and His Complete History.* With a new introduction by Rayford Logan. New York: Collier Books, 1962. The original edition appeared in 1881.

12. *The Glorious Failure: Black Congressman Robert Brown Elliott and the Reconstruction in South Carolina.* Peggy Lamson. New York: W. W. Norton, 1973.

13. *Pinckney Benton Steward Pinchback.* James Haskins. New York: Macmillan, 1973.

14. *Buffalo Soldiers: A Narrative of the Negro Cavalry in the West.* William H. Leckie. Norman, Okla.: University of Oklahoma Press, 1963.

15. *The Negro Cowboys.* Philip Durham and Everett L. Jones. New York: Dodd, Mead, 1965.

16. *The Betrayal of the Negro: From Rutherford B. Hayes to Woodrow Wilson.* Rayford Logan. New York: Collier Books, 1954. A new enlarged edition was published by Collier, 1965. Reprinted with a new introduction by Eric Foner. New York: Da Capo Press, 1997.

17. *Created Equal: The Lives and Ideas of Black American Innovators.* James Michael Brodie. New York: Morrow, 1993.

18. *Before the Mayflower: A History of Black America.* Lerone Bennett, Jr. 6th edition. New York: Penguin, 1998. Originally pubished 1962 by Johnson Publishing Company with the subtitle *A History of Black America, 1619-1962.*

19. *The Negro in New York: An Informal Social History.* Edited by Roi Ottley and William J. Weatherby. New York: New York Public Library, 1967.

20. *Crusade for Justice: The Autobiography of Ida B. Wells Barnett.*

Edited by Alfreda M. Duster. Chicago: University of Chicago Press, 1970.

21. *Up From Slavery: An Autobiograpy.* Booker T. Washington. With an introduction by Louis Lomax. New York: Doubleday, 1964. Many editions are available.

22. *Along This Way: The Autobiography of James Weldon Johnson.* James Weldon Johnson. New York: Viking Press, 1933. Reprinted by Viking, 1968; by Da Capo Press, 1973.

23. *The Negro Press in the United States.* Frederick Detweiler. Chicago: University of Chicago Press, 1922. Reprinted by McGrath Publishing Co., 1968.

24. *The Guardian of Boston: Monroe Trotter.* Stephen Fox. New York: Atheneum, 1970.

25. *The Mis-Education of the Negro.* Carter G. Woodson. Washington, D.C.: Associated Publishers, 1933. Reprinted by Africa World Press, 1990.

26. *Cane.* Jean Toomer. With a foreword by Waldo Frank. New York: Boni and Liveright, 1923. Reprinted with an introduction by Arna Bontemps, by Harper & Row, 1969.

27. *Harlem Renaissance.* Nathan Irvin Huggins. New York: Oxford University Press, 1971.

28. *Their Eyes Were Watching God.* Zora Neale Hurston. Philadelphia: Lippincott, 1937. Reprinted by New Negro Universities Press (Trenton, N.J.), 1969.

29. *Marcus Garvey and the Vision of Africa.* Edited by John Henrik Clarke. New York: Random House, 1974.

30. *100 Years of Lynchings.* Ralph Ginzburg. New York: Lancer Books, 1962. Reprinted by Black Classic Press (Baltimore), 1988.

31. *The Ways of White Folks.* Langston Hughes. New York: A. A. Knopf, 1934.

32. *The Last of the Scottsboro Boys.* Clarence Norris and Sybil Washington. New York: Putnam, 1979.

33. *The African-American Soldier.* Michael Lee Lanning. New York: Citadel Press, Kensington Publishing, 1997.

34. *Invisible Man.* Ralph Ellison. New York: Random House, 1952. Reprinted by New American Library, 1953. Reprinted

with a preface by Charles Johnson in the Modern Library (Random House), 1994.

35. *The Outsider.* Richard Wright. New York: Harper Brothers, 1953. Reprinted as Harper Perennial paperback, 1991.

36. *Here I Stand.* Paul Robeson. New York: Othello Associates, 1958. Reprinted with a preface by Lloyd D. Brown, Beacon Press (Boston), 1971. Reprinted with a new introduction by Sterling Stuckey, Beacon Press, 1988.

37. *The Autobiography of W. E. B. Du Bois.* New York: International Publishers, 1968.

38. *Stride Toward Freedom: The Montgomery Story.* Martin Luther King Jr. New York: Harper & Row, 1958.

39. *Sex and Racism in America.* Calvin Hernton. New York: Doubleday, 1965. Reprinted by Evergreen Books (Grove Press), 1966.

40. *Adam by Adam: The Autobiography of Adam Clayton Powell, Jr.* New York: Dial Press, 1971. Reprinted by Dafina Books/ Kensington Publishing Corp.: New York, 2002.

41. *Dutchman and the Slave.* Amiri Baraka. New York: Grove Press, 1964.
The Baptism and the Toilet. Amiri Baraka. New York: Grove Press, 1966.

42. *This Little Light of Mine: The Life of Fannie Lou Hamer.* Kay Mills. New York: Dutton, 1993.

43. *The Autobiography of Malcolm X.* With the assistance of Alex Haley. New York: Grove Press, 1965. Reprinted by Ballantine Books, 1992.

44. *The Making of Black Revolutionaries.* James Forman. New York: Macmillan, 1972. Reprinted with a foreword by Julian Bond by Open Hand Publishing Co., 1985.

45. *Soul on Ice.* Eldridge Cleaver. New York: McGraw Hill, 1968. Reprinted as Dell paperback, 1968.

46. *Soledad Brother: The Prison Letters of George Jackson.* With an introduction by Jean Genet. New York: Coward-McCann, 1970. Reprinted with a foreword by Jonathan Jackson, Lawrence Hill Books, 1994.

47. *And the Walls Came Tumbling Down: An Autobiography.* Ralph David Abernathy. New York: Harper & Row, 1989.

48. *The COINTELPRO Papers.* Ward Churchill and Jim Vander Wall. Boston: South End Press, 1990.

49. *Defending the Spirit: A Black Life in America.* Randall Robinson. New York: Dutton, 1998.

50. *Harlem Renaissance: Art of Black America.* Essays by David Driskell, David Levering Lewis, and Deborah Willis Ryan. Introduction by Mary Schmidt Campbell. New York: Abrams, 1987.

HONORABLE MENTIONS

There was not space to include in the main text discussions of all the deserving books by which the reader may gain fuller knowledge of African-American culture. Listed here are the titles of books that were considered for inclusion and then set aside. The adventurous reader should go read *all of them*.

The books are presented in three categories: history, biography, and fiction and poetry. Within the category they are listed by title, not author.

History

Africa's Gift to America: The Afro-American in the Making and Saving of the United States, by J. A. Rogers. New York: H. M. Rogers, 1961.

Bloods: An Oral History of the Vietnam War, by Black Veterans, edited by Wallace Terry. New York: Random House, 1984. Paperback issued by Ballantine Books, 1985, 1992.

A Century of Negro Migration, by Carter G. Woodson. Washington, D.C.: Association for the Study of Negro Life and History, 1918. Reissued by AMS Press, 1970.

Denmark Vesey's Revolt: The Slave Plot That Lit a Fuse to Fort Sumter, by John Lofton. Kent, Ohio: Kent State University Press, 1983.

The Journals of Charlotte Forten Grimké, edited by Brenda Stevenson. New York: Oxford University Press, 1988.

A Pictorial History of the Negro in America, by Langston Hughes and Milton Meltzer. New York: Crown Publishers, 1963. Fourth revised edition, edited by C. Eric Lincoln, issued 1973.

Reconstruction After the Civil War, by John Hope Franklin. Chicago: University of Chicago Press, 1944. Second edition published 1994.

A Social History of the American Negro, Being a History of the Negro Problem in the United States, Including a History and Study of the Republic of Liberia, by Benjamin Brawley. New York: Macmillan, 1921. Reprinted by, among others, Johnson Reprint Corp., 1968; AMS Press, 1970; and Collier Books, 1970.

The Southern Dream of a Caribbean Empire, 1854-1861, by Robert Evan May. Baton Rouge: Louisiana State University Press, 1973.

Three Lives for Mississippi, by William Bradford Huie. New York: WCC Books, 1965.

The Underground Railroad, by William Still. Philadelphia: Porter & Coates, 1872. Newer editions were published by Arno Press, 1968, and Johnson Publishing Co., 1970.

Biography, Journals, and Narratives

Benjamin Banneker, by Silvio A. Bedini. New York: Scribners, 1972. Second revised edition published with the subtitle *The First African-American Man of Science,* by Maryland Historical Society, 1999.

From the Mississippi Delta: A Memoir, by Endesha Ida Mae Holland. New York: Simon & Schuster, 1997.

George Washington Carver: Scientist and Symbol, by Linda O. McMurry. New York: Oxford University Press, 1981.

Ira Aldredge: The Negro Tragedian, by Herbert Marshall and Mildred Stock. New York: Macmillan, 1958. Reissued in 1993 by Howard University Press, with an introduction by Errol Hill.

The Memoirs of Chief Justice Earl Warren. New York: Doubleday, 1977.

Sojourner Truth: A Life, a Symbol, by Nell Irvin Painter. New York: W. W. Norton, 1996.

Seize the Time: The Story of the Black Panther Party and Huey P. Newton, by Bobby Seale. New York: Random House, 1970. Reissued by Black Classic Press, 1991.

Thomas Morris Chester: Black Civil War Correspondent: His Dispatches From the Virginia Front, edited by R. J. M. Blackett. Baton Rouge: Louisiana State University Press, 1989.

The Classic Slave Narratives, edited and with an introduction by Henry Louis Gates, Jr. New York: New American Library, 1987.

Live From Death Row, by Mumia Abu-Jamal. Reading, Mass.: Addison Wesley, 1995.

Malcolm X Speaks: Selected Speeches and Statements, edited by George Breitman. New York: Grove Press, 1965. Second edition issued by Pathfinder Books, 1989.

Martin Luther King, Jr.: A Profile, edited by C. Eric Lincoln, rev. ed. New York: Hill and Wang, 1970.

Muhammah Ali: His Life and Times, by Thomas Hauser. Simon & Schuster, 1991.

A Testament of Hope: The Essential Writings and Speeches of Martin Luther King, Jr., edited by James Melvin Washington. New York: Harper & Row, 1968. Reissued by HarperSanFrancisco, 1991.

Unbought and Unbossed, by Shirley Chisholm. Boston: Houghton Mifflin, 1970.

The Arts

American Negro Art, by Cedric Dover. Greenwich, Conn.: New York Graphic Society, 1960.

Black Magic: A Pictorial History of Black Entertainers in America, by Langston Hughes and Milton Meltzer. Englewood Cliffs, N.J.: Prentice-Hall, 1967.

Black Hollywood: The Negro in Motion Pictures, by Gary Null. Secaucus, N.J.: Citadel Press, 1975.

Brown Sugar: Eighty Years of American Black Female Superstars, by Donald Bogle. New York: Harmony Books, 1980. Reprinted by Da Capo Press, 1990.

Fiction, Poetry, and Drama

The Amen Corner: A Play, by James Baldwin. New York: Dial Press, 1968. Reissued by Vintage Books, 1998.

The Autobiography of an Ex-Colored Man, by James Weldon Johnson. Boston: Sherman, French & Co., 1912. Reissued by Hill and Wang, 1960, with an introduction by Arna Bontemps. Many paperback editions are available.

Black Boy: A Record of Childhood and Youth, by Richard Wright. New York: Harper & Row, 1945. Often reprinted.

Black Drama Anthology, edited by Woodie King and Ron Milner. New York: Columbia University Press, 1972. Reissued by New American Library, 1986, with a new introduction by Woodie King.

The Blacker the Berry: A Novel of Negro Life, by Wallace Thurman. New York: Scribner, 1929.

Ceremonies in Dark Old Men, by Lonne Elder III. Farrar, Straus, & Giroux, 1969. Available in a Noonday paperback edition (Farrar, Straus, & Giroux) and as a playbook from Samuel French.

The Collected Works of Phillis Wheatley, edited by John C. Shields. New York: Oxford University Press, 1988.

The Complete Poems of Paul Laurence Dunbar. New York: Dodd, Mead, 1913. Reprinted in 1980.

A Different Drummer, by William Melvin Kelley. Garden City, N.Y.: Doubleday, 1962. Reissued in Anchor Books edition, 1989.

Giovanni's Room, by James Baldwin. New York: Dial Press, 1956. Reissued by Penguin Putnam in 1998 with an introduction by Toni Morrison.

Go Tell It on the Mountain, by James Baldwin. New York: Dial Press, 1953.

Lay Bare the Heart: An Autobiography of the Civil Rights Movement, by James Farmer. New York: Arbor House, 1985.

Native Son, by Richard Wright. New York: Harper Brothers, 1940. Reissued in 1969 with an introduction by the author, "How 'Bigger' Was Born"; reissued by Harper & Row in 1998 with an introduction by Arnold Rampersad.

The Negro Caravan, edited by Sterling A. Brown, Albert P. Davis, and Ulysses Lee. New York: Dryden Press, 1941. Reissued by Arno Press, 1969. This legendary anthology is out of print, but may be found in library collections.

The New Black Poetry, edited by Clarence Major. New York: International Publisher, 1969.

The Poetry of the Negro, 1746-1949, edited by Langston Hughes and Arna Bontemps. Garden City, N.Y.: Doubleday, 1949. New updated edition with redated title *1946-1970* published in 1970.

Uncle Tom's Children, by Richard Wright. New York: Harper & Row, 1938. Reprinted as a Harper Perennial paperback, with an introduction by Richard Yarborough, 1991.

INDEX